PENGUIN ENGLISH LIBRARY

RECORDS OF SHELLEY, BYRON,
AND THE AUTHOR

David Wright, poet, is the editor of the *Penguin
Book of Romantic Verse*, *The Mid Century: English
Poetry 1940–60* and *Longer Contemporary Poems* in
the Penguin Poets and of De Quincey's *Recollections
of the Lakes and the Lake Poets* in the Penguin
English Library. He is also the author of a study of
deafness.

Scuola Grande di S. Rocco
Venezia

INGRESSO
FERIALE

L. 500

Nº   8 104

Contents

Introduction

A man who speaks neither truth nor lies but a sort of
Not Proven compound which is very relishable.

THOMAS HARDY

ONE of the oddest and most entertaining documents of the
Romantic Movement in England is Edward John Trelawny's
Records of Shelley, Byron, and the Author. Though belonging
chronologically to the high noon of the Victorian era it is in spirit
a product of the Romantic period. In 1858, when well past sixty,
Trelawny published it under the title of *Recollections of the Last
Days of Shelley and Byron*. Twenty years later the *Records of
Shelley, Byron, and the Author* appeared. This is intrinsically
the same book, greatly expanded. Trelawny, then eighty-five,
added letters, conversations, and further reminiscences to the
original text, which he otherwise subjected to very little alteration
and almost no deletions.* As much of Trelawny's new material
is too good to lose – it includes some of the most characteristic
of the Shelley anecdotes – and as the earlier version is subsumed
in the later, it is the *Records* of 1878 that I have chosen to reprint. There has in fact been no new edition of the *Records* for
more than half a century, though the *Recollections* has been
resurrected several times (its most recent appearance was an
edition prepared by J. E. Morpurgo for the Folio Society in 1952).

The *Records of Shelley, Byron, and the Author* purports to
be a memoir of three vital, not to say traumatic, years of
Trelawny's bizarre existence. In February 1822, when he had just
turned thirty, Trelawny arrived at Pisa in Italy. The foot-loose
scion of an old Cornish family of landed gentry, behind him
a broken marriage, an exotic if obscure seafaring past, and a

---

* Passages omitted from the *Recollections* are reprinted in the Notes at
the end of this book, where all significant alterations and additions to the
original version have also been indicated.

comfortable private income, he became the friend and companion
of two of the leading Romantic poets of his generation. At Pisa,
for the first six months of 1822, Trelawny was in constant contact
with Byron, Shelley, their friends and womenfolk : it was probably the happiest and most disturbing period in the whole of his
life. A man of original but uneducated mind, a character com-
bining naiveté and ruthlessness – independent, domineering,
self-willed – a man of action with all the attributes of a philistine,
yet leavened by an unexpected affinity and respect for poetry that
may have had something to do with the Celtic strain in him,
Trelawny found himself being dominated; overawed, even
hypnotized, morally, spiritually, and intellectually, by two of the
more remarkable personalities of their day. The one attracted,
the other attracted and repelled. Trelawny, fascinated by both,
must often have felt like a rabbit between two snakes. Within
the year it was Shelley, to whom he had given his spiritual
allegiance, whose drowned body Trelawny was to burn on a
beach near Viareggio. Byron, about whom Trelawny's feelings
were peculiarly ambivalent, he was soon afterwards to accompany to Greece and involuntary martyrdom on the first of those
ideological crusades that have since become endemic in our time.
Byron's death at Missolonghi in 1824 eventually became the
key that freed Greece from Turkish domination. However,
Trelawny stayed on for another year as the friend and henchman
of the Greek chieftain Odysseus Androutzos, whose thirteen-
year-old half-sister he married (an event not dwelt on in the *Records*). For months Trelawny commanded Odysseus's hide-out, a
brigand's cave in the cliffs of Parnassus. Eventually he was shot
in the back by an assassin, forced out of his romantic mountain
stronghold, and finally rescued by a British naval vessel. These
three years were scarcely uneventful.

For the rest of a long life Trelawny was to chew the cud of
the experience of his encounter with Shelley and Byron. Even
into old age he kept up a reminiscent correspondence with sur-
vivors of those halcyon months at Pisa. Almost his last act was
to arrange for his own burial at Rome in a grave next to that in
which Shelley had been interred more than half a century before.
The *Records of Shelley, Byron, and the Author* is an end-product

of an obsession: graphic, subjective, factitious, but alive.

Who was Trelawny? In 1831, nearly ten years after his first meeting with Shelley and Byron, he published an autobiography called *Adventures of a Younger Son*, a book that has been ranked as a minor classic in the genre of George Borrow's *Lavengro*. The *Adventures* begins with one of the vividly realized autobiographical set-pieces that were Trelawny's speciality as a writer. This is a brutally detailed account of the first notable event in his childhood, a battle to the death with a ferocious pet raven. It becomes evident that the raven is an objective correlative for his savage and despotic father as Trelawny goes on to paint a vigorous self-portrait of himself as an indomitably rebellious defier of paternal authority: a born freedom-fighter. But after a certain point the autobiography becomes more useful as a clue to the image Trelawny presented to his friends at Pisa than as information about his life up to his twentieth year, when the narrative ends.

In the *Adventures of a Younger Son* Trelawny describes how he was expelled from various schools till he was placed in the Navy as a midshipman. Trelawny was then thirteen; the year was 1805; and the ship in which he served only just failed to arrive in time to fight at Trafalgar. After that he was sent on several voyages to South America and the coast of Africa, and finally round the Cape of Good Hope to Bombay. Here Trelawny says he met a mysterious and romantic French privateer of Dutch descent, whom he calls De Ruyter. It is at this point that his autobiography begins to part company with the facts.

According to the *Adventures*, at Bombay Trelawny decides to desert from the Navy to join De Ruyter, who becomes his hero, and the hero of the book. De Ruyter gives the seventeen-year-old Trelawny command of a vessel in which he roams the Indian and China seas fighting with junks, Malayan proas, and even taking on the British Navy. In the course of these goings-on he rescues and marries Zella, a beautiful high-born Arab girl of thirteen, who reciprocates by saving his life on more than one occasion. Eventually she dies; stunned with grief, Trelawny dresses Zella in her richest robes, places the body on a funeral pyre built on the sea-shore, tries to throw himself into the flames but stumbles and is rescued with no more damage than the severe burning of his hands. A few weeks later De Ruyter announces that he is returning to Europe to carry despatches to Napoleon. Trelawny accompanies him as far as one of the French Channel ports, where he lingers long enough for De Ruyter to go to Paris and return with a highly interesting account of his interview with the Emperor. Upon which the twenty-year-old ex-midshipman ex-pirate slips across the Channel and finds himself back in England.

This, of course, is not quite what happened, though research has shown that the first part of the *Adventures*, up to the time of Trelawny's supposed meeting with De Ruyter, is remarkably accurate; the facts are corroborated by naval records and other evidence.*

What we know for certain is that Trelawny was born in 1792, the second son of Lt.-Col. Charles Trelawny of the famous old Cornish family ('And shall Trelawny die?'). His mother was a Hawkins; one of her grandfathers, a Manchester linen-draper, had dabbled in literature, won a mention by Steele in the *Spectator*, and even published a volume of poems. Colonel Trelawny was a ruthless character who solved the problem presented by his far from docile offspring by dumping him in the Navy when it became clear that no school would hold him. There the boy remained from 1805 to 1812. It has been established that Trelawny did not desert from the service, as he claimed in the *Adventures*. On the other hand his naval experiences appear to have been quite as interesting and exciting – though more orthodox – than those he records. Trelawny really did sail in the Java seas and fight with privateers, though these true adventures appear in reverse in the autobiography: where instead of being aboard a R.N. vessel chasing a French privateer, he depicts himself aboard the pirate vessel pursued by a British warship. The point emerges that Trelawny was not so much a Walter Mitty fantasist as an imaginative manipulator of reality.

He was discharged from the Navy on 18 August 1812, a few weeks before his twentieth birthday. A year later he married the

* *Trelawny's Family Background and Naval Career*, Anne Hill, Keats–Shelley Journal, 1956.

daughter of a colonial nabob, and a child, Maria Julia, was born in 1814. The marriage was soon on the rocks. At a Bristol lodging-house Mrs Trelawny began an affair with a fellow-boarder. Trelawny found out, left his wife, and took action for divorce. This operation must have been as expensive as it was cumbrous, for the nuptial knot was finally severed by Act of Parliament in 1819.

Disembarrassed of his wife and naval career, but with a private income of £500, Trelawny took to travelling on the continent. At the same time, rather unexpectedly for one who had received so little schooling as to be practically illiterate, and whose formative years afforded almost no contact with books or intellectual companionship, Trelawny began to interest himself in contemporary poetry. That of Byron made immediate appeal, for Trelawny's romanticism was able to identify with the moody and mysterious heroes of *Lara* and *The Corsair*. Byron's poems were, of course, famous and not difficult to come by. But while wandering in Switzerland Trelawny chanced upon a copy of *Queen Mab* by the then almost unknown Shelley. Shelley's poetry appealed to another facet of Trelawny's nature – his anti-authoritarianism, the fruit of those early battles with his tyrannous father. This anti-authoritarianism included atheism and anti-monarchic sentiments, current elements of the romantic radicalism which inclined intellectual liberals to idealize Napoleon as the heir of the French Revolution – much as, a century later, their counterparts were led to idealize Stalin as the heir of the Russian Revolution. Then at Geneva Trelawny fell in with a group of sporting young Englishmen of his own sort, like himself temporarily unoccupied. Among them were two half-pay lieutenants of the Indian Army. The first, Thomas Medwin, was a cousin of Shelley's and had been at Eton with the poet, as, indeed, had the other, a young man called Edward Ellerker Williams. Williams was living out of wedlock with the deserted wife of one of his brother-officers. This was the Jane Williams to whom Shelley was to address some of his best love-lyrics.

When the group broke up, Medwin went to Pisa while Trelawny returned to England. Soon afterwards Williams and Jane left for Italy to join Medwin. Thus began the nucleus of what came to be known as the 'Pisan Circle'. The magnet of this small coterie of young English expatriates, most of them of good family, moderately well-heeled, but in the eyes of society just a little raffish – usually because of some domestic irregularity such as a mistress or, as in the case of Williams, a common-law wife – was Medwin's cousin, Shelley. He had come to live at Pisa in order to be near Dr Vaccà Berlinghieri, an Italian doctor of international reputation. And by the end of 1821 Shelley drew to Pisa no less a personage than Lord Byron, rumbling over the Apennines from Ravenna with a baggage-train of wagons, coaches, apes, bears, and peacocks, to join his mistress, Teresa Guiccioli, and her father, Count Gamba, in a palace on the banks of the Arno that Shelley found for them. Meanwhile Williams, who had spent the summer of 1821 boating with Shelley on the Arno, occasionally corresponded with Trelawny. His news that Byron had come to Pisa determined Trelawny to join the little colony. Though in the *Records* he does his best to make out that Shelley was the attraction, it seems clear that at the time it was Byron, the cynosure of Europe, whom he really wanted to meet.

At the beginning of 1822 Trelawny arrived at Pisa, 'a kind of half-Arab Englishman', as Mary Shelley described him after their first meeting:

whose life has been as changeful as that of Anastasius, and who recounts the adventures of his youth as eloquently and well as the imagined Greek. He is clever; for his moral qualities I am yet in the dark; he is a strange web which I am endeavouring to unravel. I would fain learn if generosity is united to impetuousness, probity of spirit to his assumption of singularity and independence. He is six feet high; raven-black hair, which curls thickly and shortly like a Moor's; dark-grey expressive eyes; overhanging brows, upturned lips, and a smile which expresses good nature and kind-heartedness. ... His language as he relates the events of his life, energetic and simple, whether the tale be one of blood and horror or irresistible comedy. His company is delightful, for he excites me to think, and if any evil shade the intercourse, that time will reveal – the sun will rise or night darken all.   (Letter to Mrs Gisborne, 9 February 1822)

He was, in fact, a Romantic hero in search of an author – and the moment he set eyes on Trelawny, Byron recognized his own creation:

I have met today the personification of my Corsair. He sleeps with
the poem under his pillow, and all his past adventures and present
manners aim at this personification.

(Letter to Teresa Guiccioli)

But for Trelawny Byron was, if not a disappointment, most
decidedly a disconcertment. Trelawny in his enthusiasm expected
to meet the gloomy and intense Pilgrim of *Childe Harold*,
creator of those glamorously enigmatic Laras and Corsairs with
whom he felt kinship. But it was the ironically flippant con-
versationalist of *Don Juan*, cheerfully banging billiard-balls
about in the Palazzo Lanfranchi, to whom he was introduced.
Byron's realism and practicality, his Scotch common sense,
jolted Trelawny. 'I had come to see a solemn mystery,' he complains in the *Records*, 'and so far as I could judge from the first
it seemed to me like a solemn farce . . . Byron disenchanted me.'
Unlike Byron, but like Shelley, Trelawny had little perception
of the comic. Trelawny's romanticism, attitudinizing and line-
shooting were constantly being deflected and deflated by Byron,
who was something of a tease and obviously hugely amused by
his new friend. Though sometimes he could be exasperated : 'If
we could only make Trelawny wash his hands and speak the
truth we could make a gentleman of him.' The handsome
swashbuckling Trelawny found himself unexpectedly put out by
Byron's prowess as an athlete. To the lame poet Trelawny was
ready to yield mastery in the sphere of the philosophical and
abstract, but surely that of the physical and practical belonged
to himself. This was one reason why Trelawny took to the intellectual and dreamy Shelley, who was in most respects his
antithesis. In point of fact it was the impractical and extrava-
gantly idealistic side of Shelley that appealed to Trelawny, for
it made him think well of himself and flattered his romanticism.
Byron merely laughed at it. Shelley allowed Trelawny to play
his role of Romantic hero* and bluff, practical man of action; it

---

* Shelley even projected a drama which he never finished, one of whose
principal characters, 'A Pirate, a man of savage but noble nature', was
based on Trelawny and is thus apostrophized :

He was as is the sun in his fierce youth,
As terrible and lovely as a tempest.

was the realistic Byron who punctured the histrionics and made Trelawny feel foolish. And in one respect Trelawny and Shelley were alike. Each had, as Newman Ivey White says of Shelley, 'a perfectly amazing capacity to believe what he wished'. Apropos of which, almost fifty years later, writing about Jefferson Hogg's biography of Shelley, Trelawny remarked: 'Hogg says the Poet could never distinguish truth from falsehood – I found the Poet always truthful – his vivid imagination might occasionally delude him as it does others.' He might have been speaking of himself.

Trelawny's portraits of Byron and Shelley are far from objective. In many respects their figures are mirrors to project Trelawny's notion of himself. Despite this they remain vividly presented impressions successfully communicated – a consummation not often achieved in the memoirs of annalists of less gusto and more veracity. Trelawny's allegiance is to feelings rather than facts. Byron's one-time mistress, Claire Clairmont, with whom Trelawny had fancied himself to be in love, once burst out: 'He [Trelawny] is full of fine feelings and no principles: I am full of fine principles but never had a feeling; he receives all his impressions through his heart, I through my head. *Que voulez-vous?*' Trelawny's flair for the characteristic, spectacular, and emblematic anecdote, not subservient to fact so long as it hit the mark, has long been a crux for biographers.

There is Trelawny's story (perhaps apocryphal, we have only his word for it) of Shelley plunging into a pool where 'he lay stretched out on the bottom like a conger eel, not making the least effort or struggle to save himself', until Trelawny leapt in and fished him out. Like a cartoon that exaggerates some subliminal characteristic or idiosyncrasy to focus attention on its significance, the anecdote points a factor of Shelley's make-up – his death-wish. We know about it from other sources but Trelawny's impressionistic vignette brings it home with the immediacy of an image. Another well-known anecdote recreates Shelley's absent-minded, or rather other-minded, unworldliness and blindness to convention (a rather different thing from unconventionality, which has an element of aggression). This is the story, told only in the *Records*, of Shelley walking naked and dripping from the sea through the dining-room of the Casa Magni to get his clothes from the bedchamber beyond, quite unconcerned at the presence of a party of ladies who had been invited to dinner. Again possibly apocryphal, but convincing, because so entirely in character that, fact or no, it has become part of the truth about Shelley, if only because it is the kind of story that could be told and believed about him – an attribute that belongs to legend or myth.

The great set-piece of the *Records* is, of course, the shipwreck of the *Don Juan* in the Bay of Spezzia and the recovery and burning of the bodies of Shelley and Edward Williams on the beach at Viareggio. As a dramatic *pièce-de-resistance* the episode is a gift. Trelawny does not waste it. But though he is hardly what one would call a retiring character, there is a strange ambiguity about Trelawny's presentation of his own role in these events. He makes very little of the famous incident in which he was the undoubted protagonist – the snatching of Shelley's heart from the flames of his funeral pyre. This is dealt with in a single sentence. While making out that he was far more active in the search for the bodies of Shelley and his companion than may really have been the case, he says almost nothing about the tireless aid and comfort he extended to Jane Williams and Mary Shelley in their time of trial. There is plenty of evidence for this from almost everyone except Trelawny. Mary Shelley wrote at the time :

But the friend to whom we are eternally indebted is Trelawny. I have of course mentioned him in my letter to you – as one who wishes to be considered eccentric but who was noble and generous at bottom. ... In my outline of events, you will see how unasked he returned with Jane & I from Leghorn to Lerici, how he staid with us miserable creatures twelve days there endeavouring to keep up our spirits – how he left us, on thursday, & finding our misfortune confirmed then without rest returned on friday to us, & again without rest returned with us to Pisa on saturday. These were no common services. Since that he has gone through by himself all the annoyance of dancing attendance on consuls & governors for permission to fulfill the last duties to those gone, & attending the ceremony himself, all the disagreeable part & all the fatigue fell on him – as Hunt said – 'He worked with the meanest and felt with the best.' He is generous to a distressing degree. But after all those benefits towards us what I most thank him for is this. When on that night of agony, that friday night he returned to announce that hope was dead for us ... he did not attempt to console me, that would have been cruelly useless; but he launched forth into as it were an overflowing & eloquent praise of my divine Shelley – until I almost was happy that I was thus unhappy to be fed by the praise of him, and to dwell on the eulogy that his loss thus drew from his friend.

(Letter to Maria Gisborne, 27 August 1822)

Against this must be set Trelawny's gratuitous assertion in the *Records* that the boat in which Shelley was drowned had been designed by Edward Williams, when in fact it had been built from a model apparently procured by Trelawny himself.* Trelawny wrote no less than eight distinct accounts of the events connected with the drowning and cremation of Shelley, not including references in letters or his fragmentary, unpublished reminiscences. Seven of these narratives were written down within a month or two of the events they describe. All contain careless discrepancies and confusions, mostly of a minor sort.† Dates are muddled, as is the time of the sailing of the *Don Juan* on her last voyage, given variously as 12 noon in his early, contemporary accounts, or some time after 2 p.m. according to the narrative printed in the *Recollections* and the *Records*, written more than thirty years later. There was the temptation, which Trelawny was the last man to resist, of making a good story better. To the account in the *Records* he appends a correspondence reprinted from *The Times* of 1875 relating to an old fisherman's dying confession that he had been one of the crew of a felucca that deliberately ran down Shelley's boat because they thought Byron was on board with a bag of gold. The existence of the old sailor, who is said to have died in 1863, to say nothing of his 'confession', has never been established. All that can be said is that when the *Don Juan* was raised, the timbers of her starboard quarter were found to be stove in – evidence that she had probably been run down by another vessel during the

* see Note 28.

† One of Trelawny's on-the-spot accounts is reprinted in Appendix 3, and an extract from another in Note 42. For a detailed analysis of his various narratives, see *Trelawny on the Death of Shelley*, by Leslie A. Marchand, Keats–Shelley Memorial Bulletin No. IV, 1952.

storm in which she was lost. If so, accident would be a more likely explanation than piracy – but not to an imagination like Trelawny's.

Though the account in the *Records* is a verbatim reprint from the *Recollections* of 1858, plus the additional material provided by *The Times* correspondence, there is one deliberate and inexplicable alteration to the earlier text. It concerns the detail of Trelawny's identification of Shelley's corpse from his jacket. This he recognized by 'the volume of Aeschylus in one pocket, and Keats's poems in the other'. Thus the *Records* of 1878; but according to the *Recollections* of 1858 the first item is 'a volume of Sophocles'. In Trelawny's on-the-spot manuscript accounts and other contemporary records there is no mention of either the Aeschylus or Sophocles, only of the copy of Keats's poems. Now, if a Greek book did not exist, what was the point of inventing it – and if Trelawny were at all concerned with consistency, let alone credibility, why trouble to alter Sophocles to Aeschylus in 1878? The change must have been deliberate and not a result of accident or carelessness, because he twice refers to the Sophocles, and each time alters it to Aeschylus (cf note 20). In an appendix to the Records (see p. 306) Trelawny underlines the alteration by remarking that twenty or thirty years after the shipwreck he had presented this volume of Aeschylus to Shelley's son, Sir Percy Shelley. Five years after Trelawny's death, Professor Dowden, then writing his biography of the poet, paid a visit to the Shelley family. They showed him their most precious relics, including Trelawny's gift of the water-soaked volume found in Shelley's pocket. Examining the book, Professor Dowden discovered it to be a copy of Sophocles.*

This kind of irresponsibility has not endeared Trelawny to

---

*This book used to be exhibited among the Shelleyana at the Bodleian library but has been withdrawn. Perhaps, as Marchand suggests, it was all a devious practical joke of Trelawny's at the expense of Sir Percy Shelley, of whom he held no good opinion. Certainly Trelawny in his later years took elaborate and unscrupulous delight in passing off what are called 'associational items'. These include bits of Shelley's skull, the sofa on which he last slept, a dagger connected with the fracas at Pisa (see p. 155), Byron's sword, his cap and jacket. On each Trelawny hung a tale, probably to amuse himself – he did not sell, but gave away these miscellanea, few of which are likely to have been authentic.

biographers. In *Byron: The Last Journey* Harold Nicolson makes
no bones about calling Trelawny 'a liar and a cad', while the
entry in the index to Doris Langley Moore's recent study, *The
Late Lord Byron*, begins simply : 'Trelawny, Edward John, lies
and inaccuracies of'. Trelawny's bias against Byron wins him no
love from Byron's admirers, though his sniping is a paean of
praise compared with the exhibition of self-righteous malice in
which the egregious Leigh Hunt indulged when he published
Lord Byron and Some of his Contemporaries only four years
after the poet's death. Yet Trelawny takes up cudgels for Byron
where his marriage is concerned (not so easy to do in the nineteenth century). And with the passing of time his attitude mel-
lowed; as may be seen from the Notes at the end of this book,
most of the passages in the *Recollections* that Trelawny later
omitted from the *Records* are those containing unfriendly
references to Byron. It ought not to be forgotten that while
Trelawny was in Italy he would have heard a good deal of anti-
Byron propaganda from the Shelleys, and still more from Mary
Shelley's step-sister, Claire Clairmont, who had been Byron's
mistress.

Something must be said about the relations between Claire and
Byron, though Trelawny himself does not touch on them. It was
through Claire that Shelley and Byron had met and formed a
friendship which proved as mutually beneficial and in some ways
almost as fruitful as that between Wordsworth and Coleridge.
It was through Claire that this friendship soured. When Shelley
fell in love with her step-sister, Mary Godwin, and ran off with
her, Claire seems to have been a little in love with Shelley herself, and a little jealous of Mary for capturing a poet. As if to
show she could go one better, Claire flung herself at Byron's
head. She called on him at his home and succeeded in having
what amounted to a one-night stand with the most famous poet
in Europe. This was in the very week that Byron left England
for ever owing to the break-up of his disastrous marriage to
Annabella Milbanke. After he had gone Claire attached herself
to the Shelleys like a succubus. Byron probably imagined he
would never see the girl again; if so, he was mistaken. When the
Shelleys decided to visit the continent Claire managed to steer

the party towards Geneva, where she knew Byron was going.
Thus the two poets met. When Claire's daughter Allegra was
born in 1817 Shelley had to act as ambassador between the
parents. Byron, who could not stand the sight of Claire, undertook to rear the child on condition that it was separated from
the mother and that the mother made no attempt to communicate
with him. This proved an awkward and ungrateful task for
Shelley, often leading to coolness between him and Byron.
Naturally Claire came to look on Byron with bitter hatred,
especially after the death of Allegra, and sometimes managed to
infect Shelley with her feelings. At the time of Shelley's death
Trelawny nursed a passion for Claire – nothing came of it, but
they remained friends all their lives – and would not have been
unaffected by her attitude. Only in old age did he rebuke her:
'Your relentless vindictiveness against Byron is not tolerated by
any religion I know of.'*

What really earned Trelawny his reputation as a cad was his
portrait of Mary Shelley. She had died in 1851, seven years before
the publication of the *Recollections of the Last Days of Shelley
and Byron*. In the course of her long widowhood Mary had made
a cult of respectability, and of Shelley – two apparently irrecon-
cilable deities. But after her death her daughter-in-law, Lady
Shelley, appointed herself chief priestess at the shrine. A very
vigilant priestess too : she saw to it that Shelley's friend Jefferson
Hogg's trenchant biography of the poet (still the best there is,
as far as it goes) was stopped dead in its tracks after the publication of the second volume in 1858. In the same year Trelawny's
Recollections appeared. In this, and even more in the 1878
Records, the picture of Shelley and Mary as twin souls was
blown sky high :

Mrs Shelley had a variety of amiable qualities, but she was possessed of the green-eyed monster, jealousy ... That was an unsur-
mountable impediment to confidential intercourse with her husband.
Whenever the Poet wrote on the subject of love, however abstract or
ideal, she misconstrued this, and considered it treason to herself. She
was mournful and desponding in solitude, and panting for society. She
used every effort to make Shelley conventional, and to get him

*Letter to Claire Clairmont, 20 January 1875.

to do as others did; her moaning and complaining grieved him, and her society was no solace.

Unforgivable, doubly unforgivable from one who had sworn eternal friendship to the poet's widow and even proposed marriage (to be firmly turned down : 'You belong to womenkind in general, and Mary Shelley will never be yours'). Nevertheless Trelawny's picture of the strained relations between Shelley and Mary is a true one. Shelley himself wrote : 'I only feel the want of those who can understand me. Whether from proximity or the continuity of domestic intercourse, Mary does not.' Claire Clairmont, living with them at Florence in 1820, comments significantly in her diary : 'A bad wife is like Winter in the house,' while Mary's own journal for the same year complains : 'We have now lived five years together and if all the events of the five years were blotted out, I might be happy.'

To be fair to Mary, she had cause to write thus, and for Trelawny to think her 'moping and miserable'. Only twenty-five when Trelawny met her at Pisa, she had lived with Shelley for eight years and in that time had borne and lost three children. There had been crises and tragedies like the suicide of her half-sister, Fanny Imlay, followed within a month by that of Shelley's first wife, Harriet Westbrook, who threw herself, pregnant, into the Serpentine. She had had to endure, first the ostracism, then the relentless sponging, of her father William Godwin, not to mention the burden of her step-sister, Claire Clairmont, who followed her and Shelley wherever they went; and the never-ending financial straits, confusion and panics into which Shelley's sanguine and impractical disposition continually plunged the pair of them. Of all these crosses, the deaths of her children were the heaviest, particularly of the last, a little boy who died at Rome in 1819. This tragedy had raised a wall between her and Shelley, who found himself helpless in the face of Mary's melancholy. No wonder he was easily led into *amities amoureuses* with girls like the Contessina Emilia Viviani and Jane Williams.

But if Trelawny softened his attitude towards Byron, his treatment of Mary became more abrasive. An appendix to the *Records* launches a fresh philippic against her, though by this time she had been dead more than a quarter of a century. Some of Trelawny's additional material in the *Records* champions Shelley's first wife, Harriet Westbrook. By any standards poor Harriet, who drowned herself after Shelley's desertion, was badly treated in life and after death. Still one has the feeling that Trelawny, despite a real empathy for Harriet, is using her as a stick to beat Mary Shelley with. Trelawny's slow but deepening estrangement from Mary may have had its beginnings in her refusal to help him write a life of Shelley (a project he had to abandon because she had all the papers and documents), but it was certainly fed by her growing conformity, by the waning of her early radicalism, and by her more and more evident inclination to accept the values of society. These leanings were apparent even at Pisa. After Shelley's death, when Mary returned to England, they became pronounced. In Trelawny's eyes this backsliding was unforgivable in a daughter of the radical philosopher William Godwin and the even more radical Mary Wollstonecraft; one, moreover, who had been wife to such a man as Shelley. By 1837 the friendship between Mary and Trelawny seems to have been at an end. Not but that Mary could give as good as she got: her journal for 1831 contains this devastating analysis of the man:

A strange yet wonderful being endued with genius – great force of character and power of feeling – but destroyed by *being nothing* – destroyed by envy and internal dissatisfaction.

Yet Trelawny's view of Mary was not unshared by others. One reason why Shelley's early friend, T. L. Peacock, declined a request to write the poet's biography was his dislike of Mary, still an active dislike after half a century.

*

In the year following the death of Shelley, Trelawny accepted Byron's invitation to join him on his expedition to aid the Greeks in their war of independence against the Ottoman Empire. They had risen in 1821 after centuries of subjugation. No event since the American and French revolutions had roused so much hope and enthusiasm among European liberals and libertarians. In

March 1823 a Greek Committee had been formed in London to raise funds, munitions and supplies for the Greek insurrectionists. One of its most active members was Byron's friend, John Cam Hobhouse. But nobody on the Committee knew the precise situation or what was most needed in Greece. The object, to throw off the Turkish yoke, was clear-cut enough. Yet after some initial massacres and indecisive successes, the Greek revolutionaries had become more interested in quarrelling among themselves. On one hand there was the leader of the Westernized or civilian party, the plump bespectacled Prince Mavrocordato, who had been a friend of the Shelleys at Pisa, and who was now already fairly well established in Western Greece. On the other was the bandit Kolokontres, principal leader of the indigenous or military party, whose writ ran in the Morea (as the Peloponnese used to be called). There were innumerable splinter groups and more or less independent factions and war-lords, of whom we need only notice Odysseus Androutzos, a Klepht chieftain – the Klephts were notorious brigands – who controlled Eastern Greece and had a working understanding with Kolokontres. Byron, who had spent nearly two years travelling in Greece and Turkey between 1809 and 1811, making himself familiar not only with the country but the people and the language, and whose *Childe Harold*, and poems like *Lara* and the *Corsair*, had been largely responsible for making Philhellinism fashionable in Europe, was the obvious candidate as an emissary for the London Greek Committee. But it was the publicity value and magic of Byron's name that Edward Blaquiere, the Irish adventurer who was the driving force behind the London Greek Committee, was after when he asked Byron to join, for he realized that Byron's name was essential if the rather languid response, so far, of the British public to the Greek cause was to be stimulated. When Byron at length agreed to set out for Greece the London Committee entrusted him with money and medical supplies for the partisans, besides which he took along considerable funds from his own private purse.

Having arrived in Greece, Byron moved cautiously, much to the disgust of the impetuous and unreflective Trelawny. He spent months, apparently dawdling, on the Greek island of

Cephalonia. It was at that time under British rule, therefore neutral territory, and thus a good place to try to determine which of the various insurrectionary leaders it would be politic to back. As William St Clair has remarked in his recent study of the part played by the Philhellenes in the Greek War of Independence,* 'Byron, almost alone of the Philhellenes ... tried to inform himself about Greek institutions.' Byron made his position plain: 'I did not come here to join a faction but a nation.' This remained a policy to which he steadfastly held.

Towards the end of 1823 he was joined in Cephalonia by a co-emissary from the London Committee, Colonel the Hon. Leicester Stanhope. A follower of Jeremy Bentham, full of educational theories and democratic principles, this White Knight turned up on Byron's doorstep loaded with Bibles and printing-presses, not to mention a very determined bee in his bonnet. A free press was the surest way to end despotism : ergo, the Colonel would start a newspaper. That most of the population of Greece could not read was neither here nor there. As a contemporary observer put it, the two men did not row in the same boat. At one time Byron sardonically remarked, 'It is odd that Stanhope, the soldier, is all for writing down the Turks while I, the writer, am all for fighting them down,' and at another, 'He is like all political jobbers who mistake the accessories of civilization for its cause.'

Eventually Byron came to the conclusion, not long after Stanhope's arrival, that of the Greek leaders Prince Mavrocordato was the most responsible and offered the best hope for Greece. Byron accordingly advanced a substantial loan to his Provisional Government, and in December 1823 sailed for Missolonghi, a swampy seaport in Western Greece where Mavrocordato was established. Here Stanhope devoted himself to setting up a printing-press for his newspaper, while Byron, beset on all sides by demands for money, began trying to organize an artillery corps and prepare for an attack on Lepanto. But William Parry, the engineer in charge of the arsenal sent out by the London Committee, arrived at Missolonghi, without Congreve rockets (then the latest thing in offensive weapons; they had been used

* *That Greece Might Still Be Free*, William St Clair, O.U.P., 1972.

at Waterloo) or the means to make them. On the very eve of the
march to Lepanto Byron's Souliots, or Albanian mercenaries,
disrupted everything by a sudden demand for more pay. A few
days later one of them murdered a Swedish artillery officer, and
Missolonghi was in an uproar. Towards the end of February
1824 the 'Typographical Colonel', as Byron nicknamed Stanhope,
left for Athens to set up another of his printing-presses.

Trelawny did not accompany Byron as far as Missolonghi. He
had left Cephalonia in September 1823 with Hamilton Browne,
another member of Byron's party, to obtain information and get
in touch with the Greek leaders. Trelawny had no intention of
playing second fiddle to Byron. When eventually he and Browne
reached Athens they met a figure who at once fascinated Trelawny: the Klepht chieftain Odysseus Androutzos who at this
time controlled Athens and eastern Greece. Odysseus preferred being an independent chief and had no great belief in the
eventual success of the Greek uprising, but was ready to turn it
and anything else to account. He was a rascal though not quite
the scoundrel he has been depicted. According to St Clair,
Odysseus's domain, unlike most of Greece, 'gave the appearance
of being under an efficient government, well-policed, with
reasonably fair local administration and access to justice'. A
contemporary wrote in 1825, 'Bred as he was in the Court of
Ali Pasha [the Turkish despot], the wonder is not that Ulysses
[i.e. Odysseus] should have vices, but that he should have any
good qualities.' Odysseus was above all a man of action, a
fighter, even if most of his fighting was sheer brigandage. So
exotic figure was bound to make an immediate appeal to Trelawny's romantic susceptibilities. More Byronic than Byron – like
most of the Philhellenes who came to fight for Greek liberty – it
is no wonder that Trelawny fell for Odysseus and poured scorn,
and worse, on Byron's unromantic but realistic adherence to the
bespectacled and bourgeois-looking Prince Mavrocordato. After
Byron's death he wrote almost hysterically to Mary Shelley:
'Your wooden god, Mavrocordato ... wants kings and Con-
gresses; a poor, weak, cowardly, shuffling fellow' – whereas
Odysseus was 'a noble fellow, a gallant *soldier*, and a man of
most wonderful mind, with as little bigotry as Shelley, and nearly

as much imagination; he is a glorious being. I have lived with him – he calls me brother – wants to connect me with his family.' It is not surprising that Mary Shelley, in replying, hoped Trelawny would 'escape from the sorceries of Ulysses'.

In February 1824 Colonel Stanhope joined Trelawny and Odysseus at Athens. The latter must have been delighted. All Greeks knew that Byron had untold sums of gold at his disposal (a loan of £800,000 had been raised on the strength of his name – more than the entire revenue of Greece), and here Odysseus was with Byron's friend Trelawny, and Byron's colleague, the crackpot Colonel. Odysseus must have felt the money was as good as in the bag. Naturally he played Colonel Stanhope along, enthusiastically agreeing to the setting up of schools on the Lancastrian system, the establishment of a utilitarian society, and, of course, a free press (the Colonel's Greek newspaper eventually did come out and reached a circulation of forty). The next thing was to get hold of Byron himself. Odysseus proposed that Byron and Mavrocordato should come to a congress at Salona. Trelawny was dispatched to fetch them from Missolonghi. But he had been only two days on the road when he was met by a messenger with the news that Byron was dead. On 9 April Byron had caught a feverish chill. At Missolonghi four doctors were available. They scoured his bowels with emetics and castor oil, and further debilitated his resistance with repeated bleedings, until on 19 April he succumbed.

Torrential rains had been falling – roads were almost impassable, rivers unfordable. Trelawny, with his usual vagueness, says that he arrived at Missolonghi on 24 or 25 April, in time to see Byron's body before it was sealed up in a coffin for transportation to England, and in time to make his notorious inspection of the poet's malformed feet.* Very considerable doubt exsits whether this inspection ever took place. Doris Langley Moore, in *The Late Lord Byron*, claims that 'close study of a substantial quantity of published and unpublished Missolonghi correspondence reveals that Trelawny could not have arrived before 26

---

* In the *Records* Trelawny's description of Byron's feet differs substantially from that in the earlier *Recollections*. For a discussion of the problem see Note 77, where Trelawny's original description is printed.

April because of the state of the roads.' The date of Trelawny's arrival at Missolonghi is crucial because an official document exists (published in Harold Nicolson's *Byron, The Last Journey*) certifying that Byron's coffin was hermetically sealed in the presence of witnesses on 25 April – not the 29th as given in Moore's *Life of Byron*.* There is also the point that none of Trelawny's contemporary letters which survive make any mention of his having seen Byron's corpse. In fact there would seem to be no evidence that Trelawny ever claimed to have seen Byron's body, let alone his deformed feet, till he published the story in the *Recollections* of 1858. By then almost everyone who had been present at Missolonghi was dead and buried. There is, however, one contemporary witness to support Trelawny. A member of Byron's medical entourage, Julius Millingen, wrote in his *Memoirs of the Affairs of Greece*, published in 1831:

On the 23rd of April Mr E. Trelawney [sic] arrived at Mesolonghi. Scarcely had he been informed by Mr Finlay of Lord Byron's indisposition, than he left Salona, and hastened to visit his friend. But he arrived only to print a last kiss on his pallid lips.

Millingen's account appeared more than a quarter of a century before the publication of Trelawny's *Recollections*, and certainly substantiated his claim to have seen the body of the poet before the sealing of the coffin. There was no reason for Millingen to have invented the incident – in fact his book embodies a savage attack on Trelawny, ridiculing his conduct and excessive admiration for Odysseus, even accusing him of having set up a harem in Athens. This libel drew from Trelawny a blistering public reply couched in superb invective.†

---

*Moore probably copied a mistake in Count Pietro Gamba's *Narrative of Lord Byron's Last Journey to Greece* (1825).

† In the *London Gazette*, 12 February 1831. Unfortunately Millingen's memoirs are not exactly reliable. Millingen himself was a thoroughly nasty piece of work. Not only was he one of the doctors who helped to murder Byron but even sent in a bill of £200 to the poet's executors for his services ('Lords do not die every day'). He deserted the Greek cause to serve under the Turks and lived for fifty years at Constantinople, where he was physician to five sultans. He died in 1878.

Byron died believing that his efforts in Greece had gone for
nothing.* In fact his death at Missolonghi was the crucial event
of the Greek war of independence, for it provoked an international wave of enthusiasm for the Geeks and their cause.
Three years later a combined French, British and Russian fleet
defeated the Turks at the Battle of Navarino, and Greece was
free.

As for Trelawny, his involvement with Odysseus led to dis-
comfiture and anticlimax; eventually it nearly cost him his life.
After Byron's death he returned to Odysseus at Salona, taking
with him, despite bitter opposition from the hated Mavrocordato,
the guns and munitions that the London Greek Committee had
sent to Missolonghi. While Odysseus went off to establish communication with his lieutenants, Trelawny remained in charge
of the Klepht chieftain's stronghold, a romantic and impregnable
cavern in the cliffs of Parnassus which could be reached only by
ladders bolted to the rock. About this time Trelawny married
Odysseus' half-sister, Tersitza Kamenou, a girl of about twelve
or thirteen. It was obviously in Odysseus's interests to ally himself with an Englishman who might help him to a share of
London Committee gold. But in December 1824 Odysseus decided to change sides – or at any rate to make a temporary peace
with the Ottoman Government. Trelawny must have been disenchanted; he tried, but failed, to get Odysseus aboard a ship
bound for the British-held Ionian islands. Eventually Odysseus
was captured by his former Greek friends in April 1825, and
confined to a tower on the Acropolis, at the bottom of which,

---

*So did Trelawny at the time. His jealousy of Byron, and the spell in
which Odysseus held him, comes out in a typically immoderate outburst to
Mary Shelley, written from Odysseus' cave and dated August 1824 : 'Byron
and I took the diametrically opposite roads in Greece – I in the Eastern, he
in the Western . . . Five months he dozed away. By the gods! the lies that
are said in his praise and urge one to speak the truth. It is well for his name,
and better for Greece, that he is dead . . . the little that he did was in favour
of the aristocrats, to destroy the republic, and smooth the road for a foreign
King. But he is dead, and I now feel my face burn with shame that so weak
and ignoble a soul could so long have influenced me. It is a degrading
reflection, and ever will be. I wish that he had lived a little longer, that he
might have witnessed how I would have soared above him here, how I
would have triumphed over his mean spirit.'

a few months later, was found his dead body, probably murdered while attempting to escape. Meanwhile Trelawny himself, as he so graphically describes in the *Records*, was victim of a treacherous but unsuccessful attempt at assassination at the hands of a Scotch adventurer called Fenton, who may or may not have been in the pay of Mavrocordato's Greek Provisional Government. Though desperately wounded, Trelawny recovered, and was evacuated to Cephalonia with his Greek bride in a British naval vessel. He remained in the Ionian islands for two years, finally returning to England in 1828.

The *Records* ends with the events of 1825. But here it may be as well to give a brief sketch of the rest of Trelawny's life. He did not bring Tersitza back to England with him. They quarrelled – it is a typical Trelawny story – because he preferred her to wear the native Greek costume. When the spirited Tersitza took no notice, Trelawny threatened to cut her hair off if she disobeyed. One day he found her in a dress she had ordered from Paris. Without a word he drew his dagger and cut off her hair. Without a word Tersitza got up and left the house for good. She had borne him a daughter named Zella, and after their separation gave birth to another, which died. According to one account, when the baby was born Tersitza was living in a convent while taking divorce proceedings against Trelawny. As it was against the rules of the convent to rear a child within its walls, the Mother Superior had the baby packed in a basket and sent to the father. Feeling that its place was with its mother, Trelawny promptly sent it back; but the Mother Superior inflexibly returned the basket. On opening it Trelawny found the child dead. A less *grand guignol*, and perhaps more probable, version of the story says that Trelawny merely put the baby out to nurse; it did not live, so he returned the body to the convent. Tersitza, by the by, eventually married one of her own countrymen and died a prosperous old lady in 1870.

After his return to England in 1828 Trelawny decided that Italy was the place for him. To Florence he went, and found there a personality not unlike his own – the volcanic Walter Savage Landor – and also Charles Armitage Brown, the friend of Keats. These two persuaded him to attempt an autobiography.

With their advice and encouragement he produced the *Adventures of a Younger Son,* for which Mary Shelley helped to find a London publisher in 1831. Each chapter was headed by a quotation from Byron, Shelley, or Keats – and no others, as these three were for Trelawny 'the poets of liberty'. The book was a success, and the epigraphs must have done something to revive interest in the poetry of Keats and Shelley, an interest which hardly existed in 1831. In 1832 Trelawny returned to England with his Greek daughter, Zella.

A year later he was off again, this time to America, where he met and laid siege to the actress Fanny Kemble, with whom he paid a visit to Niagara Falls. Though fascinated, Fanny Kemble had the sense to turn him down. This is how she describes him in her journal for 1835 :

A man with the proportions of a giant for strength and agility: taller, straighter, and broader than most men; yet with the most listless, indolent carelessness of gait; and an uncertain, wandering way of dropping his feet to the ground, as if he didn't know where he was going, and didn't much wish to go anywhere. His face is as dark as a moor's; with a wild, strange look about the eyes and forehead, and a mark like a scar upon his cheek; his whole appearance giving one an idea of toil, hardship, and wild adventure.

In America Trelawny performed the last of his romantic exploits. He swam the Niagara, nearly drowning himself in the process, and commemorated the feat in one of the best of his imaginatively realized set-piece descriptions.* After that he travelled round the United States, and at Charleston bought and freed a Negro slave. But by 1835 Trelawny was back in England. He dabbled in Radical politics, becoming more and more disillusioned with Mary Shelley's growing conformism. In 1839 he eloped with a friend of hers, Lady Augusta Goring, the wife of Sir Harry Vane Goring.

Trelawny eventually married Lady Augusta after her husband had divorced her – again by Act of Parliament – in 1841. He bought an estate near Usk in Monmouthshire and set up, not unsuccessfully, as a farmer and horticulturist. But in 1858, the

---

* *A Swim in the Rapids of Niagara*, published posthumously in H. Buxton Forman's *Letters of Edward John Trelawny* (1910).

year of the publication of *Recollections of the Last Days of Shelley and Byron*, the last of his marriages came to an end. Still a law unto himself at sixty-six, Trelawny brought a young woman into the house as his mistress. Lady Augusta would not stand for it. She left him. Soon afterwards Trelawny sold the estate and returned to London.

For the next ten years he lived mostly at Putney. In London he came to know Swinburne, who was to compose a peculiarly awful elegy for Trelawny when the time came. He also met W. M. Rossetti, brother of Dante Gabriel and Christina Rossetti, and one-time secretary of the Pre-Raphaelite Brotherhood, now a civil servant and indefatigable snapper-up of literary reminiscences. Rossetti never tired of pumping Trelawny for anecdotes of Shelley and Byron. It was through Rossetti's prompting, encouragement, and assistance, that the revised and enlarged edition of the *Recollections*, retitled *Records of Shelley, Byron, and the Author*, was completed and published in 1878. In his last years Trelawny sat to Millais for his famous picture 'The North-West Passage'. He did not sit willingly, consenting only on condition that Lady Millais took a course of Turkish baths to give publicity to a company in which he had an interest. In Millais' picture Trelawny is presented as a battered old sea-dog: a grizzled ruffian with a glass of grog at one elbow and a faraway look in his eyes. A Victorian miss reads aloud to him in a room draped with charts and nautical paraphernalia. Trelawny was furious when he saw it.

From 1869 till his death Trelawny lived mainly in a cottage near Worthing with a Miss Taylor, whom he described as his niece. To the end he was as tough as old boots. Every day, till well into his eighties, he rode to the sea for a swim, dug in his garden (which he had turned into a bird sanctuary), or chopped wood. On 13 August 1881, after a short illness, he died at the age of eighty-nine. His body was cremated and brought to Rome, where it lies buried next to Shelley in the grave that he had bought for it nearly sixty years before.

A curious, unsatisfactory life, but far from dull. It is not difficult to give chapter and verse to justify Harold Nicolson's public-school verdict on Trelawny – 'a liar and a cad'. In her excellent but confessedly partisan study of Byron's posthumous reputation, Doris Langley Moore has done just that. Trelawny can be written off as a bit of a mountebank, a bit of a fraud, a bit of a ruffian, even a bit of a clown. As he wrote to Claire Clairmont when he was eighty : 'Who can look back with satisfaction? – not me – I am amazed at the vanity and folly of my past life – there is hardly an act I approve of – my first impulses were often good; but I seldom acted on them – I seldom saw things as they were – vanity and imagination deluded me.'

This is the sort of fundamental spontaneous honesty that makes it difficult to dismiss Trelawny. He was a simple soul and a complex character, the sum of the contradiction of many qualities. He had a clear head but poor judgement. A man of strong feeling, much gusto, moral and physical courage; imaginative but absolutely without compassion; coarse yet sensitive, histrionic yet commonsensical, generous, magnanimous, but perfectly ruthless. He was independent-minded, unconformist, free of cant, yet liable to the hypnosis of his own enthusiasms. Vain, almost a narcissist; yet a compulsive hero-worshipper. He was not impressed by rank, status, or even character, but owned a Celtic susceptibility to temperament and genius. Though almost uneducated (his formal schooling ended when he was thirteen), with only a rudimentary mastery of spelling or even grammar, he was gifted with a vigorous prose style and an intuitive perception that enabled him to appreciate the stature of contemporaries like Shelley, Keats, Blake, even George Eliot, well before they were awarded general recognition. All these failings and virtues go into his *Records of Shelley, Byron, and the Author*. Few books are so completely a realization of their writer's temperament and personality; that is one reason why it is alive and vivid.

As for the vexed question of Trelawny's credibility, research has established that as a record of his teens the *Adventures of a Younger Son* contains no more than one-tenth of truth. Which doesn't necessarily mean that the remainder is sheer or mere fabrication. To a great extent Trelawny's imaginary adventures in the Java seas follow his real ones, except that in the former he presents himself as a privateer eluding the British Navy when in fact he was a British naval officer chasing privateers.

And it becomes obvious that some of the more romantic incidents in the *Adventures* are based on later happenings which he was afterwards to recount in the *Records of Shelley, Byron, and the Author*. When one thinks of it, the mysterious and evidently fictitious French buccaneer, 'De Ruyter', bears an uncommon resemblance to the actual brigand chief, Odysseus Androutzos, whom Trelawny hero-worshipped when he was in Greece with Byron. The cremation of Zella's body on the sea-shore parallels the burning of Shelley on the beach at Viareggio, even to the detail of the burning of Trelawny's hands at Zella's pyre. The very name 'Zella' is not phonetically far removed from 'Shelley'. And in Greece Trelawny really married a thirteen-year-old girl – if not a high-born Arab, at any rate the half-sister of a brigand chief. Their child, by the by, was christened Zella . . .

In the matter of truth and falsehood the most controversial incident in the *Records* is probably the famous or infamous episode at Missolonghi, when Trelawny lifted the covering from the feet of Byron's corpse to ascertain the nature of their deformity. At the time that this story first appeared in the *Recollections* Trelawny seems to have been no more than mildly taken aback by the shocked reaction to the indelicacy of feeling that his action was felt to exhibit. However, twenty years later he modified his account in the *Records*; at the same time offering a different, not to say contradictory, description of the appearance of Byron's club feet.* He must have realized that the two versions would be compared. Did he set eyes on Byron's body at all? The likelihood is that Trelawny arrived at Missolonghi after Byron's coffin had been sealed, and so had no chance of even seeing the corpse – that is, if one discounts Millingen's statement that Trelawny arrived in time 'to imprint a last kiss on his pallid lips'. If Trelawny's story about the feet is pure invention, what was the purpose? The answer may be that because Byron's deformity was one of the cardinal elements of the Byronic legend, it was a story which Trelawny *had* to invent. He was a myth-maker with an eye to his audience. Byron was sensitive about his deformity, but not preoccupied with it to the same extent or in the same way that Trelawny was, and along with Trelawny,

*see Note 77.

Byron's public. On their behalf, in imagination if not in fact, Trelawny lifted up the shroud and saw 'the form and features of an Apollo, with the feet and legs of a sylvan satyr', which was exactly what Byron's public expected to see, if for no other reason than that it embodied the image of himself that Byron, in his poetry, letters and conversation, loved to project: the flawed, Romantic hero.

As H. J. Massingham remarks in his biography, *The Friend of Shelley*, 'Trelawny's contribution to the Romantic Revolution is Trelawny.' Whether from deliberate choice or from the combination of his own character, temperament, and the times in which he lived, Trelawny turned himself into an embodiment, or at least a simulacrum, of the Romantic concept of the individual, the free soul at odds with the emergent mass society produced by the industrial revolution, in dissent against its bourgeois and philistine values and conventions.

He was not only a Romantic, he was a romancer. Certainly his better anecdotes shine with the lustre of many retellings. As Roy Campbell remarks of himself in *Broken Record*: 'My memory and imagination work as one; by force of recounting them [i.e. his adventures] they have assumed more elegant shapes, and I am not one to bore you with a list of facts.' Such cavalier dealing is naturally not accounted a virtue by fact-collecting biographers. But Trelawny's attitude to truth, like Campbell's, was more than a raconteur's; it was nearer to that of a bard, of a weaver of legend. An attitude shared by T. E. Lawrence, whose *Seven Pillars of Wisdom* has been described as less history than 'imaginative reconstruction'. Indeed it was Harold Nicolson who linked Trelawny with Lawrence – and who dismissed the latter as a 'pathological fibber'. Trelawny might also be compared with his contemporary and fellow-Cornishman, George Borrow, whose *Lavengro* and *Romany Rye* belong with the *Adventures of a Younger Son* to the class of romancing autobiography, in which category might also be placed what are probably the best autobiographies of the twentieth century, George Moore's *Hail and Farewell*, and the various memoirs of Ford Madox Ford. (In parenthesis, Arthur Mizener seems demonstrably mistaken when he credits Ford with having 'practically invented a form of fictional reminiscences'.) Such writers take truth as the warp into which a weft of imagination may be woven. The web or embroidery that results is myth, but often an emblematic myth that recreates, makes explicit or at least illuminates some inherent truth or quality that strict facts may sometimes obscure.

For many of the dates and some of the facts the *Records of Shelley, Byron, and the Author* is not to be trusted; Trelawny is careless of both. His *Records*, like his *Adventures of a Younger Son*, is a Romantic novel presented as autobiography. Each celebrates a Romantic hero: De Ruyter/Odysseus, exemplar of the Romantic man of action, dominates the *Adventures*; Shelley, incarnation of the Romantic idea of a poet, is the focus of the *Records*. Yet, as Shelley's biographer Newman Ivey White says, again and again one hears in the *Records* 'the indefinable ring of truth'. Perhaps Ford Madox Ford's description of his own brand of autobiography may not be irrelevant to Trelawny's: 'Just a word to make plain the actual nature of this book. It consists of impressions. This book, in short, is full of inaccuracies as to facts, but its accuracy as to impressions is absolute.'

April 1972

Note on the Text

The text is that of the first edition of the *Records of Shelley, Byron, and the Author*, published 1878, including Trelawny's Preface and Appendix. This is substantially the same text as the *Recollections of the Last Days of Shelley and Byron*, published 1858, with few alterations and fewer omissions, but greatly expanded with additional material. All passages in the *Recollections* that do not appear in the *Records* have been reprinted in the Notes, where all significant alterations and additions to the original version are also indicated.

RECORDS OF

SHELLEY, BYRON,

AND THE AUTHOR.

BY

EDWARD JOHN TRELAWNY.

VOL. I.

ALDI

DISCIP.

ANGLVS

LONDON

BASIL MONTAGU PICKERING

196 PICCADILLY

1878

Contents

Chapter 1

Chapter 2

Chapter 3

Chapter 4

Chapter 8

Chapter 9

Chapter 10

Byron orders a yacht, and Shelley an open boat – Trelawny
and Williams go to the Gulf of Spezzia, and look over the Villa
Magni – Captain Roberts sees to building the vessels – Byron's
daily routine, and Shelley's – Shelley and Williams ardent in
the prospect of boating – The Shelleys go to Villa Magni –
Shelley's boat, the 'Don Juan' – Two letters from him to Trelawny, May and June 1822 – Prussic acid – Byron's yacht, the
'Bolivar' – Shelley and Williams inexpert in boating – Byron's
ignorance of nautical matters – Shelley's skiff upset close inshore
– He invites Mrs Williams and her children to go out in his skiff
– Proposes to 'solve the great mystery' – Mrs Williams beguiles
him to return – An instance of quasi-somnambulism in Shelley
– A visitor from Genoa arrives – Shelley enters the room un-
clothed after bathing – Trelawny, sailing to Leghorn, takes leave
of Shelley writing in the woods – Byron's villa at Monte Nero
near Leghorn – Arrival of Leigh Hunt and his family – Byron
out of humour with the household and publishing arrangements
with Hunt   p. 133

Chapter 11

Shelley and Williams arrive at Leghorn, and accompany the
Hunts to Pisa – Williams's last letter to his wife, and last entry
in Journal, July 4, 1822 – The squabble of Byron and his companions with the Sergeant-Major Masi in Pisa – Letter from
Shelley, and note from Mrs Shelley, as to this – Mrs Williams's
last letter to Shelley, July 6th – Shelley and Williams set sail from
Leghorn, July 8th – Trelawny prevented by quarantine regula-
tions from accompanying them – The squall in which Shelley
and Williams perished – An oar from the 'Don Juan' seen in an
Italian boat – Byron's emotion on hearing of Shelley's suspected
death – Trelawny searches, and finds the corpses of Shelley,
Williams, and the sailor-lad Vivian – He rides to Spezzia, and
breaks the news to the widows – The parting which had occurred
prior to Trelawny's leaving for Leghorn – Trelawny accompanies

Chapter 12

Chapter 13

Chapter 14

Chapter 15

Byron and the 'Liberal' – His disappointment and irritation –
Trelawny writes to Lieutenant Blaquiere, in London, about
Byron's interest in Greece – Blaquiere, on the part of the London
Committee, writes to Byron, and visits him – Byron resolves to
go to Greece – Conversation of Trelawny (years afterwards) with
Murray, about the sale of Byron's poems, and Moore's 'Life of
Byron' – In December 1822 Trelawny takes a riding tour in
Italy – Letter to him from Byron, June 1823 – Extracts from
letters from Capt. Roberts and Mrs Shelley regarding Byron,
May and June 1823 – Two other letters from Byron, June 1823
and August 1822 – And two others relating to a dispute of
his with Capt. Roberts, November 1822 – Incompatibility between Byron's nature and Hunt's   p. 205

Chapter 16

Trelawny starts for Genoa – Revisits Villa Magni – The bathing habits of the natives, and Shelley's comment thereon – Trelawny visits Byron at Albaro – Finds him busy over house-bills
– His arrogance and thrift – Byron, having chartered the brig
'Hercules,' takes Trelawny on board – Lumbering quality of
this vessel   p. 214

Chapter 17

Byron and Trelawny, with Count Pietro Gamba, Dr Bruno,
and suite, embark on the 'Hercules', 13 July 1823 – Delays in
getting a fair start – At Leghorn, Hamilton Browne and two
Greeks join them – Byron denounces the Neapolitan tyranny,
but, being urged to write some verses at once on the subject,
fails – His War-song for the Greeks – Conversation of Trelawny
with Byron, who would wish to be buried in the Pirates' Isle off
Maina – Another conversation : Mrs Leigh, Brougham, Southey
– Stories of ghosts and presentiment – Byron and Monk Lewis –
Stromboli, Scylla, Charybdis, Messina   p. 219

Chapter 18

Chapter 19

Chapter 20

Chapter 21

Chapter 22

Chapter 23

Appendix

Preface

'No living poet ever arrived at the fulness of his fame; the jury which sits in judgment upon a poet, belonging as he does to all time, must be composed of his peers: it must be impannelled by Time from the selectest of the wise of many generations.' – SHELLEY'S *Defence of Poetry*.

'There they saw a man clothed in white, and two men, Prejudice and Ill-will, continually casting dirt upon him. Now behold the dirt, whatsoever they cast at him would in a little time fall off again, and his garments would look as clear as if no dirt had been cast thereat.' – *Pilgrim's Progress*.

THESE two men who have left a stamp on the annals of our literature, Shelley and Byron, will interest a sect who, without priests or temples, believe in the divinity of the Muses and worship them. They alone will appreciate these records, and for them I am induced to state particulars which otherwise would die with me.

If our literature were confined to statistics and dry facts, it would be eternal winter. All our pains and aches and misadventures are dry facts, and all our pleasures spring from our imagination, which, like the sun, adorns everything. The poets create; they fill us with illusions which only Death proves delusions.

Our libraries are crammed with lives of distinguished men, and yet how rare it is to get a glimpse of the real man as he was in life. It is like unrolling an Egyptian mummy, wrapped in countless cerecloths and containing nothing but dry bones. In my brief records, first issued in 1858 and now re-issued with very large augmentations, I have endeavoured to portray men as men, as they were in their every-day lives. In public life men say and do the same things, and are as difficult to distinguish one from the other as sheep. Their writings are open to all the world; individual censure or praise should go for nothing.

Few, if any, can look back on their lives with satisfaction. Hitherto the highest mental attainments have proved incompatible with that which everyone is seeking – Happiness. Gray says: –

> 'When ignorance is bliss,
> 'Tis folly to be wise.'

The happiest human animals I have known bore the strongest affinity to house-dogs – satisfied with food and shelter, and only disturbed at the approach of beggary and rags, with stagnant brains and active instincts.

I knew Shelley the last year of his life, and Byron the last three years of his life. I was on the most intimate terms with both, and saw them almost every day. On my return to England after Shelley's death, I became more or less intimate with all the friends whom Shelley had in England, and I continued to know Mrs Shelley till her death.

That young men fresh from College and inflated with records of Greek and Roman history should rail at our humdrum life, and dissent from the institutions which had reduced us to this state, is no uncommon occurrence; but when they come in contact with the world these elevated notions are quickly rubbed off. It was not so with Shelley. Beginning at Oxford to question all things that were established in State and Church from time immemorial was considered by the orthodox as unprecedented audacity, and his being expelled from College and cast off from all his family, a just punishment. But the young reformer, with untamed energy of mind and body, fearlessly pursued his erratic course. As the pillory and imprisonment had been foolishly laid aside, there was no ready remedy to check the blasphemy spreading like a pestilence throughout the land.

If authors write their own lives, or if publishers get lives written of them, they are so anxious the author should cut a good figure that they sacrifice everything for that one object. They may tell the truth, but not the whole truth. It was so in Byron's memoirs written by himself. If Shelley had undertaken the same task, he would not have mentioned himself; he never did allude to himself, he ignored self. What the orthodox wrote against him was brief, and bitter; that soothes our self-complacency, and so we read it. If praise were as brief we could endure it; but to make an idol of a man, endowing him with every virtue, and declaring him infallible and guiltless of all human frailties, as a small sect of enthusiasts now do in chapter after chapter of eulogium, is nauseous and repulsive to every well-constituted mind. When Shelley was alive, fanatics have asked me if he was not the worst of men; now he is dead, another set of fanatics ask me if he was not perfect.

Shelley never was a boy in mind : whilst they of his age were playing marbles, he was reading. His mental hunger for knowledge was insatiable – no one ever saw him without a book in his hand or pocket.

At Eton, after an illness, the doctor who attended him took a liking to him, and Shelley borrowed his medical books and was deeply interested in chemistry from that time, and, unlike doctors, he experimented with some of the drugs on himself. The power of laudanum to soothe pain and give rest especially delighted him; he was cautioned, and knew it was wrong; the seductive power of that drug retained a hold on him during the rest of his life, used with extreme caution at first and at long intervals. People who take to opiates are enslaved and never abandon them; these may be traced in some of Shelley's flights of imagination, and fancies of supernatural appearances. On one occasion in London, and again in Italy, he so over-dosed himself that his life was only saved by those measures that are used to counteract the drug; but it must not be thought that, like De Quincey and many others, he habitually used it : he only took it on rare occasions, when in deep dejection. He was impatient of remonstrance, and so made a mystery of it. The effect of opiates is to deaden pain, but they benumb the vital powers and derange our vital organs; with Shelley they caused spasms. The professor of anatomy at the University of Pisa, Vaccà, was renowned for his skill in surgery and medicine, and he came to the conclusion that Shelley was drugging himself, and earnestly interdicted medicine in all its forms; he said that Shelley was perfectly well constituted and of a healthy and vigorous frame – he recommended his varying his diet. I often saw him in a state of nudity, and he always reminded me of a young Indian, strong-limbed and vigorous, and there were few men who would walk on broken ground at the pace he kept up; he beat us all in walking, and barring drugs and accidents, he might have lived as long as his father – to ninety.

Those desirous of knowing what Shelley really was in his natural state and habits, will find it in Jefferson Hogg's book, and in no other that I have seen. Hogg has painted him exactly as I knew him: his is the only written likeness that I have ever read of him; at the same time it is necessary to know that Hogg despised poetry, he thought it all nonsense, and barely tolerated Shakespeare. When I asked him why he did not continue the Life, he said, 'Those who asked me to write it did not want a likeness of the poet as he was, but as they thought he should be; there are literary men who undertake such jobs; Tom Moore and others, who compile Lives and will say anything that is desired; they would introduce their man as a heathen deity, with a flourish of trumpets, a big drum, and mad poets dancing, the muses singing, and the poet in a triumphal car, covered with spangles, and crowned with tinsel. I don't puff: I described him as he was, and they were shocked. It was his rare talents as a scholar that drew me to him. The greatest men are those who composed our laws and the judges who administer them, and if Shelley had put all his mind into the study of the law, instead of writing nonsensical rhapsodies, he would have been a great benefactor to the world, for he had the most acute intellect of any man I ever knew.' This being Hogg's idiosyncrasy – contempt of poets – it is unnecessary to say his criticism of Shelley's poetry was of no value; but what he says of the poet as a man is perfectly true, and so, valuable.

Leigh Hunt often said that he was the dearest friend Shelley had; I believe he was the most costly. His theory was that between friends everything should be in common; he said you could not do your friend a greater favour than constitute him your banker, and that he could receive no greater pleasure than answering your drafts: as Leigh Hunt had an ailing wife and seven children, those drafts were frequent. Mrs Shelley's father, Godwin, was another dear friend; his theory was that a man, labouring as he did for the advancement of knowledge, should be supported by those who agreed with the justness of his views. These two dear friends being heavily in debt, the poet had not the means of paying those debts, but the worldly philosopher, Godwin, having ascertained the poet's exact pecuniary position, as the heir of an entailed estate, suggested to him the antedating his inheritance, by raising money on post-obit bonds, and satisfied Shelley as to the expediency of so doing. The poet, always prepared for martyrdom, assented, and Godwin found the ready means of executing the project. Money was raised at cent. per cent; both his dear friends' debts were paid. But experience proves that this practice is not effective : those who are in the habit of allowing their expenses to exceed their earnings will not alter these habits whilst they have credit, and the debts of these claimants being paid their credit was strengthened. Shelley repeated the process in vain. Besides these dear friends, Shelley had less costly friends, who dipped their hands into his purse.

Borrowers remain borrowers as long as they can find lenders, and if this small sample of communism became general, it would rapidly lead us back to a primitive state. We all dislike work, and we are only supported in our labour by the hope of rest; but with a general system of communism there would be no urgent stimulant to compel us to work; probably we should return to cannibalism until a new beginning was made of civilization.

When Shelley had a son and heir he doubted his right to pauperize him; of himself he thought nothing, but he doubted his right to give away his son's inheritance, and so he stopped that ruinous system of post-obits, but he continued to the last to keep for himself only what was absolutely necessary, and to bestow the rest on his dear friends. Giving money without well considered, specific, and well defined objects is always foolish. It was fortunate Shelley had so few friends, for with the exception of Jefferson Hogg and Horace Smith they all used him as their purse. Schoolboys have an apt saying, if they get hold of a generous, open-handed boy, 'What's yours is mine, what's mine is my own;' and sailors say, 'Everyone for himself and the devil for us all.' This boys' saying was verified by Shelley's friends.

I one day pointed out to Shelley a picture which had great

natural beauty, a sylvan scene; there was a clear pool of water, with wild fowl, a doe and two fawns in the foreground, a timid hare with two leverets, and an impudent magpie, a ledge of rocks and a dense wood in the background; it was richly coloured, the sun just disappearing. I said, 'That's a picture that would be a pleasure for ever – all solemnity and solidity; it's a bit of heaven; any carnivorous animal, a fox, or a dog, or a man with a gun, would transform it into a semblance of hell. Why I like your poetry is, that you have none of these vermin. If you must have men or women, you create them to suit your ideal subjects. The poem you plume yourself on most is the "Prometheus Unbound."' Shelley said: 'If that is not durable poetry, tried by the severest test, I do not know what is. It is a lofty subject, not inadequately treated, and should not perish with me.' I answered: 'A man's mind must be richly stored before he can appreciate that poem. Williams and I talking of your poetry, he said he preferred the "Cenci;" I prefer the "Epipsychidion."' He opened his eyes wider. I observed: 'Our opinions are worth nothing. We both went to sea when we were eleven, and could have had no education; until near thirty we were wandering about the world, and had no leisure.' Shelley replied: 'You have the advantage; you saw the things that we read about; you gained knowledge from the living, and we from the dead.' This conversation took place in a room while we were waiting for a friend at Leghorn.

Shelley rarely read any book through; he was eager to get at the matter stripped of the verbiage. Novels were totally uninteresting to him, there was no reality or imagination in them; but he retained some of his early fondness for romances. After glancing at an old Italian romance, in which a Knight of Malta throws down the gauntlet defying all infidels, he remarked: 'I should have picked it up. All our knowledge is derived from infidels.'

There was a marked individuality in Shelley. In habits, manners, and all the ordinary occurrences of life, he never changed. He took no notice of what other people did; brave, frank, and outspoken, like a well-conditioned boy, well-bred and considerate for others, because he was totally devoid of selfishness and vanity. He did not laugh or even smile, he was always earnest. He had observed that people laughed at the misadventures of others, and therefore thought it cruel; but his eyes and face were so expressive that you could see all the workings within his mind in joy or sorrow. Beauty is said to be a fatal gift to women, and it may be added that genius is a fatal gift to men; they are born before their time and out of harmony with the things about them.

Byron, for eleven or twelve years, was the choice spirit of his age, and cheered on his way by the applause of multitudes; Shelley, on the contrary, for about the same space of time, as he himself said, was denounced as a Pariah; wherever recognized he was shunned. No two men could be more dissimilar in all ways, yet I have seldom known two men more unhappy.

I have been thus particular in describing the younger poet, as he was of a rare variety of the human species. I have met men similar to Byron, but never to Shelley; he was the ideal of what a poet should be.

E. J. T.
March 1878.

RECORDS OF
SHELLEY, BYRON, AND THE AUTHOR

Chapter 1

Thou hast like to a rock-built refuge stood
Above the blind and battling multitude:
In honoured poverty thy voice did weave
Songs consecrate to truth and liberty.

Sonnet to Wordsworth. — SHELLEY.

IN the summer of 1820 I was at Ouchy, a village on the margin of the lake of Geneva, in the Canton de Vaud. The most intelligent person I could find in the neighbourhood to talk to was a young bookseller at Lausanne, educated at a German University; he was familiar with the works of many most distinguished writers; his reading was not confined, as it generally is with men of his craft, to catalogues and indexes, for he was an earnest student, and loved literature more than lucre.

As Lausanne is one of the inland harbours of refuge in which wanderers from all countries seek shelter, his shelves contained works in all languages; he was a good linguist, and read the most attractive of them. 'The elevation of minds,' he said, 'was more important than the height of mountains (I was looking at a scale of the latter), and books are the standards to measure them by.' He used to translate for me passages from the works of Schiller, Kant, Göthe, and others, and write comments on their paradoxical, mystical, and metaphysical theories. One morning I saw my friend sitting under the acacias on the terrace in front of the house in which Gibbon had lived, and where he wrote the 'Decline and Fall'. He said, 'I am trying to sharpen my wits in this pungent air which gave such a keen edge to the great historian, so that I may fathom this book. Your modern poets, Byron, Scott, and Moore, I can read and understand as I walk along, but I have got hold of a book by one now that makes me

stop to take breath and think.' It was Shelley's 'Queen Mab.'
As I had never heard that name or title, I asked how he got the
volume. 'With a lot of new books in English, which I took in
exchange for old French ones. Not knowing the names of the
authors, I might not have looked into them, had not a pampered,
prying priest smelt this one in my lumber-room, and, after a
brief glance at the notes, exploded in wrath, shouting out, "In-
fidel, jacobin, leveller : nothing can stop this spread of blasphemy
but the stake and the faggot; the world is retrograding into
accursed heathenism and universal anarchy!" When the priest
had departed, I took up the small book he had thrown down,
saying, "Surely there must be something here worth tasting."
You know the proverb, "No person throws a stone at a tree that
does not bear fruit." '

'Priests do not,' I answered; 'so I, too, must have a bite of the
forbidden fruit. What do you think of it?'

'To my taste,' said the bookseller, 'the fruit is crude, but well-
flavoured; it requires a strong stomach to digest it; the writer is
an enthusiast, and has the true spirit of a poet; he aims at elevating, not, like Byron and Moore, levelling mankind. They say he
is but a boy, and this his first offering : if that be true, we shall
hear of him again and again.'

Some days after this conversation I walked to Lausanne, to
breakfast at the hotel with an old friend, Captain Daniel
Roberts, of the Navy. He was out sketching, but presently
came in accompanied by two English ladies, with whom he had
made acquaintance whilst drawing, and whom he brought to
our hotel. The husband of one of them soon followed. I saw by
their utilitarian garb, as well as by the blisters and blotches on
their cheeks, lips, and noses, that they were pedestrian tourists,
fresh from the snow-covered mountains, the blazing sun and
frosty air having acted on their unseasoned skins as boiling water
does on the lobster, by dyeing his dark coat scarlet. The man was
evidently a denizen of the north, his accent harsh, skin white, of
an angular and bony build, and self-confident and dogmatic in
his opinions. The precision and quaintness of his language, as
well as his eccentric remarks on common things, stimulated my
mind. Our icy islanders thaw rapidly when they have drifted

into warmer latitudes: broken loose from its anti-social system, mystic castes, coteries, sets and sects, they lay aside their purse-proud, tuft-hunting, and toadying ways, and are very apt to run riot in the enjoyment of all their senses. Besides we are compelled to talk in strange company, if not from good breeding, to prove our breed, as the gift of speech is often our principal if not sole distinction from the rest of the brute animals.

To return to our breakfast. The travellers, flushed with health, delighted with their excursion, and with appetites earned by bodily and mental activity, were in such high spirits that Roberts and I caught the infection of their mirth; we talked as loud and fast as if under the exhilarating influence of champagne, instead of such a sedative compound as *café au lait*. I can rescue nothing out of oblivion but a few last words. The stranger expressed his disgust at the introduction of carriages into the mountain districts of Switzerland, and at the old fogies who used them.

'As to the arbitrary, pitiless, Godless wretches,' he exclaimed, 'who have removed nature's landmarks by cutting roads through Alps and Apennines, until all things are reduced to the same dead level, they will be arraigned hereafter with the unjust: they have robbed the best specimens of what men should be of their freeholds in the mountains; the eagle, the black cock, and the red deer they have tamed or exterminated. The lover of nature can nowhere find a solitary nook to contemplate her beauties. Yesterday,' he continued, 'at the break of day, I scaled the most rugged height within my reach; it looked inaccessible; this pleasant delusion was quickly dispelled; I was rudely startled out of a deep reverie by the accursed jarring, jingling, and rumbling of a calèche, and harsh voices that drowned the torrent's fall.'

The stranger, now hearing a commotion in the street, sprang on his feet, looked out of the window, and rang the bell violently.

'Waiter,' he said, 'is that our carriage? Why did you not tell us? Come, lasses, be stirring, the freshness of the day is gone. You may rejoice in not having to walk; there is a chance of saving the remnants of skin the sun has left on our chins and noses – today we shall be stewed instead of barbecued.'

On their leaving the room to get ready for their journey, my friend Roberts told me the strangers were the poet Wordsworth, his wife and sister.[1]

Who could have divined this? I could see no trace, in the hard features and weather-stained brow of the outer man, of the divinity within him. In a few minutes the travellers re-appeared; we cordially shook hands, and agreed to meet again in Geneva. Now that I knew that I was talking to one of the veterans of the gentle craft, as there was no time to waste in idle ceremony, I asked him abruptly what he thought of Shelley as a poet.

'Nothing,' he replied, as abruptly.

Seeing my surprise, he added, 'A poet who has not produced a good poem before he is twenty-five, we may conclude cannot, and never will do so.'

'The Cenci!' I said eagerly.

'Won't do,' he replied, shaking his head, as he got into the carriage: a rough-coated Scotch terrier followed him.

'This hairy fellow is our flea-trap,' he shouted out as they started off.

When I recovered from the shock of having heard the harsh sentence passed by an elder bard on a younger brother of the Muses, I exclaimed,

'After all, poets are but earth. It is the old story – Envy – Cain and Abel. Professions, sects, and communities in general, right or wrong, hold together, men of the pen excepted; if one of their guild is worsted in the battle, they do as the rooks do by their inky brothers, fly from him, cawing and screaming; if they don't fire the shot, they sound the bugle to charge.'

I did not then know that the full-fledged author never reads the writings of his contemporaries, except to cut them up in a review – that being a work of love. In after years, Shelley being dead, Wordsworth confessed this fact; he was then induced to read some of Shelley's poems, and admitted that Shelley was the greatest master of harmonious verse in our modern literature.

Chapter 2

Clear, placid Leman! thy contrasted lake
With the wild world I dwelt in, is a thing
Which warns me with its stillness to forsake
Earth's troubled waters for a purer spring.
Childe Harold.

SHORTLY after I went to Geneva. In the largest country-house
(Plangeau) near that city lived a friend of mine, a Cornish
baronet, a good specimen of the old school; well-read, and
polished by long intercourse with intelligent men of many
nations. He retained a custom of the old barons, now obsolete –
his dining-table was open to all his friends; you were welcomed
at his table as often as it suited you to go there, without the
ceremony of inconvenient invitations.

At this truly hospitable house, I first saw three young men,
recently returned from India. They lived together at a pretty
villa (*Maison aux Grenades*, signifying the House of Pomegranates), situated on the shores of the lake, and at an easy walk
from the city of Geneva and the baronet's. Their names were
George Jervoice, of the Madras Artillery; E. E. Williams, and
Thomas Medwin, the two last, lieutenants on half-pay, late of
the 8th Dragoons.[2] Medwin was the chief medium that impressed
us with a desire to know Shelley; he had known him from
childhood; he talked of nothing but the inspired boy, his virtues
and his sufferings, so that, irrespective of his genius, we all
longed to know him. From all I could gather from him, Shelley
lived as he wrote, the life of a true poet, loving solitude, but by
no means a cynic. In the two or three months I was at Geneva,
I passed many agreeable days at the two villas I have mentioned.
Late in the autumn I was unexpectedly called to England; Jervoice and Medwin went to Italy; the Williamses determined on
passing the winter at Châlons sur Saône. I offered to drive them

there, in a light Swiss carriage of my own; and in the spring to rejoin them, and go on to Italy together in pursuit of Shelley.

Human animals can only endure a limited amount of pain or pleasure, excess of either is followed by insensibility. The Williamses, satiated with felicity at their charming villa on the cheerful lake of Geneva, resolved to leave it, and see how long they could exist deprived of everything they had been accustomed to. With such an object, a French provincial town was just the place to try the experiment. Châlons sur Saône was decided on. We commenced our journey in November, in an open carriage. After four days' drive through wind, rain, and mud, we arrived at Châlons in a sorry plight. The immense plain which surrounded the town was flooded; we took up our quarters at an hotel on the slimy banks of the Saône. What a contrast to the villa of pomegranates we had left, we all thought – but said nothing.

When I left them by the *malle-poste*, on my way to Paris, I felt as a man should feel when, stranded on a barren rock, he seizes the only boat and pushes off to the nearest land, leaving his forlorn comrades to perish miserably. After a course of spare diet of soupe maigre, bouilli, sour wine, and solitary confinement had restored their senses, they departed in the spring for the south, and never looked behind them until they had crossed the Alps. They went direct to the Shelleys; and amongst Williams's letters I find his first impressions of the poet, which I here transcribe:

Pisa, April 1821

My dear Trelawny,

We purpose wintering in Florence, and sheltering ourselves from the summer heat at a castle of a place, called Villa Poschi, at Pugnano, two leagues from hence, where, with Shelley for a companion, I promise myself a great deal of pleasure, sauntering in the shady retreats of the olive and chestnut woods that grow above our heads up the hill sides. He has a small boat building, only ten or twelve feet long, to go adventuring, as he calls it, up the many little rivers and canals that intersect this part of Italy; some of which pass through the most beautiful scenery imaginable, winding among the terraced gardens at the base of the neighbouring mountains, and opening into such lakes as Bientina, &c.

Shelley is certainly a man of most astonishing genius in appearance, extraordinarily young, of manners mild and amiable, but withal full of life and fun. His wonderful command of language, and the ease with which he speaks on what are generally considered abstruse subjects, are striking; in short, his ordinary conversation is akin to poetry, for he sees things in the most singular and pleasing lights; if he wrote as he talked, he would be popular enough. Lord Byron and others think him by far the most imaginative poet of the day. The style of his lordship's letters to him is quite that of a pupil, such as asking his opinion, and demanding his advice on certain points, &c. I must tell you, that the idea of the tragedy of 'Manfred,' and many of the philosophical, or rather metaphysical, notions interwoven in the composition of the fourth Canto of 'Childe Harold,' are of his suggestion; but this, of course, is between ourselves. A few nights ago I nearly put an end to the Poet and myself. We went to Leghorn, to see after the little boat, and, as the wind blew excessively hard, and fair, we resolved upon returning to Pisa in her, and accordingly started with a huge sail, and at 10 o'clock P.M. capsized her.

I commenced this letter yesterday morning, but was prevented from continuing it by the very person of whom I am speaking, who, having heard me complain of a pain in my chest since the time of our ducking, brought with him a doctor, and I am now writing to you in bed, with a blister on the part supposed to be affected. I am ordered to lie still and try to sleep, but I prefer sitting up and bringing this sheet to a conclusion. A General R., an Englishman, has been poisoned by his daughter and her paramour, a Venetian servant, by small doses of arsenic, so that the days of the 'Cenci' are revived, with this difference, that crimes seem to strengthen with keeping. Poor Beatrice was driven to parricide by long and unendurable outrages: in this last case, the parent was sacrificed by the lowest of human passions, the basis of many crimes. By the by, talking of Beatrice and the 'Cenci,' I have a horrid history to tell you of that unhappy girl, that it is impossible to put on paper : you will not wonder at the act, but admire the virtue (an odd expression, you will perhaps think) that inspired the blow. Adieu. Jane desires to be very kindly remembered, and believe me

Very sincerely yours,

E. E. Williams.

In a subsequent letter he gave me a foretaste of what I might expect to find in Lord Byron.

Pisa, December 1821

My dear Trelawny,

Why, how is this? I will swear that yesterday was Christmas Day, for I celebrated it at a splendid feast given by Lord Byron to what I call his Pistol Club – *i.e.* to Shelley, Medwin, a Mr Taaffe,[3] and myself, and was scarcely awake from the vision of it when your letter was put into my hands, dated 1st of *January*, 1822. Time flies fast enough, but you, in the rapidity of your motions, contrive to outwing the old fellow; rather take a plume or two from your mental pinions, and add them, like Mercury, to your heels, and let us see you before another year draws upon us. Forty years hence, my lad, you will treat the present with more respect than to *ante*-date the coming one. But I hope that time with you will always fly as unheeded as it now appears to do. Lord Byron is the very spirit of this place – that is, to those few to whom, like Mokannah, he has lifted his veil. When you asked me in your last letter if it was probable to become at all intimate with him, I replied in a manner which I considered it most prudent to do, from motives which are best explained when I see you. Now, however, I know him a great deal better, and I think I may safely say that that point will rest entirely with yourself. The eccentricities of an assumed character, which a total retirement from the world almost rendered a natural one, are daily wearing off. He sees none of the numerous English who are here, excepting those I have named. And of this I am selfishly glad, for one sees nothing of a man in mixed societies. It is difficult to move him, he says, when he is once fixed, but he seems bent upon joining our party at Spezzia next summer.

I shall reserve all that I have to say about the boat until we meet at the select commitee, which is intended to be held on that subject when you arrive here. Have a boat we must, and if we can get Roberts to build her, so much the better. We are settled here for the winter, perhaps many winters, for we have taken apartments and furnished them. This is a step that anchors a man at once, nay, moors him head and stern : you will find us at the Tre Palazzi, 349, Lung'Arno. Pray, remember me to Roberts; tell him he must be content to take me by the hand, though he should not discover a pipe *in* my mouth, or mustachios on it – the first makes me sick, and the last makes Jane so.

Bring with you any new books you may have. There is a Mrs B. here, with a litter of seven daughters : she is the gayest lady, and the only one who gives dances, for the young squaws are arriving at that age when, as Lord Byron says, they must waltz for their livelihood. When a man gets on this strain, the sooner he concludes his letter the better. Addio. Believe me

Very truly yours,

E. E. Williams.

Chapter 3

For nobody can write the life of a man but those who have ate and drank, and lived in social intercourse with him. — DR JOHNSON.

Men can be estimated by those who knew them not, only as they are represented by those who knew them. — IBID.

I WAS not accustomed to the town life I was then leading, and became as tired of society as townfolks are of solitude. The great evil in solitude is, that your brain lies idle; your muscles expand by exercise, and your wits contract from the want of it.

To obviate this evil and maintain the just equilibrium between the body and the brain, I determined to pass the coming winter in the wildest part of Italy, the Maremma, in the midst of the marshes and malaria, with my friends Roberts and Williams; keen sportsmen both – that part of the country being well stocked with woodcocks and wild fowl. For this purpose, I shipped an ample supply of dogs, guns, and other implements of the chase to Leghorn. For the exercise of my brain, I proposed passing my summer with Shelley and Byron, boating in the Mediterranean. After completing my arrangements, I started in the autumn by the French *malle-poste*, from Paris to Châlons, regained possession of the horse and cabriolet I had left with Williams, and drove myself to Geneva, where Roberts was waiting for me. After a short delay, I continued my journey south with Roberts in my Swiss carriage, so that we could go on or stop, where and when we pleased. By our method of travelling, we could sketch, shoot, fish, and observe everything at our leisure. If our progress was slow, it was most pleasant. We crossed Mount Cenis, and in due course arrived at Genoa. After a long stop at that city of painted palaces, anxious to see the Poet, I drove to Pisa alone. I arrived late, and after putting up my horse at the inn and dining, hastened to the Tre Palazzi, on the Lung' Arno, where the Shelleys and Williamses lived on different flats under the same roof, as is the custom on the Continent. The Williamses received me in their earnest cordial manner; we had a great deal to communicate to each other, and were in loud and animated conversation, when I was rather put out by observing in the passage near the open door, opposite to where I sat, a pair of glittering eyes steadily fixed on mine; it was too dark to make out whom they belonged to. With the acuteness of a woman, Mrs Williams's eyes followed the direction of mine, and going to the doorway, she laughingly said,

'Come in, Shelley, it's only our friend Tre just arrived.'

Swiftly gliding in, blushing like a girl, a tall thin stripling held out both his hands; and although I could hardly believe as I looked at his flushed, feminine, and artless face that it could be the Poet, I returned his warm pressure. After the ordinary greetings and courtesies he sat down and listened. I was silent from astonishment: was it possible this mild-looking beardless boy could be the veritable monster at war with all the world? – excommunicated by the Fathers of the Church, deprived of his civil rights by the fiat of a grim Lord Chancellor, discarded by every member of his family, and denounced by the rival sages of our literature as the founder of a Satanic school? I could not believe it; it must be a hoax.

It is difficult for the present generation to conceive the rancorous bigotry that existed fifty years ago.

Those who questioned the Divinity of Christ, or avowed their disbelief, were branded as felons, and every man's hand was against them.

Shelley, one of the most benevolent and humane men of his time, was shunned (as if he had a pestilential disease) from his anti-Christian writings before he was twenty-one years of age.[4]

He was habited like a boy, in a black jacket and trowsers, which he seemed to have outgrown, or his tailor, as is the custom, had most shamefully stinted him in his 'sizings'. Mrs Williams saw my embarrassment, and to relieve me asked Shelley what book he had in his hand. His face brightened, and he answered briskly.

'Calderon's "Magico Prodigioso;" I am translating some passages in it.'

'Oh, read it to us!'

Shoved off from the shore of common-place incidents that could not interest him, and fairly launched on a theme that did, he instantly became oblivious of everything but the book in his hand. The masterly manner in which he analysed the genius of the author, his lucid interpretation of the story, and the ease with which he translated into our language the most subtle and imaginative passages of the Spanish poet, were marvellous, as was his command of the two languages. After this touch of his quality I no longer doubted his identity; a dead silence ensued; looking up, I asked,

'Where is he?'

Mrs Williams said, 'Who? Shelley! Oh, he comes and goes like a spirit, no one knows when or where.'

Presently he reappeared with Mrs Shelley. She brought us back from the ideal world Shelley had left us in, to the real one, welcomed me to Italy, and asked me the news of London and Paris, the new books, operas, and bonnets, marriages, murders, and other marvels. The Poet vanished, and tea appeared. Mary Woolstonecraft (the authoress), the wife of William Godwin, died in 1797, in giving birth to their only child, Mary, married to the poet Shelley; so that at the time I am speaking of Mrs Shelley was twenty-four. Such a rare pedigree of genius was enough to interest me in her, irrespective of her own merits as an authoress. The most striking feature in her face was her calm, grey eyes; she was rather under the English standard of woman's height, very fair and light-haired, witty, social, and animated in the society of friends, though mournful in solitude; like Shelley, though in a minor degree, she had the power of expressing her thoughts in varied and appropriate words, derived from familiarity with the works of our vigorous old writers. Neither of them used obsolete or foreign words. This command of our language struck me the more as contrasted with the scanty vocabulary used by ladies in society, in which a score of poor hackneyed phrases suffice to express all that is felt or considered proper to reveal.

Chapter 4

This should have been a noble creature – he
Hath all the energy which would have made
A goodly frame of glorious elements
Had they been wisely mingled.

Manfred.

At two o'clock on the following day, in company with Shelley, I crossed the Ponte Vecchio, and went on the Lung' Arno to the Palazzo Lanfranchi, the residence of Lord Byron. We entered a large marble hall, ascended a giant staircase, passed through an equally large room over the hall, and were shown into a smaller apartment which had books and a billiard-table in it. A surly-looking bull-dog (Moretto) announced us, by growling, and the Pilgrim instantly advanced from an inner chamber, and stood before us. His halting gait was apparent, but he moved with quickness; and although pale, he looked as fresh, vigorous, and animated, as any man I ever saw. His pride, added to his having lived for many years alone, was the cause, I suppose, that he was embarrassed at first meeting with strangers; this he tried to conceal by an affectation of ease. After the interchange of common-place question and answer, he regained his self-possession, and turning to Shelley, said,

'As you are addicted to poesy, go and read the versicles I was delivered of last night, or rather this morning – that is, if you can. I am posed. I am getting scurrilous. There is a letter from Tom Moore; read, you are blarneyed in it ironically.'

He then took a cue, and asked me to play billiards; he struck the balls and moved about the table briskly, but neither played the game nor cared a rush about it, and chatted after this idle fashion:

'The purser of the frigate I went to Constantinople in called an officer *scurrilous* for alluding to his wig. Now, the day before I mount a wig – and I shall soon want one – I'll ride about with it on the pummel of my saddle, or stick it on my cane.

'In that same frigate, near the Dardanelles, we nearly ran down an American trader with his cargo of notions. Our captain, old Bathurst, hailed, and with the dignity of a Lord, asked him where he came from, and the name of his ship. The Yankee captain bellowed,

' "You copper-bottomed sarpent, I guess you'll know when I've reported you to Congress." '

The surprise I expressed by my looks was not at what he said, but that he could register such trifles in his memory. Of course with other such small anecdotes, his great triumph at having swum from Sestos to Abydos was not forgotten. I had come prepared to see a solemn mystery, and so far as I could judge from the first act it seemed to me very like a solemn farce. I forgot that great actors when off the stage are dull dogs; and that even the mighty Prospero, without his book and magic mantle, was but an ordinary mortal. At this juncture Shelley joined us; he never laid aside his book and magic mantle; he waved his wand, and Byron, after a faint show of defiance, stood mute; his quick perception of the truth of Shelley's comments on his poem transfixed him, and Shelley's earnestness and just criticism held him captive.

I was however struck with Byron's mental vivacity and wonderful memory; he defended himself with a variety of illustrations, precedents, and apt quotations from modern authorities, disputing Shelley's propositions, not by denying their truth as a whole, but in parts, and the subtle questions he put would have puzzled a less acute reasoner than the one he had to contend with. During this discussion I scanned the Pilgrim closely.

In external appearance Byron realized that ideal standard with which imagination adorns genius. He was in the prime of life, thirty-four; of middle height, five feet eight and a half inches; regular features, without a stain or furrow on his pallid skin, his shoulders broad, chest open, body and limbs finely proportioned. His small highly-finished head and curly hair had an airy and graceful appearance from the massiveness and length of his throat : you saw his genius in his eyes and lips. In short, Nature could do little more than she had done for him, both in outward form and in the inward spirit she had given to animate it. But all these rare gifts to his jaundiced imagination only served to make his one personal defect (lameness) the more apparent, as a flaw is magnified in a diamond when polished; and he brooded over that blemish, as sensitive minds will brood until they magnify a wart into a wen.

His lameness certainly helped to make him sceptical, cynical, and savage. There was no peculiarity in his dress, it was adapted to the climate: a tartan jacket braided – he said it was the Gordon pattern, and that his mother was of that race. A blue velvet cap with a gold band, and very loose nankeen trowsers, strapped down so as to cover his feet: his throat was not bare, as represented in drawings. At three o'clock, one of his servants announced that his horses were at the door, which broke off his discussion with Shelley, and we all followed him to the hall. At the outer door we found three or four very ordinary-looking horses; they had holsters on the saddles, and many other superfluous trappings, such as the Italians delight in, and Englishmen eschew. Shelley, and an Irish visitor just announced, mounted two of these sorry jades. I luckily had my own cattle. Byron got into a calèche, and did not mount his horse until we had cleared the gates of the town, to avoid, as he said, being stared at by the 'damned Englishers,' who generally congregated before his house on the Arno. After an hour or two of slow riding and lively talk – for he was generally in good spirits when on horseback – we stopped at a small *podére* on the roadside, and dismounting went into the house, in which we found a table with wine and cakes. From thence we proceeded into the vineyard at the back; the servant brought two brace of pistols, a cane was stuck in the ground, and a five-paul piece, the size of half-a-crown, placed in a slit at the top of the cane. Byron, Shelley, and I fired at fifteen paces, and one of us generally hit the cane or the coin; our firing was pretty equal; after five or six shots each, Byron pocketed the battered money and sauntered about the grounds. We then remounted. On our return homewards, Shelley urged Byron to complete something he had begun. Byron smiled and replied,

'John Murray, my patron and paymaster, says my plays won't act. I don't mind that, for I told him they were not written for the stage – but he adds, my poesy won't sell : that I do mind, for I have an "itching palm." He urges me to resume my old "Corsair style, to please the ladies." '

Shelley indignantly answered,

'That is very good logic for a bookseller, but not for an author : the shop interest is to supply the ephemeral demand of the day. It is not for him but you "to put a ring in the monster's nose" to keep him from mischief.'

Byron smiling at Shelley's warmth, said,

'John Murray is right, is not righteous : all I have yet written has been for women-kind; you must wait until I am forty, their influence will then die a natural death, and I will show the men what I can do.'

Shelley replied,

'Do it now – write nothing but what your conviction of its truth inspires you to write; you should give counsel to the wise, and not take it from the foolish. Time will reverse the judgment of the vulgar. Contemporary criticism only represents the amount of ignorance genius has to contend with.'

I was then and afterwards pleased and surprised at Byron's passiveness and docility in listening to Shelley – but all who heard him felt the charm of his simple, earnest manner; while Byron knew him to be exempt from the egotism, pedantry, coxcombry, and, more than all, the rivalry of authorship, and that he was the truest and most discriminating of his admirers.

Byron looking at the western sky, exclaimed,

'Where is the green your friend the Laker talks such fustian about,' meaning Coleridge –

> 'Gazing on the western sky,
> And its peculiar tint of yellow green.'
> *Dejection: an Ode.*

'Who ever,' asked Byron, 'saw a green sky?'

Shelley was silent, knowing that if he replied, Byron would give vent to his spleen. So I said, 'The sky in England is oftener green than blue.'

'Black, you mean,' rejoined Byron; and this discussion brought us to his door.

As he was dismounting he mentioned two odd words that would rhyme. I observed on the felicity he had shown in this art, repeating a couplet out of 'Don Juan;' he was both pacified and pleased at this, and putting his hand on my horse's crest, observed,

'If you are curious in these matters, look in Swift. I will send you a volume; he beats us all hollow; his rhymes are wonderful.'

And then we parted for that day, which I have been thus particular in recording, not only as it was the first of our acquaintance, but as containing as fair a sample as I can give of his appearance, ordinary habits, and conversation.[5]

A short time after I knew Byron I said to Shelley,

'How very unlike Byron is to what people say of him. I see no mystery about him – he is too free; he says things better not said. I shall take care what I say to him. He reads parts of letters from his London correspondents.' (Mrs Shelley smiled; she knew they cautioned Byron not to risk his popularity by coupling his name with Shelley's.) 'He is as impulsive and jealous as a woman, and may be as changeable.'

At a subsequent conversation Shelley called Mrs Shelley and said,

'Mary, Trelawny has found out Byron already. How stupid we were – how long it took us.'

'That,' she observed, 'is because he lives with the living, and we with the dead.'

I observed,

'Byron asked me if he were like the person I expected. I said, No. He went on: "They know nothing about me. How should they? My poesy is one thing, I am another. I am not such an anthropophagist as they make me. My poetry is a separate faculty. The ideal has no effect on the real character. I can only write when the *estro* is upon me; at all other times I am myself." '

Mrs Shelley was transcribing a drama of Byron's, and she repeated some lines out of it,

' "One, two, strikes the never merry clock." '

Shelley said,

'They are excellent, but he fails in the drama. He is too abstract and diffuse. We all must fail. Shakespeare is the lion in the path; he has done for the drama what the Greeks had done for sculpture – perfected it.'

MRS SHELLEY, laughing: Byron has the vanity to be jealous of Shakespeare.

SHELLEY: Byron's power is wonderful and not half wrought out. All may envy him; his wings will bear him higher; he grows stronger by every new effort.

On my mentioning a popular poem, Shelley said,

'Versifying and rhyming are very well, but they don't constitute a poem. Any subject that can be as well expressed in prose as verse is not poetry of a high class. A great portion of Pope's and Dryden's, and numerous other poets' works, would be as well in prose. Walter Scott's prose stories are excellent.'

Stopping at the entrance of his own abode on the Lung' Arno, at Pisa, Byron said,

'Can't ask you to dine, for my dinner is soda-water and biscuits; but come about nine, and we will have blue-ruin, or hock if you prefer it. There will be no one else; perhaps Medwin may come.'

TRE.: I promised the Shelleys. His banquet is less luxurious than yours – bread and unsophisticated water.

BYRON: The Snake neither eats nor drinks.

TRE.: I am not an air plant, and shall feed at the Locanda.

As the Poet was about to dismount, I said,

'You should know Medwin is taking notes of your talk.'

BYRON: He dare not publish them.

TRE.: If he outlives you he will.

BYRON: So many lies are told about me that Medwin won't be believed.

TRE.: As an Indian said to me, 'May be yes, may be no.' Medwin has no design to lie about you; he is credulous and will note your idle words.

BYRON: When I am dead I am nothing; whilst I'm alive I can keep them all in order with my pen or my pistol. If he publishes lies about me, you can say they are lies.

And so we parted.

When I mentioned this talk to the Shelleys, Mrs Shelley, smiling, said,

'That won't restrain, it will stimulate Byron; he will blab the more.'

Chapter 5

Strangers yet!
After years of life together,
After fair and stormy weather,
After travels in far lands,
After touch of wedded hands –
Why then joined – why ever met,
If they must be strangers yet?

LORD HOUGHTON.

Minds are so hardly matched, that even the first,
Though paired by God in paradise, were curst.

MEN of books, particularly Poets, are rarely men of action, their
mental energy exhausts their bodily powers. Byron has been
generally considered an exception to this rule, he certainly so
considered himself: and so he was. The idle English had become
home-keeping youths; from the long wars all over the world,
travelling had been impeded everywhere. Now that we have
peace, with the aid of steam and railroads the difficulties have
vanished.

In 1809 Byron first left England, rode on horseback through
Spain and Portugal, crossed the Mediterranean on board a
frigate, and landed in Greece; where he passed two years in
wandering through that country: this, with a trip to Smyrna,
Constantinople, Malta, and Gibraltar, generally on board our
men-of-war, where you have all the ease, comfort, and most of
the luxuries of your own homes, was at that time an adventurous
career for a Lord. Anything more luxurious than sailing on those
seas, and riding through those lands, and in such a blessed
climate, I know from experience, is not to be found in this world.
Taking into account the result of these travels as shown in his
works, he might well boast; he often said, if he had ever written
a line worth preserving, it was Greece that inspired it. After
this trip he returned to England, and remained there some years,

four or five; then abandoned it for ever, passed through the Netherlands, went up the Rhine, paused for some months in Switzerland, crossed the Alps into Italy, and never left that peninsula until the last year of his life.[6]

The Pilgrim moved about like a Pasha, with a host of attendants, and all that he and they required on the journey. So far as I could learn from Fletcher, his yeoman bold – and he had been with him from the time of his first leaving England – Byron, wherever he was, so far as it was practicable, pursued the same lazy, dawdling habits he continued during the time I knew him. He was seldom out of his bed before noon, when he drank a cup of very strong green tea, without sugar or milk. At two he ate a biscuit and drank soda-water. At three he mounted his horse and sauntered along the road – and generally the same road, – if alone, racking his brains for fitting matter and rhymes for the coming poem; he dined at seven, as frugally as anchorites are said in story-books to have done; at nine he visited the family of Count Gamba; on his return home he sat reading or composing until two or three o'clock in the morning, and then to bed, often feverish, restless, and exhausted – to dream, as he said, more than to sleep.

Something very urgent, backed by the importunity of those who had influence over him, could alone induce him to break through the routine I have described, for a day, and it was certain to be resumed on the next – he was constant in this alone.

His conversation was anything but literary except when Shelley was near him. The character he most commonly appeared in was of the free and easy sort, such as had been in vogue when he was in London, and George IV was Regent; and his talk was seasoned with anecdotes of the great actors on and off the stage, boxers, gamblers, duellists, drunkards, &c., &c., appropriately garnished with the slang and scandal of that day. Such things had all been in fashion, and were at that time considered accomplishments by gentlemen; and of this tribe of Mohawks the Prince Regent was the chief, and allowed to be the most perfect specimen. Byron, not knowing the tribe was extinct, still prided himself on having belonged to it; at nothing was he more indignant than at being treated as a man of letters, instead of as a

Lord and a man of fashion : this prevented foreigners and literary people from getting on with him, for they invariably so offended. His long absence had not effaced the mark John Bull brands his children with; the instant he loomed above the horizon, on foot or horseback, you saw at a glance he was a Britisher. He did not understand foreigners, nor they him; and, during the time I knew him, he associated with no Italians except the family of Count Gamba. He seemed to take an especial pleasure in making a clean breast to all new-comers, as if to mock their previous conceptions of him, and to give the lie to the portraits published of him.[7]

> 'The lunatic, the lover and the poet
> Are of imagination all compact,'

says our greatest Poet; and the Stoic philosophers denounced all poetry as lies. Men of genius are not to be measured by the ordinary standard of men; their organization is different; they stand higher and see farther; we hope to see the diviner part of human nature exemplified in the life of a pre-eminent poet. Byron disenchanted me. He saw it, and said, as we were riding together alone, shortly after I knew him,

'Now, confess, you expected to find me a "Timon of Athens," or a "Timur the Tartar : " or did you think I was a mere sing-song driveller of poesy, full of what I heard Braham at a rehearsal call "*Entusamusy*," and are you not mystified at finding me what I am – a man of the world – never in earnest – laughing at all things mundane?'

Then he muttered, as to himself,

> 'The world is a bundle of hay,
> Mankind are the asses who pull.'

Any man who cultivates his intellectual faculty so highly as to seem at times inspired, would be too much above us, if, on closer inspection, we should not find it alloyed with weaknesses akin to our own. Byron soon put you at your ease on this point. Godwin, in his 'Thoughts on Man,' says, 'Shakespeare, amongst all his varied characters, has not attempted to draw a perfect man;' and Pope says,

> 'A perfect man's a monster the world ne'er saw.'

At any rate I should not seek for a model amongst men of the pen; they are too thin-skinned and egotistical. The humour of the irascible poet depended on circumstances; when irritated by a recent letter from England, or memory of an old difference or by indigestion, he spared no one. Like a Malay under the influence of an overdose of his favourite drug, haschish, he ran a-muck, regardless of all consequences. In his perverse and moody humours, he would give vent to his Satanic vein. After a long silence, one day on horseback, he began,

'I have a conscience, although the world gives me no credit for it; I am now repenting, not of the few sins I have committed, but of the many I have not committed. There are things, too, we should not do, if they were not forbidden. My "Don Juan" was cast aside and almost forgotten, until I heard that the pharisaic synod in John Murray's back parlour had pronounced it as highly immoral, and unfit for publication. "Dost thou think, because thou art virtuous, there shall be no more cakes and ale?" Now my brain is throbbing, and must have vent. I opined gin was inspiration, but cant is stronger. To-day I had another letter warning me against the Snake (Shelley). He, alone, in this age of humbug, dares stem the current, as he did to-day the flooded Arno in his skiff, although I could not observe he made any progress. The attempt is better than being swept along as all the rest are, with the filthy garbage scoured from its banks.'

Taking advantage of this panegyric on Shelley, I observed, he might do him a great service at little cost, by a friendly word or two in his next work, such as he had bestowed on authors of less merit.

Assuming a knowing look, he continued,

'All trades have their mysteries; if we crack up a popular author, he repays us in the same coin, principal and interest. A friend may have repaid money lent – can't say any of mine have; but who ever heard of the interest being added thereto?'

I rejoined,

'By your own showing you are indebted to Shelley; some of his best verses are to express his admiration of your genius.'

'Ay,' he said, with a significant look, 'who reads them? If we puffed the Snake, it might not turn out a profitable investment.

If he cast off the slough of his mystifying metaphysics, he would want no puffing.'

Seeing I was not satisfied, he added,

'If we introduced Shelley to our readers, they might draw comparisons, and they are "*odorous*." '

After Shelley's death, Byron, in a letter to Moore, of the 2nd of August, 1822, says,

'There is another man gone, about whom the world was ill-naturedly, and ignorantly, and brutally mistaken. It will, perhaps, do him justice *now*, when he can be no better for it.'

In a letter to Murray, of an earlier date, he says,

'You were all mistaken about Shelley, who was without exception, the best and least selfish man I ever knew.'

And, again, he says, 'You are all mistaken about Shelley; you do not know how mild, how tolerant, how good he was.'

What Byron says of the world, that it will, perhaps, do Shelley justice when he can be no better for it, is far more applicable to himself. If the world erred, they did so in ignorance; Shelley was a myth to them. Byron had no such plea to offer.[8]

Talking of the distinguishing quality of the humans.

TRE.: Shelley says it is superstition – Landor, that we have the worst of all the animals and the best of none.

BYRON: Man is a two-legged reptile, crafty and venomous. – After a pause, coming close to me, and smiling cynically, Everybody hates everybody.

TRE.: That's in his way.

He took no notice of this; he urged his horse, and we trotted a mile or two, then resumed our talk.

BYRON: I wrote thirty-five lines of 'Don Juan' last night, or rather this morning; was stopped for a rhyme. It was in my head, there it stuck; strong waters could not loosen it, trotting has. I read it in a magazine, an old one, years ago, in a couplet quoted from Swift. He beat all the craft; he could find a rhyme for any word. To-night I shall write thirty more lines, and that will finish a canto – a thousand guineas. Murray now says pounds: I won't be stinted of my sizings. Murray told Tom Moore he was no judge of the morality; but sermons did not sell, and the 'Don' had a 'devil of a sale.' I must make him a sinner, but he shall reform and end as a saint. Who are your friends that passed us?

TRE.: A captain of the navy and his wife. He paid his ship off, and having nothing to do, spliced himself to a widow.

BYRON: Money?

TRE.: No, worse – two children.

BYRON: What marry a widow for? Could he not catch a mermaid? 'Well, God is a good man'; he supplies the widows and orphans with fools.

Another brisk trot, then a walk.

BYRON: Mrs Shelley demurs at my grammar and spelling. I am in good company – Cromwell and Napoleon, they were careless of grammar, but careful of the matter; so am I.

After ruminating, he came close, and said,

'What would you do when dared to do a thing?'

TRE.: Do it.

BYRON: Shelley was so trapped by a canting parson at the Mer de Glace; I am not to be caught by chaff. People talk of their hosts of friends: can any one name twelve intimate acquaintances? I don't feel friendship for any one, not even for Shelley. My London acquaintance I have no sympathy with.

TRE.: Tom Moore and Hobhouse?

BYRON: We have been comrades; we must have allies. Moore is the best convivial companion. Hobhouse is a good man of business, and I am the worst. If we have a good balance at our banker's, we shan't want friends. They make free with our scudi; gold is a jealous god.

TRE.: The Tuscans have a humane law; they imprison all beggars except the blind.

BYRON: They should imprison borrowers; they are the worst of beggars. Travelling in Greece, Hobhouse and I wrangled every day. His guide was Mitford's fabulous History. He had a greed for legendary lore, topography, inscriptions; gabbled in *lingua franca* to the Ephori of the villages, goatherds, and our dragoman. He would potter with map and compass at the foot of Pindus, Parnes, and Parnassus, to ascertain the site of some ancient temple or city. I rode my mule up them. They had haunted my dreams from boyhood; the pines, eagles, vultures, and owls, were descended from those Themistocles and Alexander had seen, and were not degenerated like the humans; the rocks and torrents the same. John Cam's dogged perseverance in pursuit of his hobby is to be envied; I have no hobby and no perseverance. I gazed at the stars, and ruminated; took no notes, asked no questions.

TRE.: Your memory did more than his notes. You wrote 'Childe Harold'; what have his notes produced?

BYRON: He said nature had intended him for a poet, but chance made him take to politics, and that I wrote prose better than poetry.

TRE.: That proves he has no poetry in him.

BYRON: If I am a poet – Gifford[9] says I am; I doubt it – the air of Greece made me one. I climbed to the haunts of Minerva and the Muses. – He leered at me with an ironical smile. – John Cam can plod at books twelve hours a day; one or two hours does for me, excepting Scott's – I read him through. Shelley wants me to read more and write less. My mind is vagrant; I can't do drudgery. Scott and Cobbett are the popular writers now, and their pens are never idle. You must go on; if you lag you are outstripped in the race. When a new book is sent me, I read the last chapter and then the first : if they are good, I may go through it. I like Cobbett's 'Register'; if I were Minister I would make him my Attorney-General. When Sam Rogers has hatched a stanza, he sends it round to his poetical friends for approval. His Italy has cost him thousands in illustrations; his brats are still-born. Why did you prevent his riding my black horse?

TRE.: He is a stumbler.

Byron glanced cynically.

Yes, he fell with me the second time I rode him; he is now reserved for my particular friends. A fall would do old Rogers some good; his blood is stagnant.

TRE.: He has a parboiled look; it's difficult to believe he is a poet.

BYRON: He is a banker and a poetizer. He feeds the needy critics, and they dub him poet. The black horse I bought of a captain of the Pope's guard at Ravenna, warranted. I sent for the captain and demanded my money paid. He refused; I waxed wroth. He blustered, and said he was descended from a noble

Roman family, was commander of a troop of his Holiness the Pope's Guard. 'Then I'll give you satisfaction.' I opened a chest in the hall and told him to choose his arms. I took a Spanish rapier; he had his sword. I drew my toledo, an heirloom, and went towards him. He faltered and retreated, and as I neared him, he exclaimed, 'I don't fight in the dark, and we are forbidden duelling.' As I lifted my arm to strike him he decamped in haste.

TRE.: Should you not, as a Carbonaro, have (as Iago has it) removed him by yerking him under the ribs? Your groom would have sacked him, dropped him in a hole in the yard or in the pine forest.

BYRON: You are a cool hand.

TRE.: At Ravenna they say manslaughter is not considered a heinous offence.

BYRON: It used not to be so, but it is now. Noblemen hired bravos. I am a respecter of the law. When I want to punish a man, I let an attorney loose at him – he tortures him, and so worries him to death.

Byron's great-uncle fought with swords, in a room in London, in the dusk of the evening, killed his opponent, and was tried for his life, and doubtless this was in Byron's mind when he challenged the captain to fight in the twilight, with swords, and without witnesses.

BYRON: A Frenchman visited me this morning. He said he was translating a poem of mine, and wished me to revise it. I told him I could not speak French.

TRE.: Can't you?

BYRON: I would not lower myself by speaking it like a German waiter at an hotel. The Frenchman expressed his astonishment, and then jabbered in vile English; said his wife was English, and she corrected him; asked me to refer to my poem. I told him I had no copy, that after they were sent to the publisher I saw no more of them. (If a copy were sent to him, he looked it over and gave it away directly.) I said I had never been in Paris, or any part of France. He was amazed, and asked why? When I left England, Paris was occupied by the allies. Foreigners are told that I write pretty verses, and they think I can do nothing else – that I am a literary grub. I could not endure to witness a country associated in my mind with so many and glorious deeds of art and arms so fallen, bullied by certain rascal officers, slaves in authority, the knaves of justice, her eagle chained, and the allied despots crowing over her. English money has done it!

TRE.: Shelley says he finds it far more irksome to write prose for publication than poetry.

BYRON: So do I. All this morning I was in labour at a letter to John Murray. It will be made public in his back parlour, where the rooks meet and will caw over it. They complain of my showing letters; mine go a regular circuit.

TRE.: Why do your London friends treat Shelley so cavalierly? they rarely notice him. He is as well born and bred as any of them. What are they afraid of?

BYRON, leeringly: He is not a Christian.

TRE.: Are they?

BYRON: Ask them.

TRE.: If I met the Devil at your table, I should treat him as a friend of yours.

Byron, scanning me keenly to see if I was jeering, said, 'The Devil is a Royal personage.'

Shelley, in his elegy on the death of Keats, gives this picture of himself: –

> 'Midst others of less note came one frail form,
> A phantom amongst men, companionless
> As the last cloud of an expiring storm,
> Whose thunder is its knell. He, as I guess,
> Had gazed on nature's naked loveliness
> Actæon-like; and now he fled astray
> With feeble steps o'er the world's wilderness;
> And his own thoughts along that rugged way
> Pursued, like raging hounds, their father and their prey.
> He came the last, neglected and apart,
> A herd-abandoned deer struck by the hunter's dart.
> All stood aloof.'

The next day, resuming the talk regarding Shelley –

BYRON: They don't dislike or fear Shelley; they are afraid of each other, and of poor innocent me. They spy a taint in my late writings, and think that I have fallen into bad hands. They say my orthodoxy is verging on heterodoxy. Their impression is, my popularity is declining. Cain, they opine, is a suggestion of Shelley. (Turning to me) You are the only one of my visitors they approve of. You saved Rogers[10] from a stumbling horse and a savage dog.

The dog story is this. On my nearing the passage leading to Byron's study, where Moretto was as a sentinel to give notice to his master of any stranger's approach, I heard the dog's low growl, and a voice trying to quiet him, and evidently terrified. I hastened up, and found Rogers in a fix. The dog knew me and so I convoyed the old poet through the pass. Byron was in the billiard-room, and I saw by his sinister look he had heard the row, knew it was Rogers, and maliciously enjoyed his visitor's terror. He advanced briskly towards him, saying, 'My dear Rogers, glad to see you; didn't know it was you,' went on bantering him, saying to me, 'Excuse us for five minutes,' took Rogers by the arm and led him into his *sanctum sanctorum*. He told me afterwards that on hearing Rogers's voice in the passage he was giving the finishing touches to the most savage satire on him that he had ever written, repeating the last lines. 'I had only time to put it under the sofa, and he sat on it.'

Byron's malice was caused by a London correspondent accusing Rogers as the author of scandalous stories relating to Byron. Rogers was a silent, cautious, and excessively timid man, and had the reputation of saying, in his quiet way, sarcastic things. If a man acquires this reputation, he is debited with all the ill-natured scandal that society gloats on. Byron believing this (I did not; there was no proof), he should have been on his guard in his talk. On the contrary, it excited the poet, like a perverse child, to what he designated mystifying him. This game of equivocation – *i.e.*, lying – had been in fashion with the young swells in Byron's time; to me it seemed simply perplexing people with exaggerated falsehoods. In this way Byron, to astonish and shock the demure and moral Rogers, and stock his budget, plied him with a highly-coloured catalogue of his delinquencies, glancing at me to mark his mystifications. Rogers was a good listener: his face expressed nothing, and he said nothing. My conviction was he believed nothing he had heard. Byron's intimates smiled at his vaunting of his vices, but comparative strangers stared, and noted his sayings to retail to their friends, and that is the way many scandals got abroad. George IV had made it the fashion, and the men about town were ashamed of being thought virtuous, and bragged of their profligacy. Byron, in his splenetic moods, if any one uttered moral or sentimental commonplace twaddle, sneered and scoffed, and denounced it as cant. The great poet, in the words of the greatest, 'Gave his worst of thoughts the worst of words.' Under the same provocation, I and others have done the same. Byron's words were not lost, but noted and circulated, ours forgotten. The nicknames given us in our youth are generally appropriate. Byron was designated 'Baby Byron;' it fitted him to a T – wayward, capricious, lured by glitter and false lights and his vivid imagination, ever screaming after new toys and then picking them to pieces to see what they were made of, with nothing satisfied.

Byron on one occasion said,

'What book is that?'

TRE.: The life of a Poet.

He looked at the last chapter, saying,

'If there is nothing in that, it's not worth reading.'

TRE.: There is birth, marriage, and death; a eulogy on the author's genius and tedious criticisms on his works; nothing of the individuality of the man.

BYRON: Literary lives are compiled for the bibliopolists, as puffs to sell their wares; they are nothing. When I die you will see mine, written by myself.

TRE.: Will it be published as you have written it?

BYRON: Yes; I leave it in safe hands – Tom Moore's.[11] He is pledged to publish, and omit words, but not garble facts. I have good security – he always wants money; my memoirs will bring it.

The poet could not forecast that Moore would get the money and not publish the book; that his bibliopolist's compilation – all puff and laudation to sell his stock – would be substituted – a lifeless life, giving no notion of the author, nothing told as Byron told it, and, excepting the letters it contains, unreadable and unread. Byron could not escape the poet's fate – his true life suppressed, and a bookish, elaborate eulogy of his poetry to sell his works substituted. Tom Moore, by his keen wit and continual practice, had perfected himself in the art of flattery; in his hands it was a fine art, and pleased all tastes. He deluded Byron into the belief that he was a thoroughly fearless and independent man; that he cared nothing for the world, its censure or praise; whereas Moore was the slave of forms, ceremony, and etiquette, excessively tenacious, and spoke of the big houses he frequented as if he controlled them. Moore's life is published : a sorry catalogue of lords, ladies, their dinners and parties. Where are they all? Vanished as shadows on the wall, 'alms for oblivion'. Moore will be remembered for his Irish melodies and his treachery in suppressing Byron's vindication of himself, particularly as he had read and approved of it and recommended the publication as necessary to prevent the fictitious slanders that might be spread after his death and that had been circulated during his life, and to set at rest the principal questions concerning his life. There was nothing in the memoirs that should have been omitted but the names of some people then living and some passages disconnected with his life. To these suggestions Byron readily assented.

What men say when two or three are gathered together in familiar talk I take no note of; they do not represent a man's deliberate sentiments. Byron never argued, said he could not. He admitted nothing and doubted everything; he had not made up his mind on any subject. His talk was in short sentences, generally in opposition. Mrs Shelley quoting with approval a sentiment from an Italian writer, Byron dissented, with sneers, and jibes, and irony. His reckless audacity and startling opinions made Mrs Shelley stare. Shelley, absorbed in thought, said little, and when Byron left she reproached her husband for not advocating his own opinions. She said,

'Could Byron mean what he said?'

Shelley answered,

'No, certainly not; Byron never is in earnest except in the morning, when he is talking to one person, with whom he is at his ease. I was with him at one o'clock. He told me he had been writing all night, and had had no food but biscuits for three days, but had taken strong stimulants. The long-continued strain on his nerves and brain, intensified by his capricious way of life, disorders his mind. He wants food and rest; he is feverish, and that makes him fitful.'

MRS SHELLEY:

'Great wit to madness nearly is allied.'

In company Byron talked in Don Juan's vein; with a companion with whom he was familiar he thought aloud; with strangers, as others do, but not at his ease. I have said enough to show him as he was, a thoroughly spoilt man. Lady Byron was equally spoilt in an opposite direction – self-willed, intolerant, jealous, and vindictive. She was a rigid Puritan : they are a brave and undaunted sect in self-reliance on their superiority over all other people, and fear nothing. Saints armed in righteousness prefer doing battle with great sinners, confident of their cause. Lady Byron, with the pertinacity of a zealot, plied the poet with holy texts from Scripture and moral maxims from pious writers. In his placid moments he submitted to the infliction; when her admonitions were out of season, and he was composing, or vexed with his own thoughts, he was not so passive. Most men, especially authors, are accustomed to pass their mornings in their studies, and are impatient of any intrusion, Byron excessively so. His wife, perhaps, thought that he was brooding mischief, and persistently interrupted him. He then would say things to shock and mortify her. She considered these self-accusations as his confessions, and took notes of them. Words spoken in the irritation of being interrupted were not allowed to sink into the ground, but registered, and produced in an evil hour as evidence to prove the poet was mad. This was the principal source from which all the misunderstandings arose. The lawyers said it proved him bad, not mad. We are so constructed that praise, excepting it is administered in infinitesimal globules, corrupts us. Excessive praise, such as Byron had been deluged with, no man ever bore and preserved his equanimity. If any one bestows a universal benefit on his species, and merits universal admiration, he never receives it; our loudest applause is lavished on those who amuse our idle hours.

On the disruption of Byron's marriage, the obloquy was cast on the poet; envy and malice, that lurk beneath the smiling surface of society, rejoiced in the opportunity of giving vent to their slanders. Any woman who had been strongly attached to him, and who had ordinary sense and consideration, might have lived with the poet. His lameness confined him much to the house, and made him the slave of custom and habit. He was sorely vexed if they were broken, though in everything else he was exceptionally tolerant, and of an easy, careless disposition if left to his own devices. He rarely parted with anything he was accustomed to, however useless or troublesome it became. Any one could live with him, excepting an inflexible and dogmatic saint; not that he objected to his wife's piety, for he saw no harm in that, but her inflicting it on him. The lady's theory was opposed to this: her mission was to reform him by her example and teaching. She had a smattering of science, mathematics, and metaphysics – a toy pet from her childhood, idolized by her parents and considered as a phenomenon by her country neighbours.

Women, when young, are usually pliant, and readily adapt themselves to any changes. Lady Byron was not of this flexible type: she had made up her mind on all subjects, and reversed the saying of Socrates, that 'all he had learnt was, he knew nothing.' She thought she knew everything. She was exacting, capricious, resentful, excessively jealous, suspicious, and credulous. She only lived with him one year out of her long life. Byron was not demonstrative of things appertaining to himself, especially to women, and Lady Byron judged men by her father and the country neighbours, and Byron was so dissimilar to them in all his ways as to bewilder her. She would come into his study when he was in the throes of composition, and finding he took no notice of her, say,

'Am I interrupting you?'

'Yes, most damnably.'

This was to her a dreadful shock; he thought nothing of it; he had received his greater shock in being interrupted.

She married him from vanity, and he married her to retrieve his broken fortune. They were brought together by the usual medium, lady matchmakers. There was no sympathy in choice or love, and so they parted; and although the envy and malice of the world took her part against Byron, and no justification on her part was called for, her baffled hopes rankled in her mind. During her life she kept up a confidential correspondence and intimacy with Byron's half-sister, until her death, and then gave vent to her spleen, irrespective of the injury to some still living.

A lady I had known at Florence made a short stay at Genoa.[12] She had known Lord and Lady Byron during the short time they had lived together. (This lady's husband had gone to Turin on professional business.) She enlightened me on the vexed question of Byron's wife. She said the lady was a formal, pedantic prude, ill-looking, ill-dressed, and ill-mannered; that she was peevish and jealous, and generally disliked. That Byron, elated by his excessive popularity with the public, treated men cavalierly, but was affable enough to the women, and they clustered round him; the men were sorely vexed. 'The news of his wife's leaving him they gave tongue to,' as my husband told me, 'like a pack of hounds, and would have hunted him to death. If women's voices could have been heard, they would have reversed the verdict of the men; in domestic differences they alone can see who is in the wrong.'

I observed that women gained by marriage the liberty we lost. 'As soon as they are free from durance, they try their hands on us.'

'Lady Byron,' observed the lady, 'was not, as you call it, in durance; she is said to have ruled her parents, the parson, and the school of her parish.'

I answered,

'The ancient poets were considered inspired; they were landmarks. The modern ones, shorn of their divine attributes, are yet defiant of the laws and usages that ordinary mortals submit to. The great poet of the Puritans, Milton, on his wife's leaving him, published his own divorce, and Byron, on a similar occasion, acted as if divorced.'

Having lent a friend, who was anxious to know the origin of the differences of Byron and his wife, a letter of Lady Byron's to read, these were his comments upon it : –

My dear Mr Trelawny,

I return you, with very many thanks, the copy of Lady Byron's letter, which speaks volumes, and seems to me to be in itself the strongest evidence of that incompatibility of disposition which culminated in separation. With such a woman Byron could not have lived long, and I rejoice to have at length discovered the cause of their mutual disagreement. Nothing further is needed, and I much regret that you are unable to give this letter to the world as a check to calumniation.

Yours ever sincerely,
R. E.[13]

Johnson, on being asked if marriage were natural to man, replied, 'Sir, it is so far from being natural for a man and woman to live in a state of marriage, that we find all the motive which they have for remaining in that connexion, and the restraints which society imposes to prevent separation, are hardly sufficient to keep them together.' Those who have undergone the operation will acknowledge the truth of the sage's words.

Poets, like priests, have hosts of communicants, and should be sworn to celibacy. A catalogue of the domestic grievances of the poets and their wives, from the omniscient Shakespeare and solemn Milton, to scoffing Byron and the martyr Shelley, would show that men of imagination all compact are devoid of what women call domestic virtues – that is, propriety of conduct and submission to the conventional customs of the time. Byron says : –

> 'But oh ! ye lords of ladies intellectual
> Inform us truly, have they not hen-peck'd you all ?'

and Shelley : –

> 'With one chain'd friend, perhaps a jealous foe,
> The dreariest and the longest journey go.'

Milton : –

> 'Thus they in mutual accusation spent
> The fruitless hours, but neither self-condemning;
> And of their vain contest appear'd no end.'

Shakespeare : –

> 'As for my wife,
> I would you had her spirit in such another.
> The third o' the world is yours; which, with a snaffle,
> You may pace easy, but not such a wife.'

Byron repeatedly told the story of his wife's leaving him on the plea of visiting her parents. They parted in the most friendly way, and she wrote him a playful and affectionate letter. He attributed much of the mischief to a confidential friend and maid that she had. She never returned, or assigned any reason for not doing so. She was disliked in society, from her prim and formal manners, and from assuming a moral superiority over the idle votaries of fashion, but when she parted from Byron all the envious and jealous saw that it was a good opportunity of damaging the reputation of the poet by exalting the merits of his wife. The higher they could elevate her, the lower would he sink in public estimation; so she was transformed into a suffering angel, and he covered with obloquy. Such is the envenomed malice of what is called good society. This was the cause of the turmoil made in London about so silly an affair, the real opinion remaining the same – they were all surprised that Byron could have married such an iceberg. He, after the separation, used all the means in his power to induce his wife to give her reason, publicly or privately, for leaving him. She would not speak until death had silenced the voices that would have answered her. Ask any lawyer, or person in the habit of taking evidence, if woman's or man's is the most to be relied on. Forty years after his death his wife produces notes she had taken nearly half a century past, accusing her liege lord of a heinous offence. Mrs Beecher Stowe, a New England Puritan of the deepest dye, is called into council, and these two pious and remorseless saints, after conferring, condemn the poet, and the stern Yankee lady puts on the black cap and passes sentence of death on the memory of a great man, without counsel being fee'd, or witnesses summoned on either side, and when all implicated are mouldering in their graves. If men's characters are to be thus summarily impugned and condemned, who is safe amongst the dead from being dragged from his grave and trailed in the mud as Cromwell was?

Chapter 6

Few things surpass old wine; and they may preach
    Who please, the more because they preach in vain.
Let us have wine and women, mirth and laughter,
Sermons and soda-water the day after.

                                    Don Juan.

BYRON has been accused of drinking deeply. Our universities,
certainly, did turn out more famous drinkers than scholars. In
the good old times, to drink lustily was the characteristic of all
Englishmen, just as tuft-hunting is now. Eternal swilling, and
the rank habits and braggadocio manners which it engendered,
came to a climax in George IV's reign. Since then, excessive
drinking has gone out of fashion, but an elaborate style of gas-
tronomy has come in to fill up the void; so there is not much
gained. Byron used to boast of the quantity of wine he had
drunk. He said, 'We young Whigs imbibed claret, and so saved
our constitutions: the Tories stuck to port, and destroyed theirs
and their country's.'

He bragged, too, of his prowess in riding, boxing, fencing,
and even walking; but to excel in these things feet are as necessary as hands. In the water a fin is better than a foot, and in that
element he did well; he was built for floating, – with a flexible
body, open chest, broad beam, and round limbs. If the sea were
smooth and warm, he would stay in it for hours; but as he seldom
indulged in this sport, and when he did, over-exerted himself,
he suffered severely; which observing, and knowing how deeply
he would be mortified at being beaten, I had the magnanimity
when contending with him to give in.

He had a misgiving in his mind that I was trifling with him;
and one day as we were on the shore, and the 'Bolivar' at anchor,
about three miles off, he insisted on our trying conclusions; we
were to swim to the yacht, dine in the sea alongside of her,
treading water the while, and then to return to the shore. It was

calm and hot, and seeing he would not be fobbed off, we started. I reached the boat a long time before he did; ordered the edibles to be ready, and floated until he arrived. We ate our fare leisurely, from off a grating that floated alongside, drank a bottle of ale, and I smoked a cigar, which he tried to extinguish, – as he never smoked. We then put about, and struck off towards the shore. We had not got a hundred yards on our passage, when he retched violently, and, as that is often followed by cramp, I urged him to put his hand on my shoulder that I might tow him back to the schooner.

'Keep off, you villain, don't touch me. I'll drown ere I give in.'

I answered as Iago did to Rodrigo,

' "A fig for drowning! drown cats and blind puppies." I shall go on board and try the effects of a glass of grog to stay my stomach.'

'Come on,' he shouted, 'I am always better after vomiting.'

With difficulty I deluded him back; I went on board, and he sat on the steps of the accommodation-ladder, with his feet in the water. I handed him a wine-glass of brandy, and screened him from the burning sun. He was in a sullen mood, but after a time resumed his usual tone. Nothing could induce him to be landed in the schooner's boat, though I protested I had had enough of the water.

'You may do as you like,' he called out, and plumped in, and we swam on shore.

He never afterwards alluded to this event, nor to his prowess in swimming, to me, except in the past tense. He was ill, and kept his bed for two days afterwards.[14]

He said abruptly to me one day,

'I have been reading of men's sufferings after a wreck; they were nothing to what I have gone through in a country house, imprisoned with a family of Puritans, the only divertisement prayers and discourses on propriety and morality. A wreck must stir the blood, mine stagnated. How far have you ever swum?'

TRE.: Eight knots, and I was five hours in the water off the coast of Patagonia. The heave of the sea was in my favour, there was no wind, and the water was tepid. Two others with me were drowned; it's cold that kills.

BYRON: I'll have a tussle with you.

A year after I reminded him of this at Ithaca, and proposed to cross the strait to Cephalonia. He said it was too late in the day, the sea too cold. I was in the water.

BYRON, in a cautious voice: We shan't wait four hours for you; they are waiting for us on the other side.

So I got into the boat. I challenged him without considering his inability to use his lower limbs, his soft and shrunken muscles. He was subject to cramp and spasms.

To return to his drinking propensities, after this digression about his gymnastic prowess: I must say, that of all his vauntings, it was, luckily for him, the emptiest – that is, after he left England and his boon companions, as I know nothing of what he did there. From all that I heard or witnessed of his habits abroad, he was and had been exceedingly abstemious in eating and drinking. When alone, he drank a glass of two of small claret or hock, and when utterly exhausted at night a single glass of grog; which when I mixed it for him I lowered to what sailors call 'water bewitched', and he never made any remark. I once, to try him, omitted the alcohol; he then said, 'Tre, have you not forgotten the creature comfort?' I then put in two spoonfuls, and he was satisfied. This does not look like an habitual toper. His English acquaintances in Italy were, he said in derision, all milksops. On the rare occasions of any of his former friends visiting him, he would urge them to have a carouse with him, but they had grown wiser. He used to say that little Tommy Moore was the only man he then knew who stuck to the bottle and put him on his mettle, adding, 'But he is a native of the damp isle, where men subsist by suction.'

Byron had not damaged his body by strong drinks, but his terror of getting fat was so great that he reduced his diet to the point of absolute starvation. He was of that soft, lymphatic temperament which it is almost impossible to keep within a moderate compass, particularly as in his case his lameness prevented his taking exercise. When he added to his weight, even standing was painful, so he resolved to keep down to eleven stone, or shoot himself. He said everything he swallowed was instantly converted into tallow and deposited on his ribs.

He was the only human being I ever met with who had sufficient self-restraint and resolution to resist this proneness to fatten: he did so; and at Genoa, where he was last weighed, he was ten stone and nine pounds, and looked much less. This was not from vanity about his personal appearance, but from a better motive; and as, like Justice Greedy, he was always hungry, his merit was the greater. Occasionally he relaxed his vigilance, when he swelled apace.

I remember one of his old friends saying, 'Byron, how well you are looking!' If he had stopped there it had been well, but when he added 'You are getting fat,' Byron's brow reddened, and his eyes flashed – 'Do you call getting fat looking well, as if I were a hog?' and, turning to me, he muttered, 'The beast, I can hardly keep my hands off him.' The man who thus offended him was the husband of the lady addressed as 'Genevra,' and the original of his 'Zuleika,' in the 'Bride of Abydos.' I don't think he had much appetite for his dinner that day, or for many days, and never forgave the man who, so far from wishing to offend, intended to pay him a compliment.

Byron said he had tried all sorts of experiments to stay his hunger, without adding to his bulk. 'I swelled,' he said, 'at one time to fourteen stone, so I clapped the muzzle on my jaws, and, like the hibernating animals, consumed my own fat.'

He would exist on biscuits and soda-water for days together, then, to allay the eternal hunger gnawing at his vitals, he would make up a horrid mess of cold potatoes, rice, fish, or greens, deluged in vinegar, and swallow it like a famished dog. Either of these unsavoury dishes, with a biscuit and a glass or two of Rhine wine, he cared not how sour, he called feasting sumptuously. Upon my observing he might as well have fresh fish and vegetables, instead of stale, he laughed and answered,

'I have an advantage over you – I have no palate; one thing is as good as another to me.'

'Nothing,' I said, 'disagrees with the natural man, he fasts and gorges, his nerves and brains don't bother him; but if you wish to live –'

'Who wants to live?' he replied, 'not I. The Byrons are a short-lived race on both sides, father and mother: longevity is here-ditary. I am nearly at the end of my tether. I don't care for death a damn: it is her sting I can't bear, – pain.'

His habits and want of exercise damaged him, not drink. It must be borne in mind, moreover, that his brain was always working at high pressure. The consequences resulting from his way of life were low or intermittent fevers; these last had fastened on him in his early travels in the Levant; and there is this peculiarity in malaria fevers, that if you have once had them, you are ever after peculiarly susceptible to a renewal of their attacks if within their reach, and Byron was hardly ever out of it. Venice and Ravenna are belted in with swamps, and fevers are rife in the autumn. By starving his body Byron kept his brains clear; no man had brighter eyes or a clearer voice; and his resolute bearing and prompt replies, when excited, gave to his body an appearance of muscular power that imposed on strangers. I never doubted, for he was indifferent to life, and prouder than Lucifer, that if he had drawn his sword in Greece, or elsewhere, he would have thrown away the scabbard.[15]

Mrs Shelley once observed of Byron, 'Mind what you say to him, he is a thorough blab; in his anxiety to cut a good figure he makes others cut a bad one, as most people do.'

TRE.: Is it safe to act on his suggestions?

MRS SHELLEY: They are not his, but yours; you have kindled the fire; if you don't watch, someone will throw cold water and put it out, or if you go away it will burn out.

SHELLEY: Your fresh energy and promptness are catching to a vacillating mind; he has no decision of character, he has not made up his mind, and cannot on any subject whatever. (Then standing and holding out his arms, with an expression of aston-ishment mingled with sorrow, he shrieked out) By what he said last night in talking over his 'Cain,' the best of all his undramatic dramas, I do believe, Mary (and here the poet paused to take breath, reluctant to expose his friend's weakness), I do believe, Mary, that he is little better than a Christian!

MRS SHELLEY: Hogg says that all poets are madmen, and that they should be confined in Bedlam.

SHELLEY: If Byron were inspired with Socrates' divine madness, he would eclipse all he has yet done; his faculties are dimmed by the pernicious platitudes of his London visitors.

MRS SHELLEY: His friends are amongst the great men of the day.

TRE.: Do the men of the day outlive the day – what becomes of them?

SHELLEY: They go with the day into night, darkness, oblivion.

The Poet then vanished.

TRE.: These men, who loom large in the distance, are small when you come near them; but the national song-writer, Tom Moore, and the national story-teller, Scott, will never be forgotten, for songs and tales are the earliest history of every country. Byron is as perverse as a woman. Positiveness and dogmatism irritate him; he says nothing is certain, and so he believes nothing. Shelley's earnest convictions he delights in opposing. Riding with him yesterday, to humour his incredulity, I observed to him I felt something like water running down my face, that I thought it might be raining. He perceiving my drift, looking triumphant at me, said, 'You grinned at me when I sent back my servant for my riding-cloak; you said it was certain not to rain, it had not rained for six weeks; now you are paying for your certainty!'

In after talk with Byron, I mentioned Shelley's alarm at his backsliding; he smilingly observed, 'It's all nonsense, it was to make the Snake's crest rise and shake his rattles. If I follow his counsel I shall be where he is.'

TRE.: Shelley says you should write for posterity.

BYRON: No one has ever done so – why should I? It is all cant to say they did.

During the time I knew Byron, he never talked seriously and confidentially with any person but Shelley. Shelley was disconnected from all Byron's set, and from everyone that he knew, besides being a far superior scholar. On any of his London old comrades paying him a flying visit, he suspected their mission was to observe, and that what they saw and heard would be circulated with comments, so he flared up and resumed his former dare-devil and vaunting, averting all serious talk by irony and bantering. They too were on their guard, from Byron's habit of telling people what was said of them. He had a habit of parrying questions by putting cross questions to those who questioned him, and often not very pleasant ones. He never had them staying in his house, riding if they chose with him and dining. He always, on these occasions, got Shelley if he could, but to him it was exceedingly distasteful, as there was never any topic of the slightest interest to him – deaths, elopements, marriages, scandal, &c., &c. – but Shelley had in perfection the power of closing his senses of hearing and seeing, and taking refuge within his own mind. He often left the company without exchanging a word with the guest he had been invited to meet; the instant there was an opening, like a wild animal he was off, and rushed along the Lung' Arno to his den.

Chapter 7

O thou, who plumed with strong desire
Would'st float above the earth, beware!
A shadow tracks thy flight of fire –
　　　　Night is coming!
The Two Spirits. – SHELLEY.

The enquiry in England is not whether a man has talents or genius, but whether he is passive and polite, a virtuous ass, and obedient to noblemen's opinions in art and science. If he is, he is a good man; if not, he must be starved. – WILLIAM BLAKE.

IN the annals of authors I cannot find one who wrote under so many discouragements as Shelley; for even Bunyan's dungeon walls echoed the cheers of hosts of zealous disciples on the outside, whereas Shelley could number his readers on his fingers. He said, 'I can only print my writings by stinting myself in food!' Published, or sold openly, they were not.

He had thirty copies printed of 'Queen Mab' to give to his acquaintances; the printer cut his own name from all the copies to prevent prosecution. This poem was partly written at the early age of eighteen, and printed before he was twenty-one.

The utter loneliness in which he was condemned to pass the largest portion of his life would have paralysed any brains less subtilized by genius than his were. Yet he was social and cheerful, and, although frugal himself, most liberal to others, while to serve a friend he was ever ready to make any sacrifice. It was, perhaps, fortunate he was known to so few, for those few kept him close shorn. He went to Ravenna in 1821 on Byron's business, and, writing to his wife, makes this comment on the Pilgrim's asking him to execute a delicate commission : 'But it seems destined that I am always to have some active part in the affairs of everybody whom I approach.' And so he had.[16]

Every day I passed some hours with Byron, and very often my

evenings with Shelley and Williams, so that when my memory summons one of them to appear, the others are sure to follow in his wake. If Byron's reckless frankness and apparent cordiality warmed your feelings, his sensitiveness, irritability, and the perverseness of his temper, cooled them. I was not then thirty, and the exigencies of my now full-blown vanities were unsated, and my credulity unexhausted. I believed in many things then, and believe in some now; I could not sympathize with Byron, who believed in nothing.

'As for love, friendship, and your *entusamusy*,' said he, 'they must run their course. If you are not hanged or drowned before you are forty, you will wonder at all the foolish things they have made you say and do, – as I do now.'

'I will go over to the Shelleys,' I answered, 'and hear their opinions on the subject.'

'Ay, the Snake has fascinated you; I am for making a man of the world of you; they will mould you into a Frankenstein monster : so good night !'

Göthe's Mephistopheles calls the serpent that tempted Eve, 'My Aunt – the renowned snake;' and as Shelley translated and repeated passages of 'Faust' – to impregnate, as he said, Byron's brain, – when he came to that passage, 'My Aunt, the renowned snake,' Byron said, 'Then you are her nephew,' and henceforth he often called Shelley the Snake; his bright eyes, slim figure, and noiseless movements, strengthened, if they did not suggest, the comparison.[17] Byron's wit or humour might force a grim smile, or hollow laugh, from the standers by, but they savoured more of pain than playfulness, and made you dissatisfied with yourself and him. When I left his gloomy hall, and the echoes of the heavy iron-plated door died away, I could hardly refrain from shouting with joy as I hurried along the broad-flagged terrace which overhangs the pleasant river, cheered on my course by the cloudless sky, soft air, and fading light, which close an Italian day.

After a hasty dinner at my albergo, I hastened along the Arno to the hospitable and cheerful abode of the Shelleys. There I found those sympathies and sentiments which the Pilgrim denounced as illusions believed in as the only realities.

Shelley's mental activity was infectious; he kept your brain in constant action. Its effect on his comrade was very striking. Williams gave up all his accustomed sports for books, and the bettering of his mind; he had excellent natural ability; and the Poet delighted to see the seeds he had sown, germinating. Shelley said he was the sparrow educating the young of the cuckoo. After a protracted labour, Ned was delivered of a five-act play.[18] Shelley was sanguine that his pupil would succeed as a dramatic writer. One morning I was in Mrs Williams's drawing-room, by appointment, to hear Ned read an act of his drama. I sat with an aspect as caustic as a critic who was to decide his fate. Whilst thus intent Shelley stood before us with a most woeful expression.

Mrs Williams started up, exclaiming, 'What's the matter, Percy?'

'Mary has threatened me.'

'Threatened you with what?'

He looked mysterious and too agitated to reply.

Mrs Williams repeated, 'With what? to box your ears?'

'Oh, much worse than that; Mary says she will have a party; there are English singers here, the Sinclairs, and she will ask them, and everyone she or you know – oh, the horror!'

We all burst into a laugh except his friend Ned.

'It will kill me.'

'Music, kill you!' said Mrs Williams. 'Why, you have told me, you flatterer, that you loved music.'

'So I do. It's the company terrifies me. For pity go to Mary and intercede for me; I will submit to any other species of torture than that of being bored to death by idle ladies and gentlemen.'

After various devices it was resolved that Ned Williams should wait upon the lady, – he being gifted with a silvery tongue, and sympathizing with the Poet in his dislike of fine ladies, – and see what he could do to avert the threatened invasion of the Poet's solitude. Meanwhile Shelley remained in a state of restless ecstasy: he could not even read or sit. Ned returned with a grave face; the Poet stood as a criminal stands at the bar, whilst the solemn arbitrator of his fate decides it. 'The lady,' commenced Ned, 'has set her heart on having a party, and will not be baulked;' but, seeing the Poet's despair, he added, 'it is to be limited to those here assembled, and some of Count Gamba's family; and instead of a musical feast – as we have no souls – we are to have a dinner.' The Poet hopped off, rejoicing, making a noise I should have thought whistling, but that he was ignorant of that accomplishment.

I have seen Shelley and Byron in society, and the contrast was as marked as their characters. The former, not thinking of himself, was as much at ease as in his own home, omitting no occasion of obliging those whom he came in contact with, readily conversing with all or any who addressed him, irrespective of age or rank, dress or address. To the first party I went with Byron, as we were on our road, he said,

'It's so long since I have been in English society, you must tell me what are their present customs. Does rank lead the way, or does the ambassadress pair us off into the dining-room? Do they ask people to wine? Do we exit with the women, or stick to our claret?'

On arriving, he was flushed, over-ceremonious, and ill at ease. He had learnt his manners, as I have said, during the Regency, when society was more exclusive than even now, and consequently more vulgar.

To know an author, personally, is too often but to destroy the illusion created by his works; if you withdraw the veil of your idol's sanctuary, and see him in his night-cap, you discover a querulous old crone, a sour pedant, a supercilious coxcomb, a servile tuft-hunter, a saucy snob, or at best, an ordinary mortal. Instead of the high-minded seeker after truth and abstract knowledge, with a nature too refined to bear the vulgarities of life, as we had imagined, we find him full of egotism and vanity, and eternally fretting and fuming about trifles. As a general rule, therefore, it is wise to avoid writers whose works amuse or delight you, for when you see them they will delight you no more. Shelley was a grand exception to this rule. To form a just idea of his poetry, you should have witnessed his daily life; his words and actions best illustrated his writings. If his glorious conception of Gods and men constituted an atheist, I am afraid all that listened were little better. Sometimes he would run through a great work on science, condense the author's laboured exposition, and by substituting simple words for the jargon of the schools, make the most abstruse subject transparent. The cynic Byron acknowledged him to be the best and ablest man he had ever known. The truth was, Shelley loved everything better than himself. Self-preservation is, they say, the first law of nature, with him it was the last; and the only pain he ever gave his friends arose from the utter indifference with which he treated everything concerning himself. I was bathing one day in a deep pool in the Arno, and astonished the Poet by performing a series of aquatic gymnastics, which I had learnt from the natives of the South Seas. On my coming out, whilst dressing, Shelley said, mournfully,

'Why can't I swim? it seems so very easy.'

I answered, 'Because you think you can't. If you determine, you will; take a header off this bank, and when you rise turn on your back, you will float like a duck; but you must reverse the arch in your spine, for it's now bent the wrong way.'

He doffed his jacket and trowsers, kicked off his shoes and socks, and plunged in; and there he lay stretched out on the bottom like a conger eel, not making the least effort or struggle to save himself. He would have been drowned if I had not instantly fished him out. When he recovered his breath, he said,

'I always find the bottom of the well, and they say Truth lies there. In another minute I should have found it, and you would have found an empty shell. It is an easy way of getting rid of the body.'[19]

TRE.: ' "What is truth?" said jesting Pilate, and would not stay for an answer.' What does Bacon mean by that?

SHELLEY: The truth is a jest; no one has found it.

TRE.: That is why the wise men say they know nothing. Bacon might have exposed the great lies.

SHELLEY: If we had known the great truths, they would have laid bare the great lies.

TRE.: What do they mean by the great truths?

SHELLEY: They cannot calculate time, measure distance, or say what is above or what is below us.

'What is life? What is death? What are we?'

TRE.: The knaves are the cleverest; they profess to know everything; the fools believe them, and so they govern the world.

SHELLEY: Science has done something and will do more; astronomy is working above, and geology below, and chemistry is seeking truth. In another century or two we shall make a beginning; at present we are playing the game of blind man's buff, struggling to clutch truth.

TRE.: What would Mrs Shelley have said to me if I had gone back with your empty cage?

'Don't tell Mary – not a word!' he rejoined, and then continued, 'It's a great temptation; in another minute I might have been in another planet, if old women's tales were true.'

'But as you always find the bottom,' I observed, 'you might have sunk "deeper than did ever plummet sound." Do you believe in the immortality of the spirit?'

'Certainly not; how can I? We know nothing; we have no evidence; we cannot express our inmost thoughts. They are incomprehensible even to ourselves.'

'Why,' I asked, 'do you call yourself an atheist? it annihilates you in this world.'

'It is a word of abuse to stop discussion, a painted devil to frighten the foolish, a threat to intimidate the wise and good. I used it to express my abhorrence of superstition; I took up the word, as a knight took up a gauntlet, in defiance of injustice. The delusions of Christianity are fatal to genius and originality: they limit thought.'

Shelley's thirst for knowledge was unquenchable. He set to work on a book, or a pyramid of books; his eyes glistening with an energy as fierce as that of the most sordid gold-digger who works at a rock of quartz, crushing his way through all impediments, no grain of the pure ore escaping his eager scrutiny. I called on him one morning at ten, he was in his study with a German folio open, resting on the broad marble mantelpiece, over an old-fashioned fire-place, and with a dictionary in his hand. He always read standing if possible. He had promised over night to go with me, but now begged me to let him off. I then rode to Leghorn, eleven or twelve miles distant, and passed the day there; on returning at six in the evening to dine with Mrs Shelley and the Williamses, as I had engaged to do, I went into the Poet's room and found him exactly in the position in which I had left him in the morning, but looking pale and exhausted.

'Well,' I said, 'have you found it?'

Shutting the book and going to the window, he replied, 'No, I have lost it :' with a deep sigh : ' "I have lost a day." '

'Cheer up, my lad, and come to dinner.'

Putting his long fingers through his masses of wild tangled hair, he answered faintly, 'You go, I have dined – late eating don't do for me.'

'What is this?' I asked, as I was going out of the room, pointing to one of his bookshelves with a plate containing bread and cold meat on it.

'That,' – colouring, – 'why that must be my dinner. It's very foolish; I thought I had eaten it.'

Saying I was determined that he should for once have a regular meal, I lugged him into the dining-room, but he brought a book with him and read more than he ate. He seldom ate at stated periods, but only when hungry – and then like the birds, if he saw something edible lying about, – but the cupboards of literary ladies are like Mother Hubbard's, bare. His drink was water, or milk if he could get it, bread was literally his staff of life; other things he thought superfluous. An Italian who knew his way of life, not believing it possible that any human being would live as Shelley did, unless compelled by poverty, was astonished when he was told the amount of his income, and thought he was defrauded or grossly ignorant of the value of money. He, therefore, made a proposition which much amused the Poet, that he, the friendly Italian, would undertake for ten thousand crowns a-year to keep Shelley like a grand Seigneur, to provide his table with luxuries, his house with attendants, a carriage and opera-box for my lady, besides adorning his person after the most approved Parisian style. Mrs Shelley's toilette was not included in the wily Italian's estimates. The fact was, Shelley stinted himself to bare necessaries, and then often lavished the money, saved by unprecedented self-denial, on selfish fellows who denied themselves nothing; such as the great philosopher had in his eye, when he said, 'It is the nature of extreme self-lovers, as they will set a house on fire, an' it were only to roast their own eggs.'

Byron, on our voyage to Greece, talking of England, after commenting on his own wrongs, said, 'And Shelley, too, the best and most benevolent of men; they hooted him out of his country like a mad-dog, for questioning a dogma. Man is the same rancorous beast now that he was from the beginning, and if the Christ they profess to worship reappeared, they would again crucify him.'

Chapter 8

Where the pine its garland weaves
Of sapless green and ivy dun,
Round stems that never kiss the sun,
Where the lawns and pastures be
And the sand-hills of the sea.

The Invitation. – SHELLEY.

BYRON's literary was like Alexander's military career, one great triumph; but whilst he was at the zenith of his popularity, he railed against the world's injustice. I suppose, by the 'world' he meant no more than the fashionable set he had seen squeezed together in a drawing-room; and, by all the press that attacked him, the fraction of it which took its tone from some small but active clique: as to friends deserting him, that could not be, for it was his boast that he never had attempted to make any after his school hallucinations. But in the pride of his strength, and the audacity of his youth, enemies he certainly did make, and when they saw an opportunity of getting rid of a supercilious rival, they instinctively took advantage of it. As to the Poet's differences with his wife, they must have appeared absurd to men who were as indifferent to their own wives as were the majority of Byron's enemies.

When the most worldly wise and unimpassioned marry, they take a leap in the dark, and can no more foresee the consequences, than poets, – owls blinded by the light of their vain imaginations. The worldly wise, not having risked or anticipated much, stand to their bargain 'for better, for worse,' and say nothing about it; but the irascible tribe of songsters, when they find that marriage is not exactly what they imagined it to be, 'proclaim their griefs from the house-top,' as Byron did.

Very pretty books have been written on the 'Loves of the Angels,' and 'Loves of the Poets,' and Love universal – but when lovers are paired and caged together in holy matrimony, the curtain is dropped, and we hear no more of them. It may be, they moult their feathers and lose their song. Byron's marriage must not be classed with those of the Poets, but of the worldly wise, he was not under the illusion of love, but of money. If he had left his wife and cut society (the last he was resolved on doing), he would have been content: that his wife and society should have cast him off, was a mortification his pride could never forgive nor forget. As to the oft vexed question of the Poet's separation from his wife, he has told the facts in prose and verse; but omitted to state that he treated women as things devoid of soul or sense; he would not eat, pray, walk, nor talk seriously with them. Within certain degrees of affinity marriages are forbidden; so they should be where there is no natural affinity of feelings, habits, tastes, or sympathies. It is very kind in the saints to ally themselves to sinners, but in ninety-nine cases out of one hundred, it turns out a failure; in Byron's case, it was signally so.

In all the transactions of his life, his anxiety to cut a good figure made him unjust to others. In fact, his pride mastered him, and he made no effort to conceal or to control its dominion, reckless how it marred his worldly advantages. Amidst the general homage paid to his genius, his vanity reverted to his early disappointments, when he was baffled and compelled to fly, and though Parthian-like he discharged his arrows on his pursuers, he lost the battle.

Shelley had a far loftier spirit. His pride was spiritual. When attacked, he neither fled nor stood at bay, nor altered his course, but calmly went on with heart and mind intent on elevating his species. Whilst men tried to force him down to their level, he toiled to draw their minds upwards. His words were, 'I always go on until I am stopped, and I never am stopped.' Like the Indian palms, Shelley never flourished far from water. When compelled to take up his quarters in a town, he every morning, with the instinct that guides the water-birds, fled to the nearest lake, river, or sea-shore, and only returned to roost at night. If debarred from this, he sought out the most solitary place. Towns and crowds distracted him. Even the silent and half-deserted cities of Italy, with their temples, palaces, paintings and sculpture, could not make him stay, if there was a wood or water within his reach. At Pisa, he had a river under his window, and a pine forest in the neighbourhood.

I accompanied Mrs Shelley to this wood in search of the Poet, on one of those brilliant spring mornings we on the wrong side of the Alps are so rarely blessed with. A calèche took us out of Pisa through the gate of the Cascine; we drove through the Cascine and onwards for two or three miles, traversing the vineyards and farms on the Grand Ducal estate. On approaching some farm buildings, near which were a hunting-palace and chapel, we dismissed the carriage, directing the driver to meet us at a certain spot in the afternoon. We then walked on, not exactly knowing what course to take, and were exceedingly perplexed on coming to an open space, from which four roads radiated. There we stopped until I learnt from a Contadino that the one before us led directly to the sea, which was two or three miles distant, the one on the right led to the Serchio, and that on the left, to the Arno: we decided on taking the road to the sea. We proceeded on our journey over a sandy plain; the sun being near its zenith. Walking was not included among the number of accomplishments in which Mrs Shelley excelled; the loose sand and hot sun soon knocked her up. When we got under the cool canopy of the pines, she stopped and allowed me to hunt for her husband. I now strode along; the forest was on my right hand and extensive pastures on my left, with herds of oxen, camels, and horses grazing thereon. I came upon the open sea at a place called Gombo, from whence I could see Via Reggio, the Gulf of Spezzia, and the mountains beyond. After bathing, seeing nothing of the Poet, I penetrated the densest part of the forest, ever and anon making the woods ring with the name of Shelley, and scaring the herons and water-birds from the chain of stagnant pools which impeded my progress.

With no landmarks to guide me, nor sky to be seen above, I was bewildered in this wilderness of pines and ponds; so I sat down, struck a light, and smoked a cigar. A red man would have known his course by the trees themselves, their growth, form, and colour; or if a footstep had passed that day, he would have hit upon its trail. As I mused upon his sagacity and my own stupidity, the braying of a brother jackass startled me. He was followed by an old man picking up pine cones. I asked him if he had seen a stranger?

'L'Inglese malinconico haunts the wood maledetta. I will show you his nest.'

As we advanced, the ground swelled into mounds and hollows. By-and-by the old fellow pointed with his stick to a hat, books, and loose papers lying about, and then to a deep pool of dark glimmering water, saying 'Eccolo!' I thought he meant that Shelley was in or under the water. The careless, not to say impatient, way in which the Poet bore his burden of life, caused a vague dread amongst his family and friends that he might lose or cast it away at any moment.

The strong light streamed through the opening of the trees. One of the pines, undermined by the water, had fallen into it. Under its lea, and nearly hidden, sat the Poet, gazing on the dark mirror beneath, so lost in his bardish reverie that he did not hear my approach. There the trees were stunted and bent, and their crowns were shorn like friars by the sea breezes, excepting a cluster of three, under which Shelley's traps were lying; these over-topped the rest. To avoid startling the Poet out of his dream, I squatted under the lofty trees, and opened his books. One was a volume of his favourite Greek dramatist, Æschylus – the same that I found in his pocket after death [20] – and the other was a volume of Shakespeare. I then hailed him, and, turning his head, he answered faintly,

'Hello, come in.'

'Is this your study?' I asked.

'Yes,' he answered, 'and these trees are my books – they tell no lies. In composing one's faculties must not be divided; in a house there is no solitude: a door shutting, a footstep heard, a bell ringing, a voice, causes an echo in your brain and dissolves your visions.'

I said: 'Here you have the river rushing by you, the birds chattering and the beasts bellowing.'

He answered: 'The river flows by like Time, and all the sounds of Nature harmonize; they soothe: it is only the human animal that is discordant with Nature and disturbs me. It is

difficult to conceive why or for what purpose we are here, a
perpetual torment to ourselves and to every living thing. You
are sitting on the stool of inspiration,' he exclaimed. 'In those
three pines the weird sisters are imprisoned, and this,' pointing
to the water, 'is their cauldron of black broth. The Pythian
priestesses uttered their oracles from below – now they are muttered from above. Listen to the solemn music in the pine-tops
– don't you hear the mournful murmurings of the sea? Sometimes they rave and roar, shriek and howl, like a rabble of priests.
In a tempest, when a ship sinks, they catch the despairing groans
of the drowning mariners. Their chorus is the eternal wailing
of wretched men.'

'They, like the world,' I observed, 'seem to take no note
of wretched women. The sighs and wailing you talk about
are not those of wretched men afar off, but are breathed by a
woman near at hand – not from the pine-tops, but by a forsaken
lady.'

'What do you mean?' he asked.

'Why, that an hour or two ago I left your wife, Mary Shelley,
at the entrance of this grove, in despair at not finding you.'

He started up, snatched up his scattered books and papers,
thrust them into his hat and jacket pockets, sighing, 'Poor Mary!
hers is a sad fate. Come along; she can't bear solitude, nor I
society – the quick coupled with the dead.'

He glided along with his usual swiftness, for nothing could
make him pause for an instant when he had an object in view,
until he had attained it. On hearing our voices, Mrs Shelley
joined us. To stop Shelley's self-reproaches, or to hide her own
emotions, she began in a bantering tone, chiding and coaxing
him,

'What a wild goose you are, Percy; if my thoughts have strayed
from my book, it was to the opera, and my new dress from
Florence – and especially the ivy wreath so much admired for
my hair, and not to you, you silly fellow! When I left home, my
satin slippers had not arrived. These are serious matters to gentle-
women, enough to ruffle the serenest tempered. As to you and
your ungallant companion, I had forgotten that such things are;
but as it is the ridiculous custom to have men at balls and operas,

I must take you with me, though, from your uncouth ways, you will be taken for Valentine and he for Orson.'

Shelley, like other students, would, when the spell that bound his faculties was broken, shut his books, and indulge in the wildest flights of mirth and folly. As this is a sport all can join in, we talked and laughed, and shrieked and shouted, as we emerged from under the shadows of the melancholy pines and their nodding plumes, into the now cool purple twilight and open country. The cheerful and graceful peasant girls, returning home from the vineyards and olive groves, stopped to look at us. The old man I had met in the morning gathering pine-cones passed hurriedly by with his donkey, giving Shelley a wide berth, and evidently thinking that the melancholy Englishman had now become a raving maniac. Sancho says, 'Blessings on the man who invented sleep;' the man who invented laughing deserves no less.

The day I found Shelley in the pine-forest he was writing verses on a guitar. I picked up a fragment, but could only make out the first two lines :—

> 'Ariel to Miranda : Take
> This slave of music.'

It was a frightful scrawl; words smeared out with his finger, and one upon the other, over and over in tiers, and all run together 'in most admired disorder;' it might have been taken for a sketch of a marsh overgrown with bulrushes, and the blots for wild ducks; such a dashed-off daub as self-conceited artists mistake for a manifestation of genius. On my observing this to him, he answered,

'When my brain gets heated with thought, it soon boils and throws off images and words faster than I can skim them off. In the morning, when cooled down, out of the rude sketch, as you justly call it, I shall attempt a drawing. If you ask me why I publish what few or none will care to read, it is that the spirits I have raised haunt me until they are sent to the devil of a printer. All authors are anxious to breech their bantlings.'[21]

When I first knew Shelley, I met an old friend and his wife walking by the Arno. I said to Shelley,

'That man was a gay, frank, and cheerful companion; a widow immeshed him as a spider ensnares a fly and sucks his blood. She is jealous and torments him; when I remonstrated with her, she said it was excess of love made her so.'

Shelley answered,

'Love is not akin to jealousy; love does not seek its own pleasure, but the happiness of another. Jealousy is gross selfishness; it looks upon everyone who approaches as an enemy: it's the idolatry of self, and, like canine madness, incurable.'

His eyes flashed as he spoke. I did not then know that the green-eyed monster haunted his own house.

Chapter 9

So as we rode, we talked; and the swift thought
Winging itself with laughter, lingered not,
But flew from brain to brain.

SHELLEY.

There are several kinds of divine madness. That which
proceeds from the Muses' taking possession of a tender
and unoccupied soul, awakening and bacchically in-
spiring it towards songs and other poetry, adorning
myriads of ancient deeds, instructs succeeding generations; but he who, without this madness from the Muses,
approaches the poetical gates, having persuaded himself
that by art alone he may become sufficiently a Poet, will
find in the end his own imperfection, and see the poetry
of his cold prudence vanish into nothingness before the
light of that which has sprung from divine insanity. –
SOCRATES.

AT 10 a.m. by appointment I drove to Shelley's house and hailed
him; he was always prompt as a seaman in a squall, and rushing
downstairs, was brought to by his wife on the first landing: –

'Percy, do change your cap and jacket; you promised Tre to
call on his Yankee girl and Highland beauty at Leghorn.
Caterina! bring down the padrone's coat and hat.'

The Poet, reluctantly submitting, muttered,

'Our bones should be outside, or our skins as tough as alliga-
tors'; the thing you have put on my head feels like a crown of
thorns, and the ligature round my throat a halter. I bear what
I can, and suffer what I must.'

No personal vexations could extort harsher words than these
from him, and he often used them. To avoid any further manipu-
lation he sprang down the stairs, and striding adroitly over a
fair fat child squatting on the doorstep beside its nurse, stepped
into my chaise at the door. The child cried.

SHELLEY:

>'When we are born, we cry that we are come
>To this great stage of fools.'

TRE.: Whose child is it?

POET: (looking at it): Don't know.

MRS SHELLEY (from open casement): That's too bad, not to know your own child. Why, you goose, it is Percy!

TRE.: You are not the wise man who knows his own child.

SHELLEY: The wise men have none.

TRE.: Those wise men must be in the moon; there are few such on the earth.

As we turned off the Lung' Arno, a friendly puff of wind relieved the Poet of his obnoxious head-gear, and the hat trundled along. I stopped the horse.

SHELLEY: Oh, don't stop! It will get into the river and I shall find it at Leghorn.

TRE.: That will depend on wind and current.

Two Florentine gentlemen ran and picked it up, wiped the dust off, and brought it to us.

SHELLEY: They say that beavers are nearly exterminated; if hats go too, I cannot mourn for them.

Outside of the Port, on the Leghorn road, half-a-dozen small children were clustered round a ruined building, tormenting a family of beautiful bright green-and-gold coloured lizards.

SHELLEY: The young demons!

TRE.: You are blaspheming, for is it not said, 'Of such is the kingdom of heaven'? Children, until restrained, kill everything that runs from them; but if a beetle or a mouse moves towards them they fly in terror: cruel and cowardly; and that is the nature of man.

SHELLEY: He is in process of training.

TRE.: It is very slow.

SHELLEY: The animals that subsist on herbs are docile, the flesh-eaters are untamable.

TRE.: In the tropics we can live on fruits, not in the north. The Brahmins live on grains and fruit and are docile, the flesh-eaters make serfs of them. Mrs Shelley says I am as eccentric as you; I wish I were as reasonable.

SHELLEY: Mary is under the dominion of the mythical monster 'Everybody.' I tell her I am of the Nobodies. You have been everywhere; have you seen the ubiquitous demon Everybody?

TRE.: Yes, in Egypt; a harmless and most useful beast. The loaded camels of a caravan are piloted by a donkey. His headstall is decorated with bells; he leads the way and the docile animals follow, guided by the jingling. Without him they stray always. So you see the much-abused donkey is not the most stupid of animals. 'Everybody' follows him.

SHELLEY: You have solved the mystery. You must tell Mary. Wise men in all ages have declared everything that is, is wrong; those who stray away find something that is right. A donkey decorated is a guide for those that are as stupid as camels; we stray, we are eccentric.

Soon after we passed some masons building a chapel, and women acting as bricklayers' labourers, carrying heavy stones and mortar.

SHELLEY: See the barbarism that the priests have reduced Italy to.

TRE.: It is the primitive state of things. In the earliest records of the human race the duty of men was as hunters and warriors, and women did all the drudgery – fetched the wood and water. The professor of anatomy at the university of Pisa – and he is a high authority – says that women, though not the strongest, are the toughest. He says the female of all races of animals are less highly organized than the male; they are not so subject to diseases, and wounds more readily heal with them than with the male. It is the poets, artists, and others of imagination who have reversed the natural order of things, and who have placed women where we should be.

SHELLEY: We are indebted to the poets for having transformed women from what they were to what they are – a solace and delight.

TRE.: No; they have overshot their mark. They tell us that our principal object, aim, and end is to seek in the world for a fair skin, silky hair, and bright eyes; the emptier the mind the

better; and that this is all life has to bestow. It is the old story –
the sirens luring one to the sea-beach paved with human bones.
Nature has lavished all its beauties on the male in the animal
races as well as the human. Look at the hen pheasant and the
pea-hen, and the singing birds, it is only the male that sings.
Now we search the four corners of the earth to transform a
dowdy into a fine lady. Half the world pass their lives in search-
ing for gems and silks and satins to ornament them, and what
torments does one suffer when captured by one of these dragon-
flies! Men have nothing to cover themselves with but the cast-off
winter clothing of sheep.

The poet, when he was in a placid humour, delighted in
amplifying notions the most adverse to his real opinions.

I said,

'The primitive people in the Indian Archipelago and other
countries alone preserve the natural order of things. I once put
into a bay on the eastern coast of Madagascar for fresh provisions
and water. A great chief came down to barter with a retinue of
nude followers, he himself being distinguished by having a gold-
laced cocked hat with feathers, such as worn by generals of
division, and hunting boots, otherwise as naked as Adam; his
face and body elaborately ornamented by tattooing with colours
which I had never seen before.'

SHELLEY: In youth I thought the reasoning faculties, if fairly
developed, would triumph, but passions overpower all our
faculties. The animals are guided by their instincts, we by our
cultivated cunning and blind passions.

TRE: And reason.

SHELLEY: No, that faculty is paralysed by the priests . . .

Of such stuff was our ordinary talk, to keep him awake from
his dreamy reveries, and so we reached Leghorn.

During our return I said to him,

'You had better dine with me.'

He replied,

'What for?' (I saw he was disturbed.) 'When?'

I said,

'Now,' and produced a basket of all the fresh fruit of the
season, saying,

'The Muses might dine on this food.'

He answered,

'No; they live in the blue regions of the air.'

Notwithstanding his protest, he went on picking the grapes and eating the fruit, unconscious of what he was doing. He invariably read when he was eating. He now had in his hand a monthly review, sent to him from England. He never in such cases laughed, but I saw by his eyes that he was amused. I said,

'What is it that amuses you?'

SHELLEY: The 'Epipsychidion,' that you like so much, the reviewer denounces as the rhapsody of a madman. That it may be a rhapsody I won't deny, and a man cannot decide on his own sanity. Your dry, matter-of-fact men denounce all flights of imagination as proofs of insanity, and so did the Greek sect of the Stoics. All the mass of mankind consider everyone eccentric or insane who utters sentiments they do not comprehend.

There was other abuse of him in the magazine. I said,

'The Persian poet Hafiz would have consoled you by saying, "You are like the shell of ocean that fills with pearls the hand that wounds you."'

He was delighted with the Eastern metaphors, and I repeated many others to him, talking of Eastern civilization, from which all poetry had originated.[22]

In answer to my questions Shelley once said,

'In writing the "Cenci" my object was to see how I could succeed in describing passions I have never felt, and to tell the most dreadful story in pure and refined language. The image of Beatrice haunted me after seeing her portrait. The story is well authenticated, and the details far more horrible than I have painted them. The "Cenci" is a work of art; it is not coloured by my feelings, nor obscured by my metaphysics. I don't think much of it. It gave me less trouble than anything I have written of the same length.

'I am now writing a play for the stage. It is affectation to say we write a play for any other purpose. The subject is from English history;* in style and manner I shall approach as near our great dramatist as my feeble powers will permit. "King

* Charles the First.

Lear" is my model, for that is nearly perfect. I am amazed at my presumption. Poets should be modest. My audacity savours of madness.

'Considering the labour requisite to excel in composition, I think it would be better to stick to one style. The clamour for novelty is leading us all astray. Yet, at Venice, I urged Byron to come out of the dismal "wood of error" into the sun, and to write something new and cheerful. "Don Juan" is the result. The poetry is superior to "Childe Harold," and the plan, or rather want of plan, gives scope to his astonishing natural powers.

'My friends say my "Prometheus" is too wild, ideal, and perplexed with imagery. It may be so. It has no resemblance to the Greek drama. It is original; and cost me severe mental labour. Authors, like mothers, prefer the children who have given them most trouble. Milton preferred his "Paradise Regained," Petrarch his "Africa," and Byron his "Doge of Venice."[23]

'I have the vanity to write only for poetical minds, and must be satisfied with few readers. Byron is ambitious; he writes for all, and all read his works.'

I said,

'The son of a man of genius has sent me a very silly poem to show Byron. Why are not germs of genius transmitted in a race? Their physical diseases are, but none of their mental qualities.'

Shelley answered,

'It would be a more intolerable wrong of nature than any which man has devised; the sons of foolish parents would have no hope.'

TRE.: Then the sins of parents, their diseases, should not be transmitted.

SHELLEY: With regard to the great question, the System of the Universe, I have no curiosity on the subject. I am content to see no farther into futurity than Plato and Bacon. My mind is tranquil; I have no fears and some hopes. In our present gross material state our faculties are clouded; – when Death removes our clay coverings the mystery will be solved.

He thought a play founded on Shakespeare's 'Timon' would be an excellent mode of discussing our present social and political evils dramatically, and of descanting on them.

At Leghorn, after we had done our business, I called on my Scotch friends and lured my companion in. He abhorred forcing himself on strangers – so I did not mention his name, merely observing,

'As you said you wanted information about Italy, here is a friend of mine can give it you – for I cannot.'

The ladies – for there was no man there – were capital specimens of Scotchwomen, fresh from the land of cakes, – frank, fair, intelligent, and of course, pious. After a long and earnest talk we left them, but not without difficulty, so pressing were they for us to stop to dinner.[24]

After returning with Shelley from Leghorn, I put up my chaise at the hostelry, and went in to dine with Mrs Shelley. All fixed rules of feeding the Poet looked upon as ridiculous; he grazed when he was hungry, anywhere, at any time. Mrs Shelley conformed to the ways of the world in all things that she could.

Finding no one about the house, I went into his library; the Poet was untying the bag of scudi that we brought from Leghorn. Standing up he turned out the bag on to the hearth-rug, and the glittering coins bespangled the floor. It was amusing to see him scraping them together with the shovel out of the fireplace; having adroitly got them into a lump he pressed them as flat as he could with his foot, then skilfully with the shovel divided them as nearly as possible into two equal portions; one of the halves he divided again into two equal portions by guesswork, saying to Mary,

'That half will feed the house and pay the rent,' then pointing to the smaller portion he said, 'that will do for you. This is my portion.'

Then he spoke lower to her that I might not hear, but she told me that he said,

'I will give this to poor Tom Medwin, who wants to go to Naples and has no money.'

I said to Mary as we were dining,

'Why, he has left nothing for himself.'

She said,

'No, if he wants anything he tells me to get it, and if he wants a scudo to give anyone, perhaps I lend it him (smiling), but he can't be trusted with money, and he won't have it.'

When I next visited the Scotch ladies, they were disappointed at the absence of my companion; and when I told them it was Shelley, the young and handsome mother clasped her hands, and exclaimed,

'Shelley! That bright-eyed youth; so gentle, so intelligent – so thoughtful for us. Oh, why did you not name him?'

'Because he thought you would have been shocked.'

'Shocked! – why I would have knelt to him in penitence for having wronged him even in my thoughts. If he is not pure and good – then there is no truth and goodness in this world. His looks reminded me of my own blessed baby, – so innocent – so full of love and sweetness.'

'So is the serpent that tempted Eve described,' I said.

'Oh, you wicked scoffer!' she continued. 'But I know you love him. I shall have no peace of mind until you bring him here. You remember, sister, I said his young face had lines of care and sorrow on it – when he was showing us the road to Rome on the map and the sun shone on it; – poor boy! Oh, tell us about his wife, – is she worthy of him? She must love him dearly – and so must all who know him.'

To palliate the warm-hearted lady's admiration of the Poet – as well as my own – I must observe, that all on knowing him sang the same song; and as I have before observed, even Byron in his most moody and cynical vein, joined in the chorus, echoing my monotonous notes. The reason was, that after having heard or read the rancorous abuse heaped on Shelley by the mercenary literature of the day, – in which he was described as a monster more hideous than Caliban, – the revulsion of feeling on seeing the man was so great, that he seemed as gentle a spirit as Ariel. There never has been nor can be any true likeness of him. Desdemona said, 'I saw Othello's visage in his mind,' and Shelley's 'visage' as well as his mind are to be seen in his works.

When I was at Leghorn with Shelley, I drew him towards the docks, saying,

'As we have a spare hour let's see if we can't put a girdle round the earth in forty minutes. In these docks are living specimens of all the nationalities of the world; thus we can go round it, and visit and examine any particular nation we like, observing their peculiar habits, manners, dress, language, food, productions, arts, and naval architecture; for see how varied are the shapes, build, rigging, and decoration of the different vessels. There lies an English cutter, a French chasse-marée, an American clipper, a Spanish tartan, an Austrian trabarcolo, a Genoese felucca, a Sardinian zebec, a Neapolitan brig, a Sicilian sparanza, a Dutch galleot, a Danish snow, a Russian hermaphrodite, a Turkish sackalever, a Greek bombard. I don't see a Persian dhow, an Arab grab, or a Chinese junk; but there are enough for our purpose and to spare. As you have lately written a poem, "Hellas," about the modern Greeks, would it not be as well to take a look at them amidst all the din of the docks? I hear their shrill nasal voices, and should like to know if you can trace in the language or lineaments of these Greeks of the nineteenth century A.D., the faintest resemblance to the lofty and sublime spirits who lived in the fifth century B.C. An English merchant who has dealings with them told me he thought these modern Greeks were, if judged by their actions, a cross between the Jews and gypsies – but here comes the Capitano Zarita; I know him.'

So dragging Shelley with me I introduced him, and asking to see the vessel, we crossed the plank from the quay and stood on the deck of the 'San Spiridione' in the midst of her chattering irascible crew. They took little heed of the skipper, for in these trading vessels each individual of the crew is part owner, and some share in the cargo; so they are all interested in the specula- tion – having no wages. They squatted about the decks in small knots, shrieking, gesticulating, smoking, eating, and gambling like savages.

'Does this realize your idea of Hellenism, Shelley?' I asked.

'No! but it does of Hell,' he replied.

The captain insisted on giving us pipes and coffee in his cabin, so I dragged Shelley down. Over the rudder-head facing us, there was a gilt box enshrining a flaming gaudy daub of a saint, with a lamp burning before it; this was Il Padro Santo Spiridione, the ship's godfather. The skipper crossed himself and squatted on the dirty divan. Shelley talked to him about the

Greek revolution that was taking place, but from its interrupting trade the captain was opposed to it.

'Come away!' said Shelley. 'There is not a drop of the old Hellenic blood here. These are not the men to rekindle the ancient Greek fire; their souls are extinguished by traffic and superstition. Come away!' – and away we went.

'It is but a step,' I said, 'from these ruins of worn-out Greece to the New World; let's board the American clipper.'

'I had rather not have any more of my hopes and illusions mocked by sad realities,' said Shelley.

'You must allow,' I answered, 'that graceful craft was designed by a man who had a poet's feelings for things beautiful; let's get a model and build a boat like her.'

The idea so pleased the Poet that he followed me on board her. The Americans are a social, free-and-easy people, accustomed to take their own way, and to readily yield the same privilege to all others, so that our coming on board, and examination of the vessel, fore and aft, were not considered as an intrusion. The captain was on shore, so I talked to the mate, a smart specimen of a Yankee. When I commended her beauty, he said,

'I do expect, now we have our new copper on, she has a look of the brass sarpent, she has as slick a run, and her bearings are just where they should be. We hoist up to heaven, and shoot home to hell, and cover the ocean with our canvas.'

I said we wished to build a boat after her model.

'Then I calculate you must go to Baltimore or Boston to get one; there is no one on this side the water can do the job. We have our freight all ready, and are homeward-bound; we have elegant accommodation, and you will be across before your young friend's beard is ripe for a razor. Come down, and take an observation of the state cabin.'

It was about ten and a-half feet by five or six; 'plenty of room to live or die comfortably in,' he observed; and then pressed us to have a chaw of real old Virginian cake, *i.e.* tobacco, and a cool drink of peach brandy. I made some observation to him about the Greek vessel we had visited.

'Crank as an eggshell,' he said; 'too many sticks and top

hamper, she looks like a bundle of chips going to hell to be burnt.'

I seduced Shelley into drinking a wine-glass of weak grog, the first and last he ever drank. The Yankee would not let us go until we had drunk, under the star-spangled banner, to the memory of Washington, and the prosperity of the American commonwealth.

'As a warrior and statesman,' said Shelley, 'he was righteous in all he did, unlike all who lived before or since; he never used his power but for the benefit of his fellow-creatures: –

> ' "He fought,
> For truth and wisdom, foremost of the brave;
> Him glory's idle glances dazzled not;
> 'Twas his ambition, generous and great,
> A life to life's great end to consecrate." '

'Stranger,' said the Yankee, 'truer words were never spoken; there is dry rot in all the main timbers of the Old World, and none of you will do any good till you are docked, refitted, and annexed to the New. You must log that song you sang; there ain't many Britishers that will say as much of the man that whipped them; so just set these lines down in the log, or it won't go for nothing.'

Shelley wrote some verses in the book, but not those he had quoted; and so we parted.

It was now time to return to Pisa. I never lost an opportunity of thus giving the dreamy bard glimpses of rough life. He disliked it, but could not resist my importunity. He had seen no more of the working-day world than a girl at a boarding-school, and his habit of eternally brooding on his own thoughts, in solitude and silence, damaged his health of mind and body. Like many other over-sensitive people, he thought everybody shunned him, whereas it was he who stood aloof. To the few who sought his acquaintance he was frank, cordial, and, if they appeared worthy, friendly in the extreme; but he shrank like a maiden from making the first advances. At the beginning of his literary life, he believed all authors published their opinions as he did his from a deep conviction of their truth and importance, after due investigation. When new works appeared, on any subject that interested him, he would write to the authors expressing his opinion of their books, and giving his reasons for his judgment, always arguing logically, and not for display; and, with his serene and imperturbable temper, variety of knowledge, tenacious memory, command of language, or rather of all the languages of literature, he was a most subtle critic; but, as authors are not the meekest or mildest of men, he occasionally met with rude rebuffs, and retired into his own shell.

In this way he became acquainted with Godwin, in early life; and in his first work, 'Queen Mab', or rather in the notes appended to that poem, the old philosopher's influence on the beardless boy is strongly marked. For printing these notes Shelley was punished as Ishmael is stated to have been – 'every man's hand was against him.' Southey, Wordsworth, Keats, and others he had either written to, corresponded with, or personally known; but in their literary guild he found little sympathy; their enthusiasm had burnt out whilst Shelley's had waxed stronger. Old Rothschild's sage maxim perhaps influenced them, 'Never connect yourself with an unlucky man.' However that may be, all intercourse had long ceased between Shelley and any of the literary fraternity of the day, with the exception of Peacock, Keats, Leigh Hunt, and the Brothers Smith, of the 'Rejected Addresses.'

I will now return to our drive home from visiting the ships in the docks of Leghorn. Shelley was in high glee, and full of fun, as he generally was after these 'distractions,' as he called them. The fact was his excessive mental labour impeded, if it did not paralyse, his bodily functions. When his mind was fixed on a subject, his mental powers were strained to the utmost. If not writing or sleeping, he was reading; he read whilst eating, walking, or travelling – the last thing at night, and the first thing in the morning – not the ephemeral literature of the day, which requires little or no thought, but the works of the old sages, metaphysicians, logicians, and philosophers, of the Grecian and Roman poets, and of modern scientific men, so that anything that could divert or relax his overstrained brain was of the utmost benefit to him. Now he talked of nothing but ships, sailors, and the sea; and, although he agreed with Johnson that a man who made a pun would pick a pocket, yet he made several in Greek, which he at least thought good, for he shrieked with laughter as he uttered them. Fearing his phil-Hellenism would end by making him serious, as it always did, I brought his mind back by repeating some lines of Sedley's, beginning

> 'Love still has something of the sea
> From whence his mother rose.'

During the rest of our drive we had nothing but sea yarns. He regretted having wasted his life in Greek and Latin, instead of learning the useful arts of swimming and sailoring. He resolved to have a good-sized boat forthwith. I proposed we should form a colony at the Gulf of Spezzia, and I said – 'You get Byron to join us, and with your family and the Williamses, and books, horses, and boats, undisturbed by the botherations of the world, we shall have all that reasonable people require.'

This scheme enchanted him. 'Well,' I said, 'propose this to Byron to-morrow.'

'No!' he answered, 'you must do that. Byron is always influenced by his last acquaintance. You are the last man, so do you pop the question.'

'I understand that feeling,' I observed. 'When well known neither men nor women realize our first conception of them; so we transfer our hopes to the new men or women who make a sign of sympathy, only to find them like those who have gone before, or worse.' I quoted his own lines as exemplifying my meaning –

> 'Where is the beauty, love, and truth we seek,
> But in our minds!' [25]

Byron was obstinate, but only when rubbed against the grain, or roughly handled; his body was inert, he was careless and recklessly pliant; a fresh mind, possessing the qualities he lacked, could do anything with him, for he had not made up his mind on any subject; whereas Shelley never wavered, he was unalterable. Both the poets' early deaths were hastened, if not caused, by the stubbornness of the one and the inertness of the other.

One day as the sun was setting, and I was crossing from the south to the north side of the bridge at Pisa, I ran against Williams; and, a few minutes after, caught sight of Shelley's bright eyes in the distance (I always recognized Shelley by his eyes), and said to them,

'The river has risen, and has swept the waifs and strays off its banks; they are caught by the eddies and sucked into shallows in the bends of the river. So have we three been caught here.

'On the south side of the bridge I met an old Florentine acquaintance of mine, who is a bit of an archaeologist, and I have learnt much from him. I asked him which was the healthiest place to live in – Pisa or Florence – and which was the oldest bridge across the Arno.

'He answered,

' "I return to Florence to-morrow. On Sunday evening, at half-past four, I have an antique supper at my house. There will be eight pre-Adamites – two of them are centenarians, three are ninety-five years old, and two are nonagenarians. They are live history; and if you will do us the honour to come, they will answer all your questions and many others. My party will prove the healthiness of Florence. At Pisa I do not know anyone at ninety." If Samuel Rogers arrives, as he promised on Saturday, Byron will be for sending him as a specimen of an English centenarian. My friend keeps a record of all the oldest inhabitants in Florence; he says there are sixteen above ninety whom he knows.'

Shelley said,

'He does not know me; he can put me down among the non-agenarians.'

'My host's house at Florence is very ancient, and near the Ponte Vecchio; everything in the room they sup in will be above a hundred years old, and everything on the table will be a hundred years old, except the eatables. Some of his guests are well educated, and have held high places – one as a judge. They can give you the history of everything in Florence for the last hundred and fifty years. I have not made up my mind whether I shall go. As we three castaways have met from three cross-roads, we should sit down here, open our wallets, and, when we are refreshed, tell our stories in the fashion of the old wayfarers and pilgrims. We are three birds of the same feather, same age (twenty-nine), were cast out at about the same time, and denounced as Pariahs. We are more than one thousand miles from the island we were hatched in; our affectionate parents hove us out of our nests as the birds heave their young out of theirs, on this dangerous earth. How we escaped from the ground-vermin, reptiles, and traps, and gained strength to take this long flight, we must now tell. You, Williams, will find bread in Shelley's wallet; I will dull my senses with a cigar. Neither of you has ever used the noxious weed; to me it's a solace. As Shelley says he is three times as old as either of us, he must first recount his adventures.'

SHELLEY: Mine is a life of failures. Peacock says my poetry is composed of day-dreams and nightmares; and Leigh Hunt does not think it good enough for the 'Examiner.' Jefferson Hogg [26] says all poetry is inverted sense, and consequently nonsense. Every man should attempt to do something. Poetry was the rage of the day, and I racked my imagination to be a poet. I wrote, and the critics denounced me as a mischievous visionary, and my friends said that I had mistaken my vocation, that my poetry was mere rhapsody of words; that I was soaring in the blue regions of the air, disconnected from all human sympathy. I should have liked to be a sailor; Tre says I cannot.

WILLIAMS: Why?

TRE.: Because he cannot smoke, or drink, or swear, and those are essential qualifications for a sailor.

WILLIAMS: I was in the Navy at eleven years old. I liked the sea, but detested the tyranny practised on board men-of-war. I left the Navy, went into the Dragoons, and was sent to India. My mother was a widow; a man married her for her money. Her money he would have, and he defrauded me of a large portion of my inheritance. I sold my commission, marred my prospects of rising by marrying, and drifted here. Now it is your turn, Tre: you have been as far as God has any ground.

TRE.: Well, as the sage Dogberry expresses it, 'God is a good man.' If I commence my tough yarns, the city patrol will be upon us; and, remember, you two have built your nests after the fashion of the Australian bower birds, and there will be a dire commotion at your absence; my entrance will be ever after barred; and my cigar is out, and I have no other. So we must separate.

And so we did.

Chapter 10

First our pleasures die – and then
Our hours, and then our fears – and when
These are dead, the debt is due,
Dust claims dust – and we die too.

SHELLEY.

THE following morning I told Byron our plan of going to the Gulf of Spezzia. Without any suggestion from me he eagerly volunteered to join us, and asked me to get a yacht built for him, and to look out for a house as near the sea as possible. I allowed some days to pass before I took any steps, in order to see if his wayward mind would change. As he grew more urgent I wrote to an old naval friend, Captain Roberts, then staying at Genoa, a man peculiarly fitted to execute the order, and requested him to send plans and estimates of an open boat for Shelley, and a large decked one for Byron. Shortly after, Williams and I rode along the coast to the Gulf of Spezzia. Shelley had no pride or vanity to provide for, yet we had the greatest difficulty in finding any house in which the humblest civilized family could exist.

On the shores of this superb bay, only surpassed in its natural beauty and capability by that of Naples, so effectually had tyranny paralysed the energies and enterprise of man, that the only indication of human habitation was a few most miserable fishing villages scattered along the margin of the bay. Near its centre, between the villages of San Terenzo and Lerici, we came upon a lonely and abandoned building called the Villa Magni, though it looked more like a boat or bathing-house than a place to live in. It consisted of a terrace or ground-floor unpaved, and used for storing boat-gear and fishing-tackle, and of a single storey over it divided into a hall or saloon and four small rooms which had once been whitewashed; there was one chimney for cooking. This place we thought the Shelleys might put up with for the summer. The only good thing about it was a verandah facing the sea, and almost over it. So we sought the owner and made arrangements, dependent on Shelley's approval, for taking it for six months. As to finding a palazzo grand enough for a Milordo Inglese, within a reasonable distance of the bay, it was out of the question.

Williams returned to Pisa; I rode on to Genoa, and settled with Captain Roberts about building the boats. He had already, with his usual activity, obtained permission to build them in the government dockyards, and had his plans and estimates made out. I need hardly say that though the Captain was a great arithmetician, this estimate, like all the estimates as to time and cost that were ever made, was a mere delusion, which made Byron wroth, but did not ruffle Shelley's serenity.

On returning to Pisa I found the two Poets going through the same routine of habits they had adopted before my departure; the one getting out of bed after noon, dawdling about until two or three, following the same road on horseback, stopping at the same Podere, firing his pop-guns, and retracing his steps at the same slow pace; – his frugal dinner followed by his accustomed visit to an Italian family, and then – the midnight lamp, and the immortal verses.

The other was up at six or seven, reading Plato, Sophocles, or Spinoza, with the accompaniment of a hunch of dry bread, then he joined Williams in a sail on the Arno, in a flat-bottomed skiff, book in hand, and from thence he went to the pine-forest, or some out-of-the-way place. When the birds went to roost he returned home, and talked and read until midnight. The monotony of this life was only broken at long intervals by the arrival of some old acquaintances of Byron's: Rogers, Hobhouse, Moore, Scott – not Sir Walter, – and these visits were brief.[27] John Murray, the publisher, sent out new books, and wrote amusing gossiping letters, as did Tom Moore and others. These we were generally allowed to read, or hear read, Byron archly observing, 'My private and confidential letters are better known than any of my published works.'

Shelley's boyish eagerness to possess the new toy, from which he anticipated never-failing pleasure in gliding over the azure seas, under the cloudless skies of an Italian summer, was pleasant to behold. His comrade Williams was inspired by the same spirit. We used to draw plans on the sands of the Arno of the exact dimensions of the boat, dividing her into compartments (the forepart was decked for stowage), and then, squatting down within the lines, I marked off the imaginary cabin. With a real chart of the Mediterranean spread out before them, and with faces as grave and anxious as those of Columbus and his companions, they held councils as to the islands to be visited, coasts explored, courses steered, the amount of armament, stores, water and provisions which would be necessary. Then we would narrate instances of the daring of the old navigators, as when Diaz discovered the Cape of Good Hope in 1446, with two vessels each of fifty tons burthen; or when Drake went round the world, one of his craft being only thirty tons; and of the extraordinary runs and enterprises accomplished in open boats of equal or less tonnage than the one we were building, from the earliest times to those of Commodore Bligh. Byron with the smile of a Mephistopheles standing by, asked me the amount of salvage we, the salvors, should be entitled to in the probable event of our picking up and towing Shelley's water-logged craft into port.

As the world spun round, the sandy plains of Pisa became too hot to be agreeable, and the Shelleys, longing for the sea breezes, departed to their new abode. Byron could not muster energy enough to break through his dawdling habits, so he lingered on under the fair plea of seeing the Leigh Hunts settled in his ground floor, which was prepared for them. I rode on to Genoa to hasten the completion and despatch of the long-promised boat-flotilla. I found Captain Roberts had nearly finished Shelley's boat. Williams had brought with him, on leaving England, the section of a boat as a model to build from, designed by a naval officer, and the two friends had so often sat contemplating this toy, believing it to be a marvel of nautical architecture, that nothing would satisfy them but that their craft should be built exactly on the same lines. Roberts, and the builder at Genoa, not approving, protested against it. You might as well have attempted to persuade a young man after a season of boating, or hunting, that he was not a thorough seaman and sportsman; or a youngster flushed with honours from a university that he was not the wisest of men. Williams was on ordinary occasions as humble-minded as Shelley, but having been two or three years in the Navy, and then in the cavalry, he thought there was no vanity in his believing that he was as good a judge of a boat or horse as any man. In these small conceits we are all fools at the beginning of life, until time, with his sledge-hammer, has let the daylight into our brain-boxes; so the boat was built according to his cherished model.[28] When it was finished, it took two tons of iron ballast to bring her down to her bearings, and then she was very crank in a breeze, though not deficient in beam. She was fast, strongly built, and Torbay rigged. I despatched her under charge of two steady seamen, and a smart sailor lad, aged eighteen, named Charles Vivian. Shelley sent back the two sailors and only retained the boy; they told me on their return to Genoa that they had been out in a rough night, that she was a ticklish boat to manage, but had sailed and worked well, and with two good seamen she would do very well; and that they had cautioned the gents accordingly. I shortly after received the following letter from Shelley :–

Lerici, May 16, 1822

My dear Trelawny,

The 'Don Juan' is arrived, and nothing can exceed the admiration she has excited; for we must suppose the name to have been given her during the equivocation of sex which her godfather suffered in the harem. Williams declares her to be perfect, and I participate in his enthusiasm, inasmuch as would be decent in a landsman. We have been out now several days, although we have sought in vain for an opportunity of trying her against the feluccas or other large craft in the bay; she passes the small ones as a comet might pass the dullest planet of the heavens. When do you expect to be here in the 'Bolivar?' If Roberts's 50*l.* grow into a 500*l.*, and his ten days into months, I suppose I may expect that I am considerably in your debt, and that you will not be round here until the middle of the summer. I hope that I shall be mistaken in the last of these conclusions; as to the former, whatever may be the result, I have little reason and less inclination to complain of my bargain. I wish you could express from me to Roberts how excessively I am obliged to him for the time and trouble he has expended for my advantage, and which I wish could be as easily repaid as the money which I owe him, and which I wait your orders for remitting.

I have only heard from Lord Byron once, and solely upon that subject. Tita* is with me, and I suppose will go with you in the schooner to Leghorn. We are very impatient to see you, and although we cannot hope that you will stay long on your *first* visit, we count upon you for the latter part of the summer, as soon as the novelty of Leghorn is blunted. Mary desires her best regards to you, and unites with me in a sincere wish to renew an intimacy from which we have already experienced so much pleasure.

Believe me, my dear Trelawny,
Your very sincere friend,
P. B. Shelley.

Lerici, June 18, 1822

My dear Trelawny,

I have written to Guebhard, to pay you 154 Tuscan crowns, the amount of the balance against me according to Roberts's calculation, which I keep for your satisfaction, deducting sixty, which I paid the aubergiste at Pisa, in all 214. We saw you about eight miles in the offing this morning; but the abatement of the breeze leaves us little hope that you can have made Leghorn this evening. Pray write us a full, true, and particular account of your proceedings, &c. – How Lord Byron likes the vessel; what are your arrangements and intentions for the summer; and when we may expect to see you or him in this region again; and especially whether there is any news of Hunt.

Roberts and Williams are very busy in refitting the 'Don Juan;' they seem determined that she shall enter Leghorn in style. I am no great judge of these matters; but am excessively obliged to the former, and delighted that the latter should find amusement, like the sparrow, in educating the cuckoo's young.

You, of course, enter into society at Leghorn: should you

*A servant of Byron's.

meet with any scientific person capable of preparing the *Prussic Acid, or essential oil of bitter almonds*, I should regard it as a great kindness if you could procure me a small quantity. It requires the greatest caution in preparation, and ought to be highly concentrated; I would give any price for this medicine; you remember we talked of it the other night, and we both expressed a wish to possess it; my wish was serious, and sprung from the desire of avoiding needless suffering. I need not tell you I have no intention of suicide at present, but I confess it would be a comfort to me to hold in my possession that golden key to the chamber of perpetual rest. *The Prussic Acid* is used in medicine in infinitely minute doses; but that preparation is weak, and has not the concentration necessary to medicine all ills infallibly. A single drop, even less, is a dose, and it acts by paralysis.

I am curious to hear of this publication about Lord Byron and the Pisa circle. I hope it will not annoy him; as to me I am supremely indifferent. If you have not shown the letter I sent you, don't until Hunt's arrival, when we shall certainly meet.

Your very sincere friend,

P. B. Shelley.

Mary is better, though still excessively weak.[29]

Not long after, I followed in Byron's boat, the 'Bolivar' schooner. There was no fault to find with her, Roberts and the builder had fashioned her after their own fancy, and she was both fast and safe. I manned her with five able seamen, four Genoese and one Englishman. I put into the Gulf of Spezzia, and found Shelley in ecstasy with his boat, and Williams as touchy about her reputation as if she had been his wife. They were hardly ever out of her, and talked of the Mediterranean as a lake too confined and tranquil to exhibit her sea-going excellence. They longed to be on the broad Atlantic, scudding under bare poles in a heavy sou'wester, with plenty of sea room. I went out for a sail in Shelley's boat to see how they would manage her. It was great fun to witness Williams teaching the Poet how to steer, and other points of seamanship. As usual, Shelley had a book in hand, saying he could read and steer at the same time, as one was mental, the other mechanical.

'Luff!' said Williams.

Shelley put the helm the wrong way. Williams corrected him.

'Do you see those two white objects a-head? keep them in a line, the wind is heading us.' Then, turning to me, he said: 'Lend me a hand to haul in the main-sheet, and I will show you how close she can lay to the wind to work off a lee-shore.'

'No,' I answered; 'I am a passenger, and won't touch a rope.'

'Luff!' said Williams, as the boat was yawing about. 'Shelley, you can't steer, you have got her in the wind's eye; give me the tiller, and you attend the main-sheet. Ready about!' said Williams. 'Helms down – let go the fore-sheet – see how she spins round on her heel – is not she a beauty? Now, Shelley, let go the main-sheet, and boy, haul aft the jib-sheet!'

The main-sheet was jammed, and the boat unmanageable, or as sailors express it, in irons; when the two had cleared it, Shelley's hat was knocked overboard, and he would probably have followed, if I had not held him. He was so uncommonly awkward that, when they had things ship-shape, Williams, somewhat scandalized at the lubberly manoeuvre, blew up the Poet for his neglect and inattention to orders. Shelley was, however, so happy and in such high glee, and the nautical terms so tickled his fancy, that he even put his beloved 'Plato' in his pocket, and gave his mind up to fun and frolic.

'You will do no good with Shelley,' I said, 'until you heave his books and papers overboard; shear the wisps of hair that hang over his eyes; and plunge his arms up to the elbows in a tar-bucket. And you, captain, will have no authority, until you dowse your frock coat and cavalry boots. You see I am stripped for a swim, so please, whilst I am on board, to keep within swimming distance of the land.'

The boy was quick and handy, and used to boats. Williams was not as deficient as I anticipated, but over-anxious and wanted practice, which alone makes a man prompt in emergency. Shelley was intent on catching images from the ever-changing sea and sky, he heeded not the boat. On my suggesting the addi-

tion to their crew of a Genoese sailor accustomed to the coast –
such as I had on board the 'Bolivar' – Williams, thinking I under-
valued his efficiency as a seaman, was scandalized: 'As if we
three seasoned salts were not enough to manage an open boat,
when lubberly sloops and cutters of fifty or sixty tons were
worked by as few men on the rough seas and iron-bound coast
of Scotland!'

'Yes,' I answered, 'but what a difference between those sea-
lions and you and our water-poet! A decked cutter besides, or
even a frigate, is easier handled in a gale or squall, and out-and-
out safer to be on board of than an open boat. If we had been
in a squall to-day with the main-sheet jammed, and the tiller
put starboard instead of port, we should have had to swim for
it.'

'Not I: I should have gone down with the rest of the pigs in
the bottom of the boat,' said Shelley, meaning the iron pig-
ballast.[30]

The Poet's boat was not more than thirty feet long, with a
beam in proportion; but she drew too much water to come near
the shore, and so Captain Williams, with the aid of a carpenter,
built a tiny dingey, six or seven feet long, flat-bottomed, and
very light, constructed of basket-work, covered with canvas and
tarred, exactly as the Welsh make their coracles on their rivers,
to carry one person, and, on land, one person could carry it
from the beach into the house. The Poet was delighted with this
fragile toy, and toying with it on the water, it often capsized,
and gave him many a header: standing up, or an incautious
movement, upset it. These tricks he attributed to the viciousness
of the dingey, and not to his excessive awkwardness. 'I see now,'
he said, 'the reason ships and boats are feminine; because like
women they are perverse.' He was as proud of it as a bold boy
with a skittish pony. By practice he learnt to mitigate its evils,
and vaunted that he had mastered and could do anything with
it, and recklessly went out in bad weather. Poets, not having
much on land, claim the unenclosed ocean, or, at least, the Poet
Laureateship, as their especial privilege :–

> 'The sea, the sea, the dark blue sea,
>   The bright, the pure, the ever free.'

They write in ecstasy, as they do to a mistress, and ever they love it best of all, and in all its moods it is their ideal love; but their loves and hates spring from the head, not heart. In or on it there is no beast or bird so deplorably helpless; they are qualmish at the sight of it, and sick when on it; they are, as sailors profanely say of ladies, 'the aukerd'st things as is.'

Byron by his writings would have us believe that 'a tent on shore and galley on the sea' comprised all his wants, and were indispensable to him. The first time I went on board a vessel with him I made some remark regarding her: he said, 'Tre, do what's best; it's no use asking me. Do you think we know all the things we write about? I write best on things I know the least, for then I am unprejudiced.'

Shelley liked paddling his skiff out to sea, and then letting it drift until the sea breeze came and lapped up its side over the gunwale, and drove him to the shore. 'He felt,' he said, 'independent and safe from land bores.'

On a sultry evening I heard my name called in hot haste from the verandah, Mary Shelley shrieking, 'Percy will be drowned; the boat is upset; he is struggling in the water; he can't stand, the waves knock him down.' I saw the Poët floundering; he was more anxious to save the boat than himself; was buffeting with the waves, and lay sputtering, sprawling, and floundering, imbibing the brine. I was the only water-dog of our band; neither Percy nor Captain Roberts nor the mate could swim, nor Williams well – man and his brother, the monkey, are the only animals that cannot on instinct swim; he is too clever, he must learn. I waded into the water, and convoyed the Poet and his bark to the shore. He was shrieking, not from fear, but delight, as the crisp waves curled up and over him, breaking into foam. This was the prelude to a blustering and squally night, wind, rain, and lightning; the spray swept the verandah, and dashed against the windows: it was a lively representation of being at sea in a squall.

A few years ago this superb bay of Spezzia, with its harbour and many advantages, was scarcely used, and its shores were thinly inhabited by the poorest classes, mostly fishermen's cabins, clustered and sheltered in the nooks and corners of the land. It was the policy of the Austrians to disarm, disunite, and extinguish every hope of the Italians, and the sun too, if they could. Now that the Goths are driven out, and the fiendish priests muzzled, Italy is no longer a geographical expression, but a reality, and is once more in the hands of the Italians. The sun shines on no land on which nature and art have been so lavish, and we shall see what they will do with it.

On a calm sultry evening, Jane was sitting on the sands before the villa on the margin of the sea with her two infants and watching for her husband – he was becalmed in the offing awaiting the sea breeze. Shelley came from the house dragging the skiff: after launching her he said to Jane,

'The sand and air are hot, let us float on the cool calm sea, there is room with careful stowage for us all in my barge.'

His flashing eyes and vehement eager manner determined on the instant execution of any project that took his fancy, however perilous. He overbore all opposition in those less self-willed than he was, and women are of a trusting nature and have faith in an earnest man. So Jane impulsively and promptly squatted in the bottom of the frail bark with her babies. The Poet proud of his freight triumphantly shoved off from the shore, and to exhibit his skill as a mariner rowed round a jutting promontory into deep blue water. The sea is very shallow for a considerable distance from the land in the bay, and Jane understood that Percy intended to float on the water near the shore, for the gunwale of the boat was only a hand's breadth out of the water; a puff of wind, a ripple on the water, or an incautious movement of the Poet, or herself or children, and the tub of a thing that could barely sustain the weight within it would cant over and fill and glide from under them. There was no eye watching them, no boat within a mile, the shore fast receding, the water deepening, and the Poet dreaming. As these dismal facts flashed on Jane's mind, her insane folly in trusting herself to a man of genius, but devoid of judgment, prudence, or skill, dismayed her.

After pulling out a long way, the Poet rested on his oars, unconscious of her fears and apparently of where he was, absorbed in a deep reverie, probably reviewing all he had gone through of suffering and wrong, with no present or future.

He was a brooding and silent man, feeling acutely, but never complaining – the wounds that bleed inwards are the most fatal. He took no heed of the occurrences of daily life, or men's selfish hopes or fears; his mind was so organized that it required a nice perception to know when and how to strike the chord that would excite his attention. Spellbound by terror, she kept her eyes on the awful boatman: sad and dejected, with his head leaning on his chest, his spirit seemed crushed; his hand had been for every man, and every man's hand against him. He was 'the shorn lamb, but the wind was not tempered.' At any other time or place Jane would have sympathized deeply with the lorn and despairing bard. She had made several remarks, but they met with no response. She saw death in his eyes. Suddenly he raised his head, his brow cleared and his face brightened as with a bright thought, and he exclaimed joyfully,

'Now let us together solve the great mystery.'

An ordinary lady-kind would have screamed or got up to implore, to pray, or reason, and thus herself have accomplished what she most dreaded – the Poet's suggestion; but Jane, with a true woman's instinct – a safer guide in perilous emergencies than could be found in a senate of sages – knowing Shelley was unlike all other men, felt that to be silent or strike a discordant note to his feelings might make him stamp his foot, and the leaden waters would roll over and wrap round them as a winding-sheet; that her only chance was to distract his thoughts from his dismal past life to the less dreary present – to kindle hope. In answer to his kind and affectionate proposal of 'solving the great mystery,' suppressing her terror and assuming her usual cheerful voice, she answered promptly,

'No, thank you, not now; I should like my dinner first, and so would the children.'

This gross material answer to his sublime proposition shocked the Poet, as showing his companion could not enter into the spirit of his idea.

'And look,' she continued, 'the sea breeze is coming in, the mist is clearing away, and Edward is coming on shore with Trelawny; they have been out since light and must be famished, they took nothing with them, and to-morrow you are to have the boat-race to see if you can beat the "Bolivar." I wish we were on shore; they'll be surprised at our being out at this time, and Edward says this boat is not safe.'

'Safe!' said the Poet; 'I'd go to Leghorn or anywhere in her.'

Death's demon, always attending the Poet on the water, now spread his wings and vanished. Jane felt his thoughts were veering round and continued,

'You haven't written the words for the Indian air.'

'Yes, I have,' he answered, 'long ago. I must write them out again, for I can't read what I compose and write out of doors. You must play the air again and I'll try and make the thing better.'

The weird boatman now paddled to where our boat had landed. Williams, not finding his wife in the house, came down to the beach in dismay, when I pointed her out to him in the skiff: the fisherman's boat that landed us had shoved off.

The Poet, deluded by the wiles of a woman into postponing his voyage to solve the great mystery, paddled his cockle shell of a boat into shallow water.

As soon as Jane saw the sandy bottom, she snatched up her babies and clambered out so hurriedly that the punt was capsized. Edward and I picked them up; the bard was underneath the boat and rose with it partly on his back, and was not unlike a turtle, or a hermit crab that houses itself in any empty shell it can find. Edward, surprised at his wife's lubberly way of getting out of the boat, said,

'We would have hauled the boat up, if you had waited a moment.'

'No, thank you. Oh, I have escaped the most dreadful fate; never will I put my foot in that horrid coffin. Solve the great mystery? Why, he is the greatest of all mysteries. Who can predict what he will do? – and he casts a spell over everything. You can form some notion of what other people will do as they partake of our common nature – not what he will do. He is seeking after what we all avoid, death. I wish we were away, I shall always be in terror.'

Leaving them to their cogitation, I went to make my toilet, the sea my washing-basin – there was no other. As usual we had a fish dinner. Jane ate nothing; the sight of the natives of the deep was enough. Condemned men can eat, but not the suddenly reprieved.

'You won't catch me in a boat with Shelley alone,' said Jane.[31]

The Poet hearing his name – for all his faculties were marvellously acute – glided into the room, with his boyish face and radiant expression. He seized some bread and grapes – his usual food. He fed his brain as well as body; he was then reading the Spanish dramas. His body was with us but his brain in Spain. His young face looked as innocent of all guile as a cherub, and so he was. Simple, frank, and confiding, any one would trust him at sight. His mild, earnest manners won all hearts, gentle and simple. There was no limit to his generosity and self-negation to serve a friend, and he considered all the poor and oppressed as his friends. But then he avowed that he did not believe the State religion, and repeated what many have said before him and more have thought, that priests of all denominations only consider religion as the means of obtaining that which all are desirous of – power. When Lord Eldon was Chancellor, the Church of England excommunicated unbelievers more effectually than the Church of Rome.

The ground floor of the Poet's villa was appropriated, as is often done in Italy, for stowing the implements and produce of the land, as rent is paid in kind there. In the autumn you find casks of wine, jars of oil, tools, wood, occasionally carts, and, near the sea, boats and fishing-nets. Over this floor there were a large saloon and four bedrooms, and nothing more; there was an out-building for cooking, and a place for the servants to eat and sleep in. The Williamses had one room and Shelley and his wife occupied two more, facing each other.

Events not worth narrating in the lives of ordinary men are interesting as regards our Poet; they illustrate the character and the working of an over-excited brain, kept in continual action by a fervid imagination and metaphysical studies.

On a moonless and gloomy night, the wind and sea and rain making such a hubbub without that Mrs Williams was kept awake, ruminating and longing for daylight, she was startled by a heavy weight from the saloon falling against her door and moaning. It awoke her husband, and they sprang out of their nest. On opening the door Mrs Shelley, in her night-dress, tumbled into their room, helpless and tongue-tied by terror. The Poet, unconscious of everything, his eyes wide open, with no speculation in them, stood over her, upright and motionless, holding a lighted candle at arm's length. On Mrs Shelley recovering her senses she told Mrs Williams she had been awakened by the glare of a light. On opening her eyes she beheld Shelley holding a lighted candle over her. She spoke but he did not answer. His eyes were wide open, but misty; he resembled a statue. She got out of bed and crossed the saloon; he followed, and she fainted, falling against the Williams' door. Williams watched the sleep-walker; he stalked to the door leading out to the verandah, seemingly listening to the crashing of the waves, then walked into his room, put the candle on the table, and stretched himself on his bed.

The Poet often got up at night to write or read, and talked in sleep, but he was not a somnambulist.

> 'Our simple life wants little, and true taste
> Hires not the pale drudge Luxury to waste
> The scene it would adorn.'

A visitor from Genoa was expected. Shelley, anxious to do him honour, and conscious that their anchorite way of living would not suit ordinary mortals, caused a considerable commotion at the villa. After a council had been held on their commissariat, it was determined that Williams should go out in the offing to fish, another to forage on horseback. The women folks were to set their wits and hands to work. As on all such occasions, the Poet disappeared, but not until Mrs Shelley had extorted from him a promise to be at home at the appointed hour to don a coat – his usual costume was a black jacket – and she added, archly, 'I'll brush his hair and smarten him up.'

The absurd womenkind proceeded to their business indoors and the others to theirs out. Their short notice for preparations was no detriment, as in the hot weather in southern climes things that are killed must be instantly cooked. Notwithstanding the bother and turmoil the ladies, as is their wont, seemed to enjoy it. They so rarely had an opportunity of exhibiting and comparing their drapery and dressmaking capabilities, that, corrupted by our example of negligence, they hardly knew themselves from the Contadine around. There were no milliners or maids or shops to help them; their wardrobes were scant, but they were young and good-looking, and had their wits and taste to help them. There was one serious drawback – they knew each the other's wardrobe. Men are so wrapt up in their own vanity and self-conceit as to believe that women adorn themselves exclusively to captivate them, whereas in general the desire of women is to astonish, eclipse, and excite the envy of their own sex : –

> 'My sister is a goodly portly lady,
> A lady of a presence, she spreads satin
> As king's ships do canvas, everywhere.'

When they speak of the handsomest, they mean the woman most costly-attired; men are of a grosser nature and estimate them by their flesh and faces. The visitor came, and he was most anxious to see the Poet, with whose works he was enchanted, and of whose great knowledge and simple habits he had heard so much from me and others; however, they knew how uncertain the Poet was, and never waited for him. The dinner was served with more precision than was usual, and, as sailors have it, 'Compliments pass when gentlefolks meet.'

The stranger told them the news of the outer world from which they were isolated, for newspapers at that period were a mere farrago of Austrian lies. From German humbug they got into literature. The visitor said the German students of English literature considered Shelley as a metaphysical and moral philosopher, a writer of transcendent imagination; that he awakened all the dormant faculties of his readers, was the Poet of the inner mind, that he surpassed our popular poets in depth of thought and refinement. One of the party remarked that genius purifies: the naked statues of the Greeks are modest, the draped ones of the moderns are not. The talk was here interrupted by a concussion of glass and crockery, and a vehement exclamation, 'Oh my gracious !' from one of the trio of ladies, drew all eyes her way. Appalled by the sight, the ladies instantly averted their gaze and held up their hands, not having fans, in mute despair. Had it been a ghoul, he would have been scoffed at, as they prey on the dead; if it had been a spectre or phantom he would have been robed, and therefore welcome, for they are shadowy and refined spirits; but the company were confronted by an apparition not tolerated in our chaste and refined age even in marble – by our poet, washed, indeed, for he was just out of the sea, not in an evening costume, nor was his hair dressed, as his wife had promised it should be; but, like Adam before the fall –

> 'Such of late
> Columbus found the Americans, so girt
> With feathered cincture; naked else, and wild.'

The brine from his shock of hair trickling down his innocent nose; if he were girt with a feathered cincture or anything else, it was not visible; small fragments of seaweed clung to his hair, and he was odorous of the salt brine – he scorned encumbering himself with combs or towels. He was gliding noiselessly round the two sides of the saloon to his room, and might possibly have succeeded unnoticed, or certainly unchallenged – as the Italian maid, with accustomed tact, had walked by his side, carefully screening him from the company – but for the refined and excitable lady calling attention to such an unprecedented licence even in a poet.

The simple and innocent bard, grieved at having given pain by his alleged breach of etiquette, felt bound to explain his case, so stopping beside the complainant, and drawing himself up (as the novelists have it) to his full height, with the air and accent of a boy wrongfully accused, said,

'How can I help it? I must go to my room to get my clothes; there is no way to get to it but through this. At this hour I have always found this place vacant. I have not altered my hour of bathing, but you have changed yours for dining. The skittish skiff has played me one of her usual tricks by upsetting all my clothes in the water; the land breeze is getting up, and they will be drifting out to sea again, if I don't make haste to recover them.'

His blushing wife could not bandy words with a sea monster. Having thus refuted to his own satisfaction the implied censure on his manners, he, without noticing any one else, glided from out the puddle he had made on the floor into his dormitory. The dinner circle were thus indebted to the sensitive lady, not only for a full view of our poet in his character of a merman, but for an oration.

In a few minutes he reappeared, rushing down to secure his former attire. Speedily coming back, he held up a book, saying,

'I have recovered this priceless gem from the wreck' (Æschylus).

He then took his place, unconscious of having done anything that could offend any one.

All strangers were astonished at his boyish appearance. The guest could not believe it was the poet whose writings he had read five or six years back. He said,

'Why, he is not more than eighteen or twenty! The thing that impressed me most in what I read of his writings was his knowledge of the mind and display of our deepest feelings. Young writers write of outward and visible objects. When I was translating German poetry into English, I got more rare words out of Shelley's and Milton's works than from all the rest of the English poets.'

This strong sensation scene spoilt the order, formality, and propriety of the banquet, but added to its mirth. To confine Shelley within the limits of conventional or any other arbitrary laws of society was out of the question; he retained his simple, boyish habits. In the last year of his life I lived in close alliance with him. To those he liked and that liked him he was cordial and confiding; to those he did not like the oracle was dumb.

I left Shelley at Spezzia, and sailed to Leghorn. He was writing in the woods. He told me he always wrote best in the open air, in a boat, under a tree, or on the bank of a river. There was, he said, an undivided spirit which reigns abroad, a sympathizing harmony amongst the works of nature, that made him better acquainted with himself and them.

'If,' said he, 'I have passed a day in a city, as I have done this one on this lovely spot, I should accuse myself of having lost rather than gained a day, by not having applied myself to any kind of improvement.'

When I took my departure for Leghorn on board the 'Bolivar,' Shelley and Williams accompanied me out of the bay, and then we parted. I arrived at Leghorn the same night. I found my Lord Inglese had at last mustered sufficient energy to move from Pisa to Monte Nero, near Leghorn; I condoled with him on the change, for his new, flimsy-built villa – not unlike the suburban verandahed cockney boxes on the Thames – was ten times hotter than the old solid palace he had left, with its cool marble halls, and arched and lofty floors that defied the sun. He was satisfied with his boat, but by no means with its cost; he took little interest in her, and I could not induce him to take a cruise; he always had some excuse. The first time he came on board, he said in answer to something I pointed out in the rigging : –

'People think I must be a bit of a sailor from my writings. All the sea-terms I use are from authority, and they cost me time, toil, and trouble to look them out; but you will find me a land-lubber. I hardly know the stem from the stern, and don't know the name or use of a single rope or sail; I know the deep sea is blue, and not green, as that greenhorn Shakespeare always calls it.'

This was literally true; in regard to Byron, he neither knew nor cared to know, nor ever asked a question (excepting when writing) about sea-terms or sea-life.

Towards the end of June, 1822, the long-expected family of the Hunts arrived by sea from England.

Byron observed, 'You will find Leigh Hunt[32] a gentleman in dress and address; at least he was so when I last saw him in England, with a taint of cockneyism.'

I found him a gentleman and something more; and with a quaint fancy and cultivated mind. He was in high spirits, and disposed to be pleased with others. His anticipated literary projects in conjunction with Byron and Shelley were a source of great pleasure to him – so was the land of beauty and song. He had come to it as to a new home, in which, as the immortal Robins the auctioneer would have said : 'You will find no nuisance but the litter of the rose-leaves and the noise of the nightingales.' The pleasure that surpassed all the rest, was the anticipation of seeing speedily his friend Shelley. But alas! all those things which seemed so certain –

> 'Those juggling fiends
> That keep the word of promise to our ear,
> And break it to our hope.'

so kept – and so broke – it with Leigh Hunt.[33]

The first visit I paid to Byron after the Hunts' arrival I found Mrs Hunt was confined to her room, as she generally was, from bad health. Hunt too was in delicate health – a hypochondriac; and the seven children, untamed, the eldest a little more than ten and the youngest a yearling, were scattered about playing on the large marble staircase and in the hall. Hunt's theory and practice were that children should be unrestrained until they were of an age to be reasoned with. If they kept out of his way he was satisfied. On my entering the Poet's study, I said to him, 'The Hunts have effected a lodgment in your palace;' and I was thinking how different must have been his emotion on the arrival of the Hunts from that triumphant morning after the publication of 'Childe Harold,' when he 'awoke and found himself famous.'

Usually meeting him after two or three days' absence his eyes glistened; now they were dull and his brow pale. He said,

'I offered you those rooms. Why did you not take them? Have you seen Hunt?'

'Not this morning,' I replied; 'he is in labour for an article in the new Review.'

Byron said,

'It will be an abortion. I shall have nothing to do with it. Gifford and Jeffrey will run him down as you say Shelley's boat was run down. Why did not he stick to the 'Examiner?' He is in Italy, but his mind is in Hampstead, Highgate, and Covent Garden.'

When I took my leave he followed me into the passage, and patting the bull-dog on the head he said, 'Don't let any Cockneys pass this way.'

Byron could not realize till the actual experiment was tried the nuisance of having a man with a sick wife and seven disorderly children interrupting his solitude and his ordinary customs, and then Hunt did not conceal that his estimate of Byron's poetry was not exalted. At that time Hunt thought highly of his own poetry and under-estimated all other, as is the wont of the literary guilds. Shelley he thought would have made a great poet if he had written on intelligible subjects. He was smitten with the old rhymesters' quaintness, punning, and playing battledore and shuttlecock with words. Shelley soared too high for him and Byron flew too near the ground. There was not a single subject on which Byron and Hunt could agree.

Chapter 11

Alas! what is life, what is death, what are we,
That when the ship sinks, we no longer may be?

SHELLEY.

SHELLEY, with his friend Williams, soon came in their boat, scudding into the harbour of Leghorn. They went with the Hunts to Pisa, and established them in Lord Byron's palace, Shelley having furnished a floor there for them. In a few days Shelley returned to Leghorn, and found Williams eager to be off. We had a sail outside the port in the two boats. Shelley was in a mournful mood; his mind depressed by a recent interview with Byron.

Byron, at first, had been more eager than Shelley for Leigh Hunt's arrival in Italy to edit and contribute to the proposed new Review, and so continued until his English correspondents had worked on his fears. They did not oppose, for they knew his temper too well, but artfully insinuated that he was jeopardizing his fame and fortune, &c., &c., &c. Shelley found Byron irritable whilst talking with him on the fulfilment of his promises with regard to Leigh Hunt. This was doomed to be their last meeting.

On Saturday, the 6th, Williams wrote the following letter to his wife at the Villa Magni: –

I HAVE just left the quay, my dearest girl, and the wind blows right across to Spezzia, which adds to the vexation I feel at being unable to leave this place. For my own part, I should have been with you in all probability on Wednesday evening, but I have been kept day after day waiting for Shelley's definitive arrangements with Lord B. relative to poor Hunt, whom, in my opinion, he has treated vilely. A letter from Mary, of the most gloomy kind, reached S. yesterday, and this mood of hers aggravated my uneasiness to see you; for I am proud, dear girl, beyond words to express, in the conviction, that *wherever* we may be together you could be cheerful and contented.

Would I could take the present gale by the wings and reach you to-night; hard as it blows, I would venture across for *such* a reward. However, to-morrow something decisive shall take place; and if I am detained, I shall depart in a felucca, and leave the boat to be brought round in company with Trelawny in the 'Bolivar'. He talks of visiting Spezzia again in a few days. I am tired to death of waiting – this is our longest separation, and seems a year to me. Absence alone is enough to make me anxious, and indeed unhappy; but I think if I had left you in our own house in solitude, I should feel it less than I do now. – What can I do? Poor S. desires that I should return to you, but I know secretly wishes me not to leave him in the lurch. He too, by his manner, is as anxious to see you almost as I could be, but the interests of poor H. keep him here; – in fact, with Lord B. it appears they cannot do anything, – who actually said as much as that he did not wish(?) his name to be attached to the work, and of course to theirs.

In Lord Byron's family all is confusion; – the cut-throats he is so desirous to have about him, have involved him in a second row; and although the present banishment of the Gambas from Tuscany is attributed to the first affair of the dragoon, the continued disturbances among his and their servants is, I am sure, the principal cause for its being carried into immediate effect. Four days (commencing from the day of our arrival at Leghorn) were only given them to find another retreat; and as Lord B. considers this a personal, though tacit attack upon himself, he chooses to follow their fortunes in another country. Genoa was first selected, – of that government they could have no hope; – Geneva was then proposed, and this proved as bad if not worse. Lucca is now the choice, and Trelawny was despatched last night to feel their way with the governor, to whom he carried letters. All this time Hunt is shuffled off from day to day, and now heaven knows when or how it will end.

Lord B.'s reception of Mrs H. was – as S. tells me – most shameful. She came into his house sick and exhausted, and he scarcely deigned to notice her; was silent, and scarcely bowed.[34]

This conduct cut H. to the soul; but the way in which he received our friend Roberts, at Dunn's door, shall be described when we meet: – it must be acted. How I long to see you; I had written *when*, but I will make no promises, for I too well know how distressing it is to both of us to break them. Tuesday evening, at furthest, unless kept by the weather, I *will* say, 'Oh, Jane! how fervently I press you and our little ones to my heart.'

Adieu! – Take body and soul; for you are at once my heaven and earth; – that is all I ask of both.

E. Elk. W—.

S. is at Pisa, and will write to-night to me.

The last entry in Williams's Journal is dated July 4, 1822, Leghorn: –

Processions of priests and religiosi have been for several days past praying for rain: but the gods are either angry, or nature too powerful.

The affair of the dragoon alluded to in Williams's letter, as connected with the Gambas, was this: – As Byron and his companions were returning to Pisa on horseback, the road being blocked up by the party, – a serjeant-major on duty in their rear trotted his horse through the cavalcade. One of the awkward literary squad, – a resolute bore, but timid rider, – was nearly spilt, from his nag shying.[35] To divert the jeers from his own bad riding, he appealed pathetically to Byron, saying: –

'Shall we endure this man's insolence?'

Byron said: – 'No, we will bring him to an account;' and instantly galloped after the dragoon into Pisa, his party following. The guard at the gate turned out with drawn swords, but could not stop them. Some of the servants of Byron and the Gambas were idling on the steps of his palace; getting a glimpse of the row, one of them armed himself with a stable-fork, rushed at the dragoon as he passed Byron's palace, and wounded him severely in the side. This scene was acted in broad daylight on the Lung' Arno, the most public place in the city, scores of people looking on! yet the police, with their host of spies and backed by the power of a despotic government, could never ascertain who struck the blow.

Not liking to meddle with the Poet, they imprisoned two of his servants, and exiled the family of Count Gamba. Byron chose to follow them. Such is the hatred of the Italians to their rulers and all who have authority over them, that the blind beggars at the corners of the streets, – no others were permitted to beg in Tuscany, – hearing that the English were without arms, sidled up to some of them, adroitly putting into their hands formidable stilettos, which they had concealed in the sleeves of their ragged gaberdines.

Shelley wrote me the following note about the dragoon: –

My dear T.,

Gamba is with me, and we are drawing up a paper demanded of us by the police. Mary tells me that you have an account from Lord Byron of the affair, and we wish to see it before ours is concluded. The man is severely wounded in the side, and his life is supposed to be in danger from the weapon having grazed the liver. It were as well if you could come here, as we shall decide on no statement without you.

Ever yours truly,
Shelley.

Mrs Shelley, writing an account of the row, says: –

'Madame G. and I happened to be in the carriage, ten paces behind, and saw the whole. Taaffe kept at a safe distance during the fray, but fearing the consequence, he wrote such a report that Lord Byron quarrelled with him; and what between insolence and abject humility he has kept himself in hot water, when, in fact, he had nothing to fear.'[36]

Here is a letter – the last – addressed to Shelley by Mrs Williams: –[37]

July 6th

My Dearest Friend,

Your few melancholy lines have indeed cast your own visionary veil over a countenance that was animated with the hope of seeing you return with far different tidings. We heard yesterday that you had left Leghorn in company with the 'Bolivar,' and would assuredly be here in the morning at five o'clock; therefore I got up, and from the terrace saw (or I dreamt it) the 'Bolivar' opposite in the offing. She hoisted more sail, and went through the Straits. What can this mean? Hope and uncertainty have made such a chaos in my mind that I know not what to think. My own Neddino does not deign to lighten my darkness by a single word. Surely I shall see him to-night. Perhaps, too, you are with him. Well, *pazienza!*

Mary, I am happy to tell you, goes on well; she talks of going to Pisa, and indeed your poor friends seem to require all her assistance. For me, alas! I can only offer sympathy, and my fervent wishes that a brighter cloud may soon dispel the present gloom. I hope much from the air of Pisa for Mrs Hunt.

Lord B.'s departure gives me pleasure, for whatever may be the present difficulties and disappointments, they are small to what you would have suffered had he remained with you. This I say in the spirit of prophecy, so gather consolation from it.

I have only time left to scrawl you a hasty adieu, and am

Affectionately yours,

J. W.

Why do you talk of never enjoying moments like the past? Are you going to join your friend Plato, or do you expect I shall do so soon? *Buona notte.*

P. B. Shelley, Esq.,
  Ferma in Posta,
    Pisa.

On Monday, the 8th of July, 1822, I went with Shelley to his bankers, and then to a store. It was past one P.M. when we went on board our respective boats, – Shelley and Williams to return to their home in the Gulf of Spezzia; I in the 'Bolivar,' to accompany them into the offing. When we were under weigh, the guard-boat boarded us to overhaul our papers. I had not got my port clearance, the captain of the port having refused to give it to the mate, as I had often gone out without. The officer of the Health Office consequently threatened me with fourteen days' quarantine. It was hopeless to think of detaining my friends. Williams had been for days fretting and fuming to be off; they had no time to spare, it was past two o'clock, and there was very little wind.

Sullenly and reluctantly I re-anchored, furled my sails, and with a ship's glass watched the progress of my friends' boat. My Genoese mate observed, – 'They should have sailed this morning at three or four A.M., instead of three P.M. They are standing too much in shore; the current will set them there.'

I said, 'They will soon have the land-breeze.'

'Maybe,' continued the mate, 'she will soon have too much breeze; that gaff topsail is foolish in a boat with no deck and no sailor on board.' Then pointing to the S.W., 'Look at those black lines and the dirty rags hanging on them out of the sky – they are a warning; look at the smoke on the water; the devil is brewing mischief.'

There was a sea-fog, in which Shelley's boat was soon after enveloped, and we saw nothing more of her.

Although the sun was obscured by mists, it was oppressively sultry. There was not a breath of air in the harbour. The heaviness of the atmosphere and an unwonted stillness benumbed my senses. I went down into the cabin and sank into a slumber. I was roused up by a noise over-head and went on deck. The men were getting up a chain cable to let go another anchor. There was a general stir amongst the shipping; shifting berths, getting down yards and masts, veering out cables, hauling in of hawsers, letting go anchors, hailing from the ships and quays, boats sculling rapidly to and fro. It was almost dark, although only half-past six o'clock. The sea was of the colour, and looked as solid and smooth as a sheet of lead, and covered with an oily scum. Gusts of wind swept over without ruffling it, and big drops of rain fell on its surface, rebounding, as if they could not penetrate it. There was a commotion in the air, made up of many threatening sounds, coming upon us from the sea. Fishing-craft and coasting vessels under bare poles rushed by us in shoals, running foul of the ships in the harbour. As yet the din and hubbub was that made by men, but their shrill pipings were suddenly silenced by the crashing voice of a thunder squall that burst right over our heads. For some time no other sounds were to be heard than the thunder, wind, and rain. When the fury of the storm, which did not last for more than twenty minutes, had abated, and the horizon was in some degree cleared, I looked to seaward anxiously, in the hope of descrying Shelley's boat, amongst the many small craft scattered about. I watched every speck that loomed on the horizon, thinking that they would have borne up on their return to the port, as all the other boats that had gone out in the same direction had done.

I sent our Genoese mate on board some of the returning craft to make inquiries, but they all professed not to have seen the English boat. So remorselessly are the quarantine laws enforced in Italy, that, when at sea, if you render assistance to a vessel in distress, or rescue a drowning stranger, on returning to port you are condemned to a long and rigorous quarantine of fourteen or more days. The consequence is, should one vessel see another in peril, or even run it down by accident, she hastens on her course, and by general accord, not a word is said or reported on the subject. But to resume my tale. I did not leave the 'Bolivar' until dark. During the night it was gusty and showery, and the lightning flashed along the coast: at daylight I returned on board, and resumed my examinations of the crews of the various boats which had returned to the port during the night. They either knew nothing, or would say nothing. My Genoese, with the quick eye of a sailor, pointed out, on board a fishing-boat, an English-made oar that he thought he had seen in Shelley's boat, but the entire crew swore by all the saints in the calendar that this was not so. Another day was passed in horrid suspense. On the morning of the third day I rode to Pisa. Byron had returned to the Lanfranchi Palace. I hoped to find a letter from the Villa Magni: there was none. I told my fears to Hunt, and then went upstairs to Byron. When I told him, his lip quivered, and his voice faltered as he questioned me. I sent a courier to Leghorn to despatch the 'Bolivar' to cruise along the coast, whilst I mounted my horse and rode in the same direction. I also despatched a courier along the coast to go as far as Nice. On my arrival at Via Reggio, I heard that a punt, a water keg, and some bottles had been found on the beach. These things I recognized as having been in Shelley's boat when he left Leghorn. Nothing more was found for seven or eight days, during which time of painful suspense I patrolled the coast with the coast-guard, stimulating them to keep a good look-out by the promise of a reward. It was not until many days after this that my worst fears were confirmed. Two bodies were found on the shore, – one near Via Reggio, which I went and examined. The face and hands, and parts of the body not protected by the dress, were fleshless. The tall slight figure, the jacket, the volume of Æschylus[38] in one pocket, and Keats's poems in the other, doubled back, as if the reader, in the act of reading, had hastily thrust it away, were all too familiar to me to leave a doubt on my mind that this mutilated corpse was any other than Shelley's. The other body was washed on shore three miles distant from Shelley's, near the tower of Migliarino, at the Bocca Lericcio. I went there at once. This corpse was much more mutilated; it had no other covering than, – the shreds of a shirt, and that partly drawn over the head, as if the wearer had been in the act of taking it off, – a black silk handkerchief, tied sailor-fashion round the neck, – socks, – and one boot, indicating also that he had attempted to strip. The flesh, sinews, and muscles hung about in rags, like the shirt, exposing the ribs and bones. I had brought with me from Shelley's house a boot of Williams's, and this exactly matched the one the corpse had on. That, and the handkerchief, satisfied me that it was the body of Shelley's comrade. Williams was the only one of the three who could swim, and it is probable he was the last survivor. It is likewise possible, as he had a watch and money, and was better dressed than the others, that his body might have been plundered when found. Shelley always declared that in case of wreck he would vanish instantly, and not imperil valuable lives by permitting others to aid in saving his, which he looked upon as valueless. It was not until three weeks after the wreck of the boat that a third body was found – four miles from the other two. This I concluded to be that of the sailor boy, Charles Vivian, although it was a mere skeleton, and impossible to be identified. It was buried in the sand, above the reach of the waves. I mounted my horse, and rode to the Gulf of Spezzia, put up my horse and walked until I caught sight of the lone house on the sea-shore in which Shelley and Williams had dwelt, and where their widows still lived. Hitherto in my frequent visits – in the absence of direct evidence to the contrary – I had buoyed up their spirits by maintaining that it was not impossible but that the friends still lived; now I had to extinguish the last hope of these forlorn women. I had ridden fast, to prevent any ruder messenger from bursting in upon them. As I stood on the threshold of their house, the bearer, or rather confirmer, of news which would rack every fibre of their quivering frames to the utmost, I paused, and, looking at the sea, my memory reverted to our joyous parting only a few days before.

The two families, then, had all been in the verandah, overhanging a sea so clear and calm that every star was reflected on the water, as if it had been a mirror; the young mothers singing some merry tune, with the accompaniment of a guitar. Shelley's shrill laugh – I heard it still – rang in my ears, with Williams's friendly hail, the general *buona notte* of all the joyous party, and the earnest entreaty to me to return as soon as possible, and not to forget the commissions they had severally given me. I was in a small boat beneath them, slowly rowing myself on board the 'Bolivar,' at anchor in the bay, loth to part from what I verily believed to have been at that time the most united, and happiest, set of human beings in the whole world. And now by the blow of an idle puff of wind the scene was changed. Such is human happiness.

My reverie was broken by a shriek from the nurse Caterina, as, crossing the hall, she saw me in the doorway. After asking her a few questions, I went up the stairs, and, unannounced, entered the room. I neither spoke, nor did they question me. Mrs Shelley's large grey eyes were fixed on my face. I turned away. Unable to bear this horrid silence, with a convulsive effort she exclaimed –

'Is there no hope?'

I did not answer, but left the room, and sent the servant with the children to them. The next day I prevailed on them to return with me to Pisa. The misery of that night and the journey of the next day, and of many days and nights that followed, I can neither describe nor forget. It was ultimately determined by those most interested that Shelley's remains should be removed from where they lay, and conveyed to Rome, to be interred near the bodies of his child, and of his friend Keats, with a suitable monument, and that Williams's remains should be taken to England. To do this, in their then far advanced state of decomposition, and to obviate the obstacles offered by the quarantine laws, the ancient custom of burning and reducing the body to ashes was suggested. I wrote to our minister at Florence, Dawkins, on the subject, and solicited his friendly intercession with the Lucchese and Florentine governments, that I might be furnished with authority to accomplish our purpose.

The following was his answer : –

Dear Sir,

An order was sent yesterday from hence to the Governor of Via Reggio, to deliver up the remains of Mr Shelley to you, or any person empowered by you to receive them.

I said they were to be removed to Leghorn for interment, but that need not bind you. If they go by sea, the governor will give you the papers necessary to insure their admittance elsewhere. If they travel by land, they must be accompanied by a guard as far as the frontier – a precaution always taken to prevent the possibility of infection. Quicklime has been thrown into the graves, as is usual in similar cases.

With respect to the removal of the other corpse, I can tell you nothing till I hear from Florence. I applied for the order as soon as I received your letter, and I expect an answer to my letter by tomorrow's post.

I am very sensible of Lord Byron's kindness, and should have called upon him when I passed through Pisa, had he been anybody but Lord Byron. Do not mention trouble; I am here to take as much as my countrymen think proper to give me; and all I ask in return is fair play and good humour, which I am sure I shall always find in the S. S. S.

> Believe me, dear sir,
> Yours very faithfully,
> W. Dawkins.

Such was his subsequent influence and energy, that he ultimately overcame all the obstacles and repugnance of the Italians to sanction such an unprecedented proceeding in their territories.[39]

What was the real cause of the catastrophe whereby Shelley and Williams came to their end? I shall here insert without further comment the correspondence which took place on this subject, beginning, towards the end of 1875, with a letter from my daughter.[40] The several communications were published towards their respective dates in the 'Times.'

> *Rome, Nov. 22, 1875*

My dear Father,

I have just heard something that will interest you. A little while ago there died at Spezzia an old sailor who, in his last confessions to the priest (whom he told to make it public), stated that he was one of the crew that ran down the boat containing Shelley and Williams, which was done under the impression that the rich 'milord Byron' was on board with lots of money.

They did not intend to sink the boat, but to board her and murder Byron. She sank, he said, as soon as she was struck.

This account was sent to my friends the K—s by a person they are intimate with, and who lives at Spezzia, and, I believe, knows the priest.

My comment on the above letter was as follows: —

'This account so exactly corresponds with the event that I think it solves that which for half a century has been a mystery to me and others.'

To the Editor of the 'Times.'

Sir,

    With reference to the recent letters and comments which have appeared regarding the death of Shelley in connection with the story of the fisherman, as related by Miss Trelawny, I think it right to clear up, as far as seems practicable, the present mystification which surrounds it. This seems to be all the more necessary in the interests of truth since the publication in the 'Times,' on the 24th of December, of the letter from Professor de Gubernatoris (quoted from the 'Athenæum'), wherein the whole story is treated as the canard of some 'wag of a sailor.' A perusal of the following particulars will, perhaps, better enable your readers to judge for themselves on which side probability leans. In May of the present year I chanced to be on a visit in a charming villa overlooking the Bay of Spezzia, and the romantic spot where Shelley spent the last few months of his life. Guided by my hostess, who is an old friend of the Shelley family, I made a morning pilgrimage to the Poet's former abode, and, having recently stood on the very shore where his body was discovered and consumed by flames, I naturally questioned my companion regarding such particulars of the tragical tale as might have come to her knowledge from her intimacy with the family, and it was with intense interest that I then listened to the story of the fisherman, of which a somewhat garbled version has now appeared in print.

    The old fisherman died so far back as 1863, and appears to have made no particular secret on his deathbed of the crime that weighed on his conscience; and as his name seems to have been withheld by the priest to whom allusion has been made, there would appear to have been no 'betrayal of the confessional' in the case; indeed, the very fact of the story having transpired may be accepted as proof that it was but the overflowing of the dying man's conscience to all who were around him. The priest confided what had thus come to his knowledge to an Italian noble residing in the vicinity, who was known to be on terms of intimacy with the deceased Poet's friends, and by him it was made known to my informant for a similar reason. She forthwith communicated it to 'the person most interested,' who seems to have refrained from publicity; and meanwhile the old noble has died, and the mention of his name would serve no useful purpose. But it seems evident that neither he nor the priest could have had any possible motive in concocting such a story some forty years after the Poet's death, when all excitement on the subject had ceased; and to those conversant with the actual facts of the disaster it will seem like a revelation of the probable truth. It should not be forgotten that Mr Trelawny, after a careful investigation on the spot, came to the conclusion that there had been foul play. The boat wherein Shelley sailed was evidently not capsized, but run down by another craft. I will now give the story itself in the very words of my friend : –

'A boatman dying near Sarzana, confessed, about twelve years ago, that he was one of five who, seeing the English boat in great danger, ran her down, thinking milord Inglese was on board, and they should find gold.'

My informant has resided during the last twenty years in the neighbourhood of Spezzia, and has always placed entire faith in the truth of the above. But it has crept into the papers without my agency, although I am responsible for having mentioned it as an interesting anecdote to some friend of the Trelawny family in Rome, and I have obtained the permission of my original informant to offer this explanation. I enclose my card, and should my name be considered of any consequence, I place it at your disposal, although it seems quite immaterial to the object in view.

Yours faithfully,

V. E.

Rome, December 28th, 1875.

To the Editor of the 'Times.'

Sir,

When I received the news from Rome of an old sailor at Spezzia having confessed he was one of the crew of the felucca who ran down Shelley's boat, I believed it, and do so still, as it exactly corresponded with the event. The Italian fishing feluccas on that part of the coast are long, low, heavy-decked vessels, carrying from seven to ten men, lateen sails, sharp in the bows, and very fast sailers. Shelley's was an undecked open boat, schooner rigged. She was so light that she had three tons and a half of iron ballast to bring her down to her bearings. At midday on the 8th of July, 1822, Shelley came from his banker's at Leghorn with a canvas bag full of Tuscan crown pieces. Byron, Shelley, Williams, and myself could not be distinguished by the sailors at the harbour, and Byron's and Shelley's boats had their sails loose ready for sea. It was a light land breeze when we weighed our anchors and started at two P.M. I was on board Byron's boat, and was hailed at the entrance of the harbour by the captain of the port, asking if I had my port clearances and bill of health. On my answering I had not, that I was going to return that night, he replied that I should be put in quarantine. I was therefore obliged to re-anchor, and Shelley's boat proceeded alone. Two feluccas went out of port at the same time, in the same direction as Shelley's boat. I remained on board. Some hour after the squall came on; the wind and the sea mist veiled everything from sight at any distance, and the first thing we saw was several feluccas returning for refuge into the harbour.

When the first vessel anchored I sent a mate on board of her, a Genoese, to see what tidings he could get of Shelley's boat. The crew declared they had seen nothing of her. The Genoese said, 'Why, there are some of her spars on board you,' pointing to an English oar, 'that belongs to her.' This they all denied. On his reporting the circumstance to me, he expressed his suspicions that they knew more than they would acknowledge. I thought that we should know more the next day. If I had reported to the captain of the port what the Genoese said, their vessel would have been put in quarantine for fourteen days. That restrained me. I had no suspicion at that time of the disaster which had happened, and the light spars of Shelley's boat might have been thrown overboard.[41] Hearing nothing for several days I became alarmed; but everything was conjecture. I then rode along the coast line to Via Reggio, and collected evidence that Shelley's boat had been wrecked. At length the bodies of the crew were found, and every effort was made to detect where the boat had sunk. After a course of dredging she was found in ten fathoms water, about two miles off the coast of Via Reggio. The cause of her loss was then evident. Her starboard quarter was stove in, evidently by a blow from the sharp bows of a felucca; and, as I have said, being undecked and having three tons and a half of iron ballast, she would have sunk in two minutes. Had she been decked it would have been otherwise. So that the man in his confession saying that 'the moment they struck she went down, 'impressed me with the truth of his revelation. That this had been her fate had been the general opinion of the Spezzia dockyard authorities and of all who saw her. The Italian professor's endeavour to exculpate his countrymen is patriotic. We English are not so credulous; we are better acquainted with Italy and the Italians than they are with us. And whom is there to hoax about an occurrence which has never been commented upon, which happened two generations ago, and in which few persons are interested?

Yours obediently,
E. J. Trelawny.

Sompting, near Worthing,
    Dec. 27, 1875.

Chapter 12

All things that we love and cherish,
Like ourselves, must fade and perish;
Such is our rude mortal lot;
Love itself would, did they not.

SHELLEY.

I GOT a furnace made at Leghorn, of iron-bars and strong sheet-iron, supported on a stand, and laid in a stock of fuel, and such things as were said to be used by Shelley's much loved Hellenes on their funeral pyres.

On the 13th of August, 1822, I went on board the 'Bolivar,' with an English acquaintance, having written to Byron and Hunt to say I would send them word when everything was ready, as they wished to be present. I had previously engaged two large feluccas, with drags and tackling, to go before, and endeavour to find the place where Shelley's boat had foundered; the captain of one of the feluccas having asserted that he was out in the fatal squall, and had seen Shelley's boat go down off Via Reggio, with all sail set. With light and fitful breezes we were eleven hours reaching our destination – the tower of Migliarino, at the Bocca Lericcio, in the Tuscan States. There was a village there, and about two miles from that place Williams was buried. So I anchored, landed, called on the officer in command, a major, and told him my object in coming, of which he was already apprised by his own government. He assured me I should have every aid from him. As it was too late in the day to commence operations, we went to the only inn in the place, and I wrote to Byron to be with us the next day at noon. The major sent my letter to Pisa by a dragoon, and made arrangements for the next day. In the morning he was with us early, and gave me a note from Byron, to say he would join us as near noon as he could. At ten we went on board the commandant's boat, with a squad of soldiers in working dresses, armed with mattocks and spades, an officer of the quarantine service, and some of his crew. They had their peculiar tools, so fashioned as to do their work without coming into personal contact with things that might be infectious – long-handled tongs, nippers, poles with iron hooks and spikes, and divers others that gave one a lively idea of the implements of torture devised by the holy inquisitors. Thus freighted, we started, my own boat following with the furnace, and the things I had brought from Leghorn. We pulled along the shore for some distance, and landed at a line of strong posts and railings which projected into the sea – forming the boundary dividing the Tuscan and Lucchese States. We walked along the shore to the grave, where Byron and Hunt soon joined us; they, too, had an officer and soldiers from the tower of Migliarino, an officer of the Health Office, and some dismounted dragoons, so we were surrounded by soldiers; but they kept the ground clear, and readily lent their aid. There was a considerable gathering of spectators from the neighbourhood, and many ladies richly dressed were amongst them. The spot where the body lay was marked by the gnarled root of a pine tree.

A rude hut, built of young pine-tree stems, and wattled with their branches, to keep the sun and rain out, and thatched with reeds, stood on the beach to shelter the look-out man on duty. A few yards from this was the grave, which we commenced open-ing – the Gulf of Spezzia and Leghorn at equal distances of twenty-two miles from us. As to fuel I might have saved myself the trouble of bringing any, for there was an ample supply of broken spars and planks cast on the shore from wrecks, besides the fallen and decaying timber in a stunted pine forest close at hand. The soldiers collected fuel whilst I erected the furnace, and then the men of the Health Office set to work, shovelling away the sand which covered the body, while we gathered round, watching anxiously. The first indication of their having found the body was the appearance of the end of a black silk hand-kerchief – I grubbed this out with a stick, for we were not allowed to touch anything with our hands – then some shreds of linen were met with, and a boot with the bone of the leg and the foot in it. On the removal of a layer of brushwood, all that now remained of my lost friend was exposed – a shapeless mass of bones and flesh. The limbs separated from the trunk on being touched.

'Is that a human body?' exclaimed Byron; 'why, it's more like the carcass of a sheep, or any other animal, than a man : this is a satire on our pride and folly.'

I pointed to the letters E. E. W. on the black silk handkerchief.

Byron looking on, muttered, 'The entrails of a worm hold together longer than the potter's clay of which man is made. Hold! let me see the jaw,' he added, as they were removing the skull, 'I can recognize any one by the teeth, with whom I have talked. I always watch the lips and mouth : they tell what the tongue and eyes try to conceal.'[42]

I had a boot of Williams's with me; it exactly corresponded with the one found in the grave. The remains were removed piecemeal into the furnace.

'Don't repeat this with me,' said Byron; 'let my carcass rot where it falls.'

The funereal pyre was now ready; I applied the fire, and the materials being dry and resinous the pine-wood burnt furiously, and drove us back. It was hot enough before, there was no breath of air, and the loose sand scorched our feet. As soon as the flames became clear, and allowed us to approach, we threw frankincense and salt into the furnace, and poured a flask of wine and oil over the body. The Greek oration was omitted, for we had lost our Hellenic bard. It was now so insufferably hot that the officers and soldiers were all seeking shade.

'Let us try the strength of these waters that drowned our friends,' said Byron, with his usual audacity. 'How far out do you think they were when their boat sank?'

'If you don't wish to be put into the furnace, you had better not try; you are not in condition.'

He stripped, and went into the water, and so did I and my companion. Before we got a mile out, Byron was sick, and persuaded to return to the shore. My companion, too, was seized with cramp, and reached the land by my aid. At four o'clock the funereal pyre burnt low, and when we uncovered the furnace, nothing remained in it but dark-coloured ashes, with fragments of the larger bones. Poles were now put under the red-hot furnace, and it was gradually cooled in the sea. I gathered together the human ashes, and placed them in a small oak-box, bearing an inscription on a brass plate, screwed it down, and placed it in Byron's carriage. He returned with Hunt to Pisa, promising to be with us on the following day at Via Reggio. I returned with my party in the same way we came, and supped and slept at the inn. On the following morning we went on board the same boats, with the same things and party, and rowed down the little river near Via Reggio to the sea, pulled along the coast towards Massa, then landed, and began our preparations as before.*

Three white wands had been stuck in the sand to mark the Poet's grave, but as they were at some distance from each other, we had to cut a trench thirty yards in length, in the line of the sticks, to ascertain the exact spot, and it was nearly an hour before we came upon the grave.

In the meantime Byron and Leigh Hunt arrived in the carriage, attended by soldiers, and the Health Officer, as before. The lonely and grand scenery that surrounded us so exactly harmonized with Shelley's genius, that I could imagine his spirit soaring over us. The sea, with the islands of Gorgona, Capraja, and Elba, was before us; old battlemented watch-towers stretched along the coast, backed by the marble-crested Apennines glistening in the sun, picturesque from their diversified outlines, and not a human dwelling was in sight. As I thought of the delight Shelley felt in such scenes of loneliness and grandeur whilst living, I felt we were no better than a herd of wolves or a pack of wild dogs, in tearing out his battered and naked body from the pure yellow sand that lay so lightly over it, to drag him back to the light of day; but the dead have no voice, nor had I power to check the sacrilege – the work went on silently in the deep and unresisting sand, not a word was spoken, for the Italians have a touch of sentiment, and their feelings are easily excited into sympathy. Byron was silent and thoughtful. We were startled and drawn together by a dull hollow sound that followed the blow of a mattock; the iron had struck a skull, and the body was soon uncovered. Lime had been strewn on it; this, or

* For an account of the cremation of Shelley, written down by me at the time, see the Appendix.

decomposition, had the effect of staining it of a dark and ghastly indigo colour. Byron asked me to preserve the skull for him; but remembering that he had formerly used one as a drinking-cup, I was determined Shelley's should not be so profaned. The limbs did not separate from the trunk, as in the case of Williams's body, so that the corpse was removed entire into the furnace. I had taken the precaution of having more and larger pieces of timber, in consequence of my experience of the day before of the difficulty of consuming a corpse in the open air with our apparatus. After the fire was well kindled we repeated the ceremony of the previous day; and more wine was poured over Shelley's dead body than he had consumed during his life. This with the oil and salt made the yellow flames glisten and quiver. The heat from the sun and fire was so intense that the atmosphere was tremulous and wavy. The corpse fell open and the heart was laid bare. The frontal bone of the skull, where it had been struck with the mattock, fell off; and, as the back of the head rested on the red-hot bottom bars of the furnace, the brains literally seethed, bubbled and boiled as in a cauldron, for a very long time.

Byron could not face this scene, he withdrew to the beach and swam off to the 'Bolivar.'[43] Leigh Hunt remained in the carriage. The fire was so fierce as to produce a white heat on the iron, and to reduce its contents to grey ashes. The only portions that were not consumed were some fragments of bones, the jaw, and the skull; but what surprised us all was that the heart remained entire. In snatching this relic from the fiery furnace, my hand was severely burnt; and had any one seen me do the act I should have been put into quarantine.[44]

After cooling the iron machine in the sea, I collected the human ashes and placed them in a box, which I took on board the 'Bolivar.' Byron and Hunt retraced their steps to their home, and the officers and soldiers returned to their quarters.[45] I liberally rewarded the men for the admirable manner in which they behaved during the two days they had been with us.

As I undertook and executed this novel ceremony, I have been thus tediously minute in describing it. A sage critic remarks that I performed this cremation in a bungling manner, that I should have used a gas retort. My answer is that neither gas nor retorts were then known in Italy. He further remarks that bodies washed on shore were obliged to be burnt; that is an error. Bodies washed on shore were buried in the sand above the wash of the sea, and as the Inquisition no longer burnt heretics, I followed the practice of the Hindoos in using a funeral pyre.

In all cases of death from suffocation the heart is gorged with blood; consequently it is the more difficult to consume, especially in the open air.

Byron's idle talk during the exhumation of Williams's remains did not proceed from want of feeling, but from his anxiety to conceal what he felt from others. When confined to his bed and racked by spasms, which threatened his life, I have heard him talk in a much more unorthodox fashion, the instant he could muster breath to banter. He had been taught during his town-life that any exhibition of sympathy or feeling was maudlin and unmanly, and that the appearance of daring and indifference denoted blood and high breeding.

VOLUME II

Chapter 13

An old, mad, blind, despised, and dying king, –
Princes, the dregs of their dull race, who flow
Through public scorn – mud from a muddy spring, –
Rulers who neither see, nor feel, nor know,
But leech-like to their fainting country cling,
Till they drop blind in blood.

England in 1819 – SHELLEY.

Physician. Are many simples operative whose power
Will close the eye of anguish.

SHAKESPEARE.

WHEN I arrived at Leghorn, as I could not immediately go on to Rome, I consigned Shelley's ashes to our Consul at Rome, Mr Freeborn, requesting him to keep them in his custody until my arrival. When I reached Rome, Freeborn told me that to quiet the authorities there, he had been obliged to inter the ashes with the usual ceremonies in the Protestant burying-place. When I came to examine the ground with the man who had the custody of it, I found Shelley's grave amidst a cluster of others. The old Roman wall partly enclosed the place, and there was a niche in the wall formed by two buttresses – immediately under an ancient pyramid, said to be the tomb of Caius Cestius. There were no graves near it at that time. This suited my taste, so I purchased the recess, and sufficient space for planting a row of the Italian upright cypresses. As the souls of Heretics are foredoomed by the Roman priests, they do not affect to trouble themselves about their bodies. There was no 'faculty' to apply for, nor Bishop's licence to exhume the body. The custode or guardian who dwelt within the enclosure, and had the key of the gate, seemed to have uncontrolled power within his domain, and scudi, impressed with the image of Saint Peter with the two keys, ruled him. Without more ado, masons were hired, and two tombs built in the recess. In one of these, when completed, I deposited the box, with Shelley's ashes, and covered it in with solid stone, inscribed with a Latin epitaph, written by Leigh Hunt. I received the following note at Leghorn previous to burning the body : –

Pisa 1st August, 1822

Dear Trelawny,

You will of course call upon us in your way to your melancholy task; but I write to say, that you must not reckon upon passing through Pisa in a very great hurry, as the ladies particularly wish to have an evening, while you are here, for consulting further with us; and I myself mean, at all events, to accompany you on your journey, if you have no objection.

I subjoin the inscriptions – mere matter-of-fact memorandums – according to the wish of the ladies. It will be for the other inscriptions to say more.

Yours sincerely,
Leigh Hunt.

P.S. – Mrs Shelley wishes very much that Capt. Roberts would be kind enough to write to his uncle about her desk, begging it to be forwarded as speedily as possible. If it is necessary to be opened, the best way will be to buy a key for that purpose; but if a key is not to be had, of course it must be broken open. As there is something in the secret drawers, it will be extremely desirable that as few persons meddle with it as possible.

PERCY BYSSHE SHELLEY, ANGLUS, ORAM ETRUSCAM LEGENS IN NAVIGIOLO INTER LIGURNUM PORTUM ET VIAM REGIAM, PROCELLÂ PERIIT VIII. NON. JUL. MDCCCXXII. ÆTAT. SUÆ XXX.

EDVARDUS ELLIKER WILLIAMS, ANGLICÂ STIRPE ORTUS, INDIÂ ORIENTALI NATUS, A LIGURNO PORTU IN VIAM REGIAM NAVIGIOLO PROFICISCENS, TEMPESTATE PERIIT VIII. NON. JUL. MDCCCXXII. ÆTAT SUÆ XXX.

Io, sottoscritta, prego le Autorità di Viga Reggio o Livorno di consegnare al Signore Odoardo Trelawny, Inglese, la Barca nominata Il Don Juan, e tutta la sua carica, appartenente al mio marito, per essere alla sua disposizione.

Maria Shelley.

*Genova 16 Sett*bre, *1822*

To the first inscription (which has not been exactly followed)
I added two lines from Shelley's favourite play 'The Tempest,'

> 'Nothing of him that doth fade,
> But doth suffer a sea change
> Into something rich and strange.'

The other tomb, built merely to fill up the recess, was likewise
covered in in the same way – but blank without as within. I
planted eight seedling cypresses. When I last saw them, in 1844,
the seven which remained were about thirty-five feet in height.
I added flowers as well. The ground I had purchased, I enclosed, and so ended my task.[46]

Shelley, who was born in 1792, came of a long-lived race, and,
barring accidents, there was no reason why he should not have
emulated his forefathers in attaining a ripe age. His father lived
till he was past ninety. The Poet had no other complaint than
occasional spasms, and these were probably caused by the excessive and almost unremitting strain on his mental powers, the
solitude of his life, and his long fasts, which were not intentional,
but proceeded from the abstraction and forgetfulness of himself
and his wife. If food were near him he ate it, if not he fasted, and
it was after long fasts that he suffered from spasms.

From the slight scenes and fragments I have given, some
notion of the man and his way of life may be formed. His life
illustrated his writings: his brain absorbed him. As I am the
last man that knew him, I record my last impressions. He was
tall – 5 feet 11 inches – slim, and bent from eternally poring over
books. This habit had contracted his chest. In common with
enthusiastic students he had put his whole strength into his mind.
The body he looked upon as a self-acting piece of mechanism.
He had never played at boys' games or joined in men's sports,
but was a bookworm from childhood. His limbs were well-
proportioned, strong, and long; his head was remarkably small,
and his features were expressive of great sensibility and decidedly
feminine; his softness of expression and mild bearing were decep-
tive, as you soon found out he was a resolute, self-sustaining
man. There was nothing about him outwardly to attract notice,
except his extraordinarily juvenile appearance. When he was at

a distance among others you knew him by his eyes; they were like a stag's amongst a herd of deer. The guileless, fearless expression, as well as his dress and address, were so boyish that it was impossible to believe he had been guilty of any greater offences than neglecting to attend the chapel at Oxford, and feeling that he knew much more than his father, and avowing that he would not be guided by his father's counsel or walk in his path, but follow his own course. At twenty-nine he still retained on his tanned and freckled cheeks the fresh look of a boy, although his long wild locks were coming into blossom, as a polite hairdresser once said to me whilst cutting mine. It was not until he spoke that you could discern anything uncommon in him, but the first sentence he uttered when excited by his subject riveted your attention, and at once the boy was transformed into a man. He was thoroughly masculine in act, prompt in reply, and bold in his opinions. The light from his very soul streamed from his eyes, and every mental emotion of which the human mind is susceptible was expressed in his pliant and ever-changing features. He left the conviction on the minds of his audience that however great he was as a Poet, he was greater as an orator. There was another and most rare peculiarity in Shelley, – his intellectual faculties completely mastered his material nature, and hence he unhesitatingly acted up to his own theories, if they only demanded sacrifices on his part, – it was where they implicated others that he forbore. Mrs Shelley has observed, 'Many have suggested and advocated far greater innovations in our political and social system than Shelley; but he alone practised those he approved of as just.' [47]

This young man's voice was drowned by the howling of priests, and yet the founders of all religions from Buddha to Christ, judging him by his deeds, would have welcomed and crowned him with glory in their elysiums, and condemned his uncharitable persecutors to the lowest depths of the infernal regions. He was unlike the poetasters whom I had seen gowned and slippered in soft chairs, dawdling over slops all the morning, with a halo of foolish faces anointing them with flattery. Shelley's study was in the woods, amongst the rocks, or in his boat; he never sauntered or lounged. All his motions were energetic and rapid. He was very well on a horse, but better on foot. He was a famous walker. In going up rugged paths or steep hills he was at the top whilst we strong men were not half way up.

I have a strong taint of the mule in my blood, with his redeeming qualities of sure-footedness, endurance, toughness, and longevity; but Mrs Shelley and those who knew us decided that Shelley's will was the most inflexible. Witness all his acts. He was a rebel at his early school; he was expelled from college; he defied all authority, and left his paternal home and went his own way ever after. Then he defied the world's opinions in his writings from first to last. He said, 'Everybody saying a thing does not make it right.' In his outward life he was misled by his impulsive and vehement nature. His imagination coloured everything, and when heated deluded him. The gross and sensual passions and feelings that link men together had no hold on him. In benevolence and friendship none could excel him. My slight sketch is of the end of his brief life; the beginning and middle will doubtless furnish the critic with ample material for darkening the picture if it is too bright. Excessive laudation is nauseous. I am only induced to narrate the facts I have given, in the conviction that all 'properly constituted' minds will consider my facts regarding him as heinous sins, indicating insanity or something worse.

In the early part of this century a man opened a small bookseller's and publisher's shop in Skinner Street; he had been a Methodist preacher and teacher, but finding that too narrow and obscure a vocation to suit the aspirations of his mind, he ascended to higher ground.

The first French Revolution had stirred men's minds and made them think. This man might be considered as the earliest of the philosophical Radicals; he wrote vigorously against the arbitrary acts of those who were in power, he advocated moral and not physical force to correct abuses, he said 'mob oratory and secret societies frightened the timid and gave strength to the Government.' He acquired considerable fame and power by his writings.

He was sitting in his study over the shop with his family, five children; two of them his, and others his wife's, who had been a widow. He was about middle age, with a large face, and features, and body. His face was of a leaden hue, without shadow or colour to relieve it; he was reading something to his daughter (who was sitting next to him) in a dogmatic manner, which his former habit of preaching gave him. His daughter bore such a resemblance to him, on a reduced scale, that there could be no doubt as to her paternity, and they were all hushed as if in a chapel, when the door was opened. A tall, thin young man entered; his radiant face and lustrous eyes dispelled the gloom like sunshine. The contrast was striking between him and the family group; he was evidently of another type. The master of the house got up and introduced him to his daughter Mary. Whilst sitting, the master of the house appeared of the middle height, but when he stood it added so little to his stature that you saw Nature had stinted him of his fair proportions. His daughter inherited the same disadvantage; they were both redeemed from being commonplace by having bright and intelligent eyes.

The Poet's face – for such he was – flushed at seeing the daughter of Mary Woolstonecraft, her portrait being in the room, and the daughter so dissimilar in every minute particular that no one but a Poet with a double vision could have believed there was any relationship existing. He was soon engaged in talking earnestly to Mary, but the philosopher, impatient at playing the part of a dummy, interrupted them by saying,

'I have been puzzling myself over the poem you last sent me, asking my opinion. I wrote to you this morning: perhaps you have not received the letter? I hoped to find a beginning of what it was about. I could find nothing but high-sounding words. I could discover no clue to the subject, or middle, or end. It was like a discharged cartridge in a sham battle: there was noise, clamour, and some fury in the words, but what it portended I could not discover except that poetry is not your vocation. You should write prose; your letter to the Lord Chancellor on Eaton's case was admirable, logical, argumentative, and convincing. Prose is your forte.'

The Poet then essayed to explain the argument and design of

his poem. Mary, knowing her father's contempt of all poetry, except dramatic, from his being devoid of imagination, diverted the conversation to the topics of the day, in which they could all join. This was the first meeting of Mary Godwin and Percy Shelley, as near as I could gather from words dropped from Mary at different times; and the letter here alluded to by Godwin, Mary gave me, in which the sentiments herein expressed are written.

The conversation was interrupted by the widow Godwin had married – his second wife – one of the robust, bustling, shrewd women of whom there are thousands, approaching middle age. Three of the youngest children were hers; nothing could escape the vigilance of her glances, she saw in a minute the state of things.

The Poet took no other notice of her than slightly bowing, and what displeased her more, no notice whatever of her children; he was absorbed with Mary, and doubtless with his inward eye saw a resemblance to her mother in her mind.

The widow had won Godwin by the two great accomplishments of flattery and cooking, which will win most men, and especially those called philosophers; but she had the great merit, which is very rare, of continuing to exercise these faculties after she had attained her object, retaining these to the last, and thus securing his regards.

Shelley had long thought that Godwin was the most persistent and able political reformer of his time, and, when he was in town, frequently went to Godwin's house. Mary Woolstonecraft was his ideal of what a woman should be, both from her writings and portrait; he was entranced by meeting a child of that celebrated woman.

Mrs Shelley said her father, William Godwin, studied and ruminated, but never wrote from his feelings or passions; they were very faint; for love or sentiment he consulted authority. He professed to be guided by reason in all things. Pathetic and sentimental passages in books he skipped as nonsense. Dryden and Pope he admired, but metaphysical poetry was to him incomprehensible.

Well-constituted minds, not influenced by personal considerations, are shocked at every act of injustice committed in the world; and as I see indications that the reputation of Harriet Shelley, the first wife of the Poet, will be slandered by an evil tongue, to remove the only great error in that Poet's life, I desire, as I am the last person who can do so, to leave on record what evidence I could collect regarding the separation that ensued between Shelley and his first wife.

And first as to their marriage. Shelley had one or two of his sisters at a boarding-school in London. He often visited them, and found a girl named Harriet Westbrook with them. In one of these visits the girls were discussing the difficulty that her father had with her; the arbitrary tyranny of his own father caused Shelley to sympathize with her. The perplexed girls not seeing their way out of the difficulty, Shelley said abruptly, 'I will marry her.' They were both startled, for Shelley had shown no symptoms of individual liking for the girl, nor any special interest regarding her. The thought had flashed from his mind to meet a sudden emergency. As both were under age, Shelley with his usual impetuosity posted to Scotland, and there this boarding-school Miss and the expelled Oxford boy were married, and, as the novelists would end their story by saying, they were ever after happy. Harriet and Shelley were both thoroughly ignorant of life as it is, and essentially different in their minds and bringing up. Harriet was made of plastic clay and could be readily stamped into any form; but her elder sister Eliza was of the fire-brick clay, and once pressed into a form was unalterable.

I was assured by the evidence of the few friends who knew both Shelley and his wife – Hookham, who kept the great library in Bond Street; Jefferson Hogg, Peacock, and one of the Godwins – that Harriet was perfectly innocent of all offence.[48] Shelley had early been a convert to Godwin's and Mary Woolstonecraft's theories regarding marriage: that the sexes should not be held together when their minds become thoroughly estranged. In five or ten thousand years this theory may be practicable; it is not so now. Shelley indoctrinated his wife with these impracticable theories. Harriet felt Shelley's great superiority to herself, and placed implicit confidence in his judgment. She was innocent of all knowledge, beyond the ordinary routine of a boarding-school education. The poet, at the date of his marriage, was nineteen years of age, and his bride sixteen.

Harriet, as already intimated, was of an easy, trusting, and pliant nature, that any person could have lived with. Her sister Eliza – so admirably described by Jefferson Hogg in his 'Life of Shelley' – was a woman composed of all those ingredients which constitute a she-devil, that no man can live with. She was a perpetual torment to the Poet. Shelley knew that animals can't alter their nature. He could not reason with his tormentor, because she was devoid of reasoning faculty. Eliza was much older than Harriet; and, when the latter was not at school, Eliza domineered over her. Eliza considered Shelley and her sister as young people utterly ignorant of the ways of the world, and deemed it her duty to set them right. Their irregular habits, and neglect of all forms and ceremonies, as practised by well-conducted families, perplexed and irritated Eliza, and she was perpetually lecturing the Poet on proper behaviour. Harriet, from being used to her admonitions, was callous to them; Shelley's sensitive nature could not endure the process, and it generally ended in driving him out of the room.

If our universities cannot teach our boys how to act their parts as men, our female schools do not teach our girls how to act *their* parts as women; otherwise Harriet would have seen that the only prudent course was to get rid of her sister. Shelley's excessive toleration was dangerous, and misled unobservant people; but an observer could see by his face how much he suffered in consequence of what he considered ungenerous or unjust assertions. His indignation was suppressed; he never contradicted or used harsh words to his opponent, and sometimes foolish opponents were absurd enough to think they were converting him to their opinions. He retreated into his burrow to avoid them.

Thus Eliza became a perpetual torment to him with her platitudes and commonplaces. She was bristling all over with knowledge of the ways of the world; and what the world did she thought must be as orthodox as the Gospel. She looked upon

Shelley and Harriet as infants who knew little or nothing. She tried her hand upon Shelley, but considered that he was incorrigibly perverse, and was making her sister as bad as himself. She complained to her friends bitterly of the mean way in which they had been married in Scotland, saying that the great event of a girl's life was the marriage ceremony, and of this Harriet had been defrauded; that she had been taken away like a piece of smuggled goods into a strange country where they had no relatives or friends, no one to give her away, no wedding dress of silk or satin, no wreath of orange flowers, no presents of trinkets, no public breakfast, or wedding cake, or chaise-and-four with postillions, white gloves, and favours, and nowhere to go to but a paltry lodging. It was a pauper wedding: this grievance rankled in Eliza's mind, and often found vent. Girls look to a triumphant marriage as the great event of their lives; but Harriet was so simple-minded that she laughed at the affair, and thought it good fun.

Eliza was arbitrary and energetic. Harriet had the difficult task of pacifying her sister, and following in the footsteps of her husband. They wandered into the Northern Lake district, then into Ireland and Wales, and back to London – as Eliza said, like tramps or gipsies – for nearly three years; then the Poet, lured by a new light, broke his chain, and fled. Harriet sought a refuge with her father. The father at last was confined to his room by sickness, and the sister refused her entrance there. Friendless, and utterly ignorant of the world and its ways, deserted by her husband and family, Harriet was the most forlorn and miserable of her sex – poor and outcast. It is too painful to trace her faltering steps. She made one effort to hold on to life. A man professed to be interested and to sympathize in her fate. He was a captain in the army, and was suddenly ordered to join his regiment abroad. He promised to correspond with her. Her poverty compelled her to seek a refuge in a cheaper lodging; her former landlady refused to forward her letters to her new address. In this deplorable state, fancying that no human being could take the least interest in her, and believing in Shelley's doctrine – that when our last hopes are extinguished, and life is a torment, our only refuge is death – blighted, benighted, and crushed, with hurried steps she hastened into the Park, and threw herself off the bridge into the Serpentine.

Shelley had lately been on the Continent, and knew nothing of this train of events, supposing Harriet was with her family. The calamity very much changed his character, and was a torment to him during the rest of his life.

The first time I met Thomas Medwin, shortly after Shelley's death, was at Florence. He called to thank me for some service I had done him. He then said,

'You ought to write Shelley's life. You and Williams were his inseparable companions the last and important year of his life. He loved Williams, but Williams died with him. I was at Naples; you alone did all that could be done to the very last. He liked you exceedingly from the first of his seeing you; your enthusiasm and unselfishness charmed him; the same qualities made him like Williams. I have two or three letters of his, and might have had more; but I have been careless of letters, and when moving about I burn them. I will write down things I remember, and give them to you. The public are quite ignorant of him, and now he is gone, they will perhaps listen to the truth.'

I asked,

'Why cannot his wife write? She has been with him for some years.'

Medwin said,

'No, women cannot write men's lives and characters – they don't know them: much less his – he was so different from ordinary men. She told me she could never get him to speak of the past. He disliked being questioned, was impatient, left the room whenever she attempted it; and never spoke of himself. She knows very little of his early life, except what I and others have told her.'

TRE.: There are his early friends, Godwin, Peacock, Hogg, and Hunt.

MEDWIN: They were his book-friends, fellow-students. They admired his great abilities, his generosity of character; but they had no sympathy with his writings, they laughed at his transcendentalism and enthusiasm. Shelley said that men herding in great cities might differ widely in theory, but all of them did the same things in their daily life, and though they denounced abuses and clamoured for reform, any changes that interrupted their habits they would have abhorred; they exhausted their strength in words. They will grieve at Shelley's death, some of them, because of his many amiable qualities.

I now (1878) publish at the end of this chapter the four and a half letters that Medwin gave me; when I wrote before, I had left some of my papers in Italy. Hogg and Peacock were good classical scholars. They read the same books with Shelley, but drew perfectly opposite conclusions from the text, – that furnished them with disputations; this led to endless discussions, which delighted Shelley, for he was imperturbable in argument. His other London friends were merely men of the day.

Mrs Shelley had a variety of amiable qualities, but she was possessed of the green-eyed monster, jealousy,

> 'That follows still the changes of the moon
> With fresh suspicions.'

That was an insurmountable impediment to confidential intercourse with her husband.

Whenever the Poet wrote on the subject of love, however abstract or ideal, she misconstrued this, and considered it treason to herself. She was mournful and desponding in solitude, and panting for society. She used every effort to make Shelley conventional, and to get him to do as others did; her moaning and complaining grieved him, and her society was no solace. The Poet never sought acquaintance with others: very few suited him: his life was entirely solitary, almost without a parallel.

In his inexhaustible thirst for knowledge, chemical and medical books had not escaped him; and seeking to allay the perturbation of his seething brain he had from early life tampered with opiates. He used them in the shape of laudanum. He had always a bottle of that, which he endeavoured to conceal from everyone, disliking to be remonstrated with. He used it with caution at first, but, in times of extreme dejection or in paroxysms of passion, was heedless, and on more than one occasion his life was only preserved by remedies to counteract the poison. Whether he intended to destroy himself or no, is not clear. He differed from other writers who speak of Death as a malignant deity. He writes –

> 'She met me, stranger, upon life's rough way,
> And lured me towards Sweet Death.'
>
> *Epipsychidion.*

And again:

> 'Death, and his brother Sleep.'
>
> *Queen Mab.*

In short, he hardly mentioned death except with love of it, and said no man should complain of life when he had the disposal of it in his own hands.

This habit of taking laudanum accounts for all his visions and occasional delusions, but startled his wife and friends, and was one cause of the pains he had in his side: for it is the effect of opiates, if not counteracted by other means, to paralyse the stomach and other vital organs.

The Professor of Anatomy at Pisa, Vaccà, had ordered him never to take any medicine of any description, and recommended him occasionally to eat animal food.

The last year of his life was, by the evidence of Mrs Shelley and others, the happiest he had passed in Italy.

Williams and his wife exactly suited him – Williams as a playmate, and his boat as a plaything. Then he had daily conferences on poetry with Byron, and one or two friends who sympathized with him.[49]

Godwin observed to me, – 'that Byron must occasionally have said good things, though not capable, as Shelley was, of keeping up a long conversation or argument; and that Shelley must have been of great use to Byron, as from the commencement of their intimacy at Geneva, he could trace an entirely new vein of thought emanating from Shelley, which ran through Byron's subsequent works, and was so peculiar that it could not have arisen from any other source.' This was true. Byron was but superficial on points on which Shelley was most profound; and the latter's capacity for study, the depth of his thoughts as well as their boldness, and his superior scholarship, supplied the former with exactly what he wanted: and thus a portion of Shelley's aspirations were infused into Byron's mind. Ready as Shelley always was with his purse or person to assist others, his purse had a limit, but his mental wealth seemed to have none; for not only to Byron, but to any one disposed to try his hand at literature, Shelley was ever ready to give any amount of mental labour. Every detail of the life of a man of genius is interesting, and Shelley's was so pre-eminently, as his life harmonized with his spiritual theories. He fearlessly laid bare those mysterious feelings and impulses of which few dare to speak, but in a form so purified from earthly matter that the most sensitive reader is never shocked. Shelley says of his own writings in the preface to the 'Cenci,' 'they are little else than visions which impersonate my own apprehensions of the beautiful and the just – they are dreams of what ought to be, or may be.' Whilst he lived, his works fell still-born from the press; he never complained of the world's neglect, or expressed any other feeling than surprise at the rancorous abuse wasted on an author who had no readers. 'But for the reviewers,' he said, laughing, 'I should be utterly unknown.' 'But for them,' I observed, 'Williams and I would never have crossed the Alps in chase of you. Our curiosity as sportsmen was excited to see and have a shot at so strange a monster as they represented you to be.'

It must not be forgotten that Shelley lived in the good old times, under the paternal government of the Tories, when liberal opinions were prohibited and adjudged as contraband of war. England was then very much like what Naples was in King Bomba's time.

Sidney Smith [50] says,

'From the beginning of the century to the death of Lord Liverpool was an awful period for any one who ventured to maintain liberal opinions. He was sure to be assailed with all the Billingsgate of the French Revolution; "Jacobin," "Leveller," Atheist," "Incendiary," "Regicide," were the gentlest terms used, and any man who breathed a syllable against the senseless bigotry of the two Georges was shunned as unfit for social life. To say a word against any abuse which a rich man inflicted, and a poor man suffered, was bitterly and steadily resented,' and he adds, that 'in one year, 12,000 persons were committed for offences against the Game Laws.'

Shelley's life was a proof that the times in which he lived were awful for those who dared to maintain liberal opinions. These caused his expulsion from Oxford, and for them his parents discarded him, every member of his family disowned him, and the savage Chancellor Eldon deprived him of his children.

Sidney Smith says of this Chancellor, that he was 'the most heartless, bigoted, and mischievous of human beings, who passed a long life in perpetuating all sorts of abuses, and in making money of them.'[51]

*

Shelley to Medwin at Geneva.

Florence, Jan. 17th, 1820

My dear Medwin,

The winter at Florence has been, for the climate, unusually severe, and yet I imagine you must have suffered enough in Switzerland to make you regret that you did not come further South. At least I confidently expect that we shall see you in the Spring. We are fixed for the ensuing year in Tuscany, and you will always find me by addressing me at Leghorn.

Perhaps you belong to the tribe of the hopeless, and nothing shocks or surprises you in politics.

I have enough of unrebuked hope remaining to be struck with horror at the proceedings in England; yet I reflect, as a last consolation, that oppression which authorizes often produces resistance. These are not times in which one has much spirit for writing poetry, although there is a keen air in them that sharpens the wits of men, and makes them imagine vividly even in the midst of despondence.

I dare say the lake before you is a plain of solid ice, bounded by the snowy hills, whose white mantles contrast with the aerial rose-colour of the eternal glaciers – a scene more grand, yet like the recesses of the Antarctic circle. If your health allows you to skate, this plain is the floor of your Paradise, and the white world seems spinning backwards as you fly. The thaw may have arrived, or you may have departed, and this letter reach you in a very different scene.

This Italy, believe me, is a pleasant place, especially Rome and Naples. Tuscany is delightful eight months of the year; but nothing reconciles me to the slightest indication of winter, much less such infernal cold as my nerves have been racked upon for the last ten days. At Naples all the worst is over in three weeks. When you come hither, you must take up your abode with me, and I will give you all the experience which I have bought, at the usual market price, during the last year and a half residence in Italy.

You used, I remember, to paint very well, and you were remarkable, if I do not mistake, for a peculiar taste and knowledge of the *belle arti*. Italy is the place for you, the very place – the Paradise of exiles, the retreat of Pariahs. But I am thinking of myself rather than of you. If you will be glad to see an old friend, who will be very glad to see you – if this is any inducement – come to Italy.

To Medwin at Geneva.

Pisa, April 16th, 1820

My dear Medwin,

I have delayed answering your letter and sending you my ideas on its valuable accompaniment in consequence of an inexplicable *impiccio* of the Genoese post, which got hold of your last communication, and which yet rests to be cleared up. I determined, so soon as I found that the measures for obtaining it from them were drawn out to a hopeless length, to write immediately, and entreat you to send me a duplicate by Dejean's Diligence which goes to Florence, and addressed to me at Mr Klieber's the banker there, who will immediately forward it to me. I conjecture that it must be the printed book which you mention in your letter; I am consoled by reflecting that the loss and annoyance is less than if it had been a MS.

The volume of which you speak, if it resemble the 'Pindarus,' I cannot doubt is calculated to produce a considerable sensation.

That poem is highly fit for popularity, considered in its subject; there being a strong demand in the imagination of our contemporaries for the scenery and situations which you have studied. I admire equally the richness and variety of the imagery with the ease and profusion of language in which it is expressed.

Perhaps the severe criticism of a friend, jealous of every error, might discern some single lines and expressions which may be conceived to be changed for the better. But these are few, and I by no means conceive myself qualified to do more than point them out; and if I should incur, as is probable, the charge of hypercriticism, you will know to what motives and feelings to impute it. I will enclose your 'Pindarus' by the next post, with a list of these, and such corrections, since you ask me for them, as I can best make. But remember, I will not vouch for their not being much inferior to the passages they supplant. The only general error, if it be such, in your poem, seems to me to be the employment of Indian words, in the body of the piece, and the relegation of their meaning to the notes. Strictly, I imagine, every expression in a poem ought to be in itself an intelligible picture. But this practice, though foreign to that of the great poets of former times, is so highly admired by our contemporaries that I can hardly counsel you to dissent. And then you have Moore and Lord Byron on your side, who, being much better and more successful poets than I am, may be supposed to know better the road to success than one who has sought and missed it. I am printing some things which I am vain enough to wish you to see. Not that they will sell; they are the reverse, in this respect, of the razors in Peter Pindar. A man like me can in fact only be a poet by dint of stinting himself of meat and drink to pay his printer's bills; that is, he can only print poems on this condition. But there is every reason to hope better things for you.

You will find me at Pisa in the autumn. Pisa until December will be an excellent climate for you, nor am I aware that Naples or Sicily would be more favourable, all things considered. The sun is certainly warmer, but unless you fit up a house expressly for the purpose of warmth, the Tramontana will enter by a thousand crevices, charged with frozen and freezing atoms. I suffered dreadfully at Naples from the cold, far more than at

Florence, where I had a warm room, spending two successive winters in those cities. We shall at all events be at Pisa in the autumn, and I am almost certain we shall remain during the whole winter in a pleasant villa outside the gates. We will make you as comfortable as we can, but our *ménage* is too philosophic to abound in much external luxury. The rest must be made up in good-will. Mrs Shelley desires me to say how acceptable your visit will be to her. If you should come before the autumn, we shall be at the Baths of Lucca, a delightful place, about thirty miles from this town.

You will find me a wretched invalid unless a great change should take place.

As to the expense of Italy – why, it is a very cheap place. A crown here goes as far as a pound note in England in all affairs of eating and drinking. The single article of clothes is the same. Geneva seems to me about as dear as England; but I may have been horribly cheated.

I ought to tell you that we do not enter into society. The few people we see are those who suit us, and I believe nobody but us. I find saloons and compliments too great bores; though I am of an extremely social disposition. I hope if they come to Italy I may see the lovely lady and your friend. Though I have never had the ague, I have found these sort of beings, especially the former, of infinite service in the maladies to which I am subject; and I have no doubt, if it could be supposed that anyone would neglect to employ such a medicine, that the best physicians would prescribe them, although they have been entered in no pharmacopœia.

Forgive my joking on what all poets ought to consider a sacred subject. Courage : when we meet we will sit upon our melancholy and disorders, bind them like an evil genius and bury them in the Tyrrhene sea, nine fathoms deep. Adieu.

Affectionately yours,
P. B. S.

To Medwin at Geneva. (*Fragment*.)

'No antidote could know.'

Suppose you erase line twenty-four, which seems superfluous, as one does not see why Oswald shunned the *chase* in particular. So, you will put in what you think are amendments, and which I have proposed because they appeared such to me. The poem is certainly very beautiful. I think the conclusion rather morbid; that a man should kill himself is one thing, but that he should live on in the dismal way that poor Oswald does is too much. But it is the spirit of the age, and we are all infected with it. Send me as soon as you can copies of your printed poems.

I have just published a tragedy called the 'Cenci,' and I see they have reprinted it at Paris at Galignani's. I dare say you will see the French edition, full of errors of course, at Geneva. The people from England tell me it is liked. It is dismal enough. My chief endeavour was to produce a delineation of passions which I had never participated in, in chaste language, and according to the rules of enlightened art. I don't think very much of it; but it is for you to judge.

Particularly, my dear friend, write to me an account of your motions, and when and where we may expect to see you. Are you not tempted by the Baths of Lucca?

I have been seriously ill since I last wrote to you, but I am now recovering.

Affectionately yours,
P. B. S.

Pisa, May 1st, 1820

*

To Medwin at Milan (re-addressed to Geneva).

My dear Medwin,

I wrote to you a day or two ago at Geneva. I have since received your letter from the mountains. How much I envy you, or rather how much I sympathize in the delights of your wandering. I have a passion for such expeditions, although partly the capriciousness of my health, and partly the want of incitement of a companion, keep me at home. I see the mountains, the sky, and the trees from my windows, and recollect, as an old man does the mistress of his youth, the raptures of a more familiar intercourse, but without his regrets, for their forms are yet living in my mind. I hope you will not pass Tuscany, leaving your promised visit unpaid. I leave it to you to make the project of taking up your abode with such an animal of the other world as I am, agreeable to your friend; but Mrs Shelley unites with me in assuring both yourself and him that, whatever else may be found deficient, a sincere welcome is at least in waiting for you.

I am delighted with your approbation of my 'Cenci,' and am encouraged to wish to present you with 'Prometheus Unbound,' a drama also, but a composition of a totally different character. I do not know if it be wise to affect variety in compositions, or whether the attempt to excel in many ways does not debar from excellence in one particular kind. 'Prometheus Unbound' is in the merest spirit of ideal poetry, and not, as the name would indicate, a mere imitation of the Greek drama; or, indeed, if I have been successful, is it an imitation of anything. But you will judge. I hear it is just printed, and I probably shall receive copies from England before I see you. Your objection to the 'Cenci' – as to the introduction of the name of God – is good, inasmuch as the play is addressed to a Protestant people; but *we* Catholics speak eternally and familiarly of the First Person of the Trinity, and, amongst *us*, religion is more interwoven with, and is less extraneous to, the system of ordinary life. As to Cenci's curse, I know not whether I can defend it or no. I wish I may be able; and, as it often happens respecting the worst part of an author's work, it is a particular favourite with me. I prided myself – as since your approbation I hope that I had just cause to do – upon the two concluding lines of the play. I confess I cannot approve of the squeamishness which excludes the exhibition of such *subjects* from the scene – a squeamishness the produce, as I firmly believe, of a lower tone of the public mind, and foreign to the majestic and confident wisdom of the golden age of our country. What think you of my boldness? I mean to write a play, in the spirit of human nature, without prejudice or passion, entitled 'Charles the First.' So vanity intoxicates people; but let those few who praise my verses, and in whose approbation I take so much delight, answer for the sin.

I wonder what in the world the Queen has done. I should not wonder, after the whispers I have heard, to find that the green bag contained evidence that she had imitated Pasiphae, and that the Committee should recommend to Parliament a Bill to exclude all Minotaurs from the succession. What silly stuff is this to employ a great nation about. I wish the King and the Queen, like Punch and his wife, would fight out their disputes in person.

What is very strange, I can in no manner discover your parcels; I never knew anything more unfortunate. Klieber sends me your letters regularly (which, by-the-bye, I wish in future you would direct to Pisa, as I have no money business now in Florence), but he has heard of no parcel or book.

This warm weather agrees excellently with me; I only wish it would last all the year. Many things both to say and to hear be referred until we meet.

Your affectionate friend,

P. B. S.

Pisa, July 20, 1820

To Medwin at Geneva.

Pisa, August 22nd, 1821

My dear Medwin,

How do you know that there are not seven distinct letters, patiently waiting with the Williams's, seven lost letters, in the seven distinct post offices of Italy, whose contents you have never unveiled? To write to you hitherto would have been such an enterprise as if the oyster might undertake a correspondence with the eagle, with orders that the billets should be left until called for on every promontory, thunder cloud, or mountain, where the imperial bird might chance to pass.

I have read with pleasure your elegant stanzas on Tivoli. What have you done with the compositions you have sent to England? I am particularly interested in the fate of the stanzas on the lake of Geneva, which seemed to me the best you ever wrote. Have you any idea, according to my counsel, of disciplining your powers to any more serious undertaking? It might at once contribute to your happiness and your success; but consider that poetry, although its source is native and involuntary, requires in its development severe attention.

I am happy to hear that 'Adonais' pleased you; I was considering how I could send you a copy; nor am I less flattered by your friend Sir John's approbation. I think I shall write again. Whilst you were with me, that is, during the latter period, and after you went away, I was harassed by some severe disquietudes, the causes of which are now I hope almost at an end. What were the speculations which you say disturbed you? My mind is at peace respecting nothing so much as the constitution and mysteries of the great system of things; my curiosity on this point never amounts to solicitude. Williams's play, if not a dramatic effort of the highest order, is one of the most manly, spirited, and natural pieces of writing I ever met with. It is full of observation, both of nature and of human-nature; the theatrical effect and interest seems to be strong and well kept up. I confess that I was surprised at his success, and shall be still more so if it is not universally acknowledged on the stage. It is worth fifty such things as Cornwall's 'Mirandola.'

I am just returned from a visit to Lord Byron at Ravenna, whom I have succeeded in rousing to attack the 'Quarterly.' I believe he is about to migrate to this part of the world.

We see the Williams every day, and my regard for them is every day increased; I hardly know which I like best, but I know Jane is your favourite.

We are yet undecided for Florence or Pisa this winter, but in either of these places I confidently expect that we shall see you. Mary unites with me in best regards, and I remain, my dear Medwin,

Faithfully and affectionately yours,

P. B. Shelley.

I am delighted to hear that you have so entirely recovered your health; I hardly dared hope so last winter.

P.S. – I think you must have put up by mistake a MS. translation of the 'Symposium' of Plato; if so, pray contrive to send it me. I have one or two of your books which I keep till you give me instructions.

I add also a letter –

From Mrs Shelley.

At Jane's request I enclose you this letter. Of course, the horse is useless to her; nor could she keep it in any way, nor can she in her state of mind attend to it. If nothing else can be done with it, you can sell it to pay its expenses, but you will be so kind as to attend to the affair yourself.

I ought to say something more about that which has left us in desolation. But why should I *attrister* you with my despair? I will only mention Jane, since you will be interested and anxious, perhaps. She is not well, she does not sleep; but I hope with care she may get better. God knows! She must have struggles, and no one is more unfit for them. No woman had ever more need of a protector; but we shall be together, and until she joins either her mother or Edward's brother, who is expected next year, I shall be with her. Seven or six weeks ago – just three weeks before this blank moral death visited me – I was very ill, near dying; but I have got through it all. I had not been out of the house from illness when Jane and I posted to Leghorn from Lerici to get intelligence of them; and without intelligence, without rest, we returned, to wait ten days for the confirmation of our sentence of a life of eternal pain. Yet not eternal: I think we are all short-lived. But for my child, I would take up my abode at Rome. Rome is a good nurse, and soon rocks to a quiet grave those who seek death. I scrawl all this nonsense, I know not why. I intended to have written two words only; but grief makes my mind active, and, my pen in my hand, I run on by instinct. I could do so for sheets.

Adieu! I hope you will be happy.

> Yours very truly,
> Mary W. Shelley.

July 29th, 1822

S. and I were united exactly eight years ago yesterday. On the 4th of August he would have been thirty. Except that his health was getting better and better, I would not selfishly desire that his angelic spirit should again inhabit that frame which tormented it. He is alive and often with me now. Everyone feels the same; all say that he was an elemental spirit, imprisoned here, but free and happy now. I am not now, one day I hope to be, worthy to join him. My life is chalked out to me : it will be one of study only, except for my poor boy. The children are in excellent health.

Chapter 14

It is mentioned in my narrative, that when I left Leghorn, in the 'Bolivar,' to burn the bodies, I despatched two large feluccas, with ground-tackling to drag for Shelley's foundered boat, having previously ascertained the spot in which she had been last seen afloat. This was done for five or six days, and they succeeded in finding her, but failed in getting her up. I then wrote the particulars to my friend Capt. Roberts, who was still at Genoa, asking him to complete the business. He did so, whilst I went on to Rome, and, as will be seen by the following letters, he not only found, but got her up, and brought her into the harbour of Leghorn.

Pisa, Sept. 1822

Dear T.

We have got fast hold of Shelley's boat, and she is now safe at anchor off Via Reggio. Everything is in her, and clearly proves that she was not capsized. I think she must have been swamped by a heavy sea; we found in her two trunks, that of Williams, containing money and clothes, and Shelley's, filled with books and clothes.

Yours, very sincerely,
Dan Roberts.

Sept. 18, 1822

Dear T.

I consulted Ld. B., on the subject of paying the crews of the felucca employed in getting up the boat. He advised me to sell her by auction, and to give them half the proceeds of the sale. I rode your horse to Via Reggio. On Monday we had the sale, and only realized a trifle more than two hundred dollars.

The two masts were carried away just above board, the bowsprit broken off close to the bows, the gunwale stove in, and the hull half full of blue clay, out of which we fished clothes, books, spyglass, and other articles. A hamper of wine that Shelley bought at Leghorn, a present for the harbour-master of Lerici, was spoilt, the corks forced partly out of the bottles, and the wine mixed with the salt-water. You know, this is effected by the pressure of the cold sea-water.

We found in the boat two memorandum-books of Shelley's, quite perfect, and another damaged; a journal of Williams's, quite perfect, written up to the 4th of July. I washed the printed books: some of them were so glued together by the slimy mud that the leaves could not be separated: most of these things are now in Ld. B.'s custody. The letters, private papers, and Williams's journal, I left in charge of Hunt.

Ld. B. has found out that you left at Genoa some of the ballast of the 'Bolivar,' and he asked me to sell it for him.

P.S. – On a close examination of Shelley's boat, we find many of the timbers on the starboard quarter broken, which makes me think for certain that she must have been run down by some of the feluccas in the squall.

Dan Roberts.

Byron's spirit was always fretting for action, but his body was a drag that held him back. One of his pleas for hoarding money was that he might buy a province in Chili or Peru, to which he once added, archly, 'of course with a gold or silver mine to pay usance for my monies:' at another time it was Mexico and copper; and when savage with the Britishers, he would threaten to go to the United States and be naturalized; he once asked me to apply to the American consul at Leghorn, and Commodore Jones of the American navy, then in the harbour, offered him a passage. Byron visited the ship, and was well pleased with his reception; there was a beginning but no middle or end to his enterprises. The under-current of his mind was always drifting towards the East; he envied the free and independent manner in which Lady Hester Stanhope[52] lived in Syria, and often reverted to it. He said he would have gone there if she had not forestalled him.

Then his thoughts veered round to his early love, the Isles of

Greece, and the revolution in that country – for before that time he never dreamt of donning the warrior's plume, though the peace-loving Shelley had suggested and I urged it. He asked me to get him any information I could amongst my friends at Leghorn of the state of Greece; but as it was a common practice of his to make such inquiries without any serious object, I took little heed of his request.

We were then at Pisa in the old palace, which he was about giving up, Mrs Shelley having gone to Genoa, and taken for him the Casa Saluzzi at Albaro, near Genoa; the Hunts too were about moving to the same destination. I had determined to return to Rome, but stopped to convoy them in the 'Bolivar.'

When a lazy and passive master who has never learnt, or if he may have learnt has forgotten, how to put on his trousers, shave, or brush his hair, in a sudden ecstasy or impulse resolves to do everything for himself and everybody else, as Byron now attempted to do, the hubbub, din, and confusion that ensue are frightful. If the Casa Lanfranchi had been on fire at midnight it could not have been worse, nor I more pleased at escaping from it, as I did, under the plea of getting the flotilla ready at Leghorn.

In September we all left Tuscany, Byron by land, the Hunts in one felucca; and Byron's servants, and what the Yankee would have called a freight of notions, in another; for as Byron never sold or gave away anything he had acquired, there was all the rubbish accumulated in the many years he had lived in Italy, besides his men, women, dogs, and monkeys, and all that was theirs. In the 'Bolivar' I had only a few things, such as plate, books, and papers; we put into Lerici, and there all met again. I took Hunt to the Villa Magni where Shelley had lived. Byron came on board the 'Bolivar,' we had a sail and a swim (as mentioned in my sixth Chapter), after which he was seized with spasms and remained two days in bed. On my visiting him and questioning him as to his ailments, he said he was always 'bedevilled for a week after moving.'

'No wonder,' I answered, 'if you always make such a dire commotion before it.'

'Look in that book,' pointing to one on the table, Thomas's 'Domestic Medicine,' 'look for a prescription.'

'For what? what is your complaint?' I said. 'How do you feel?'

'Feel? why, just as that damned obstreperous fellow felt chained to a rock, the vultures gnawing my midriff, and vitals too, for I have no liver.' As the spasms returned, he roared out, 'I don't care for dying, but I cannot bear this! It's past joking, call Fletcher; give me something that will end it – or me! I can't stand it much longer.'

His valet brought some ether and laudanum, and we compounded a drench as prescribed in the book, with an outward application of hot towels, and other remedies. Luckily, the medico of Lerici was absent, so in two or three days our patient was well enough to resume his journey, and we all started for Genoa, where we arrived without further accident.

All that were now left of our Pisan circle established themselves at Albaro – Byron, Leigh Hunt, and Mrs Shelley. I took up my quarters in the city of palaces. The fine spirit that had animated and held us together was gone. Left to our own devices, we degenerated apace.[53]

Chapter 15

It is the same – For be it joy or sorrow,
 The path of its departure still is free
Man's yesterday may ne'er be like his morrow
 Naught may endure but Mutability.

SHELLEY.

Even I, least thinking of a thoughtless throng,
Just skilled to know the right and choose the wrong;
Freed at that age when reason's shield is lost,
To fight my course through passion's countless host;
Whom every path of pleasure's flowery way
Has lured in turn, and all have led astray.

English Bards and Scotch Reviewers.

BYRON[54] considered it indispensable to the preservation of his popularity that he should keep continually before the public; and thought an alliance with an able and friendly newspaper would be an easy way of doing so. Not that he would or could submit to the methodical drudgery of continually writing for one, but that he might occasionally use it for criticizing and attacking those who offended him, as a vent for his splenetic humours. Shelley opposed the scheme; still, Byron had a hankering to try his powers in those hand-to-hand conflicts, then in vogue even in the great Reviews.

The appetites of actors, authors, and artists for popularity, are insatiable. The craving to be noticed is general; it begins at birth and ends in death. It grows by what it feeds on. This morbid yearning in some minds for notoriety, or to make a sensation, is such, that, rather than be unnoticed, they invent crimes, and lay claim to the good or evil deeds of others.

'The aspiring fool that fired the Ephesian dome
Outlives, in fame, the pious fool that raised it.'

SHAKESPEARE.[55]

When he consented to join Leigh Hunt and others in writing for the 'Liberal,' I think Byron's principal inducement was in the belief that John and Leigh Hunt were proprietors of the 'Examiner;' – so when Leigh Hunt at Pisa told him he was no longer connected with that paper, Byron was taken aback, finding that Hunt would be entirely dependent on the success of their hazardous project, while he would himself be deprived of that on which he had set his heart, – the use of a weekly paper in great circulation.

The death of Shelley, and the failure of the 'Liberal,' irritated Byron; the cuckoo-note, 'I told you so,' sung by his friends, and the loud crowing of enemies, by no means allayed his ill-humour. In this frame of mind he was continually planning how to extricate himself.[56] His plea for hoarding was that he might have a good round tangible sum of current coin to aid him in any emergency, as 'money,' he observed, 'is the only true and constant friend a wise man puts his trust in. They used to call me spendthrift, now they call me miser. Spending don't turn to account, so I am trying what saving will do. I want a sum of money independent of income. £30,000 will do – £10,000 I have – to buy a principality in one of the South American States – Chili or Peru. Lady Hester Stanhope's way of life in Syria would just suit my humour.'

I replied,

'They are not habitable for strangers yet. Better buy one of the Greek islands; the Turks would sell them cheap now.'

Byron answered,

'We shall see. Prudent people talk of a middle course; I am always for extremes. A short cut; all or nothing.'

He exhausted himself in planning, projecting, beginning, wishing, intending, postponing, regretting, and doing nothing: the unready are fertile in excuses, and his were inexhaustible; so I determined to be off. At this time a committee was formed in London to aid the Greeks in their war of independence, and shortly after I wrote to one of the most active movers in it, Lieut. Blaquiere, to ask information as to their objects and intentions, and mentioned Byron as being very much interested on the subject of Greece; the Lieutenant wrote, as from the committee, direct to Byron, in the grandiloquent style which all authorities, especially self-constituted ones, delight in. In the early part of 1823 Blaquiere on his way to the Ionian Islands stopped at Genoa, and saw Byron, whom he informed of his intention to visit Greece, in order to see how matters were progressing. He said that his lordship had been unanimously elected a member of the Greek Committee, and that his name was a tower of strength; he brought Byron's credentials, and a mass of papers. The propositions of the committee came at the right moment; the Pilgrim was dissatisfied with himself and his position. Greece and its memories warmed him, a new career opened before him. His first impulses were always ardent, but if not acted on instantly, they cooled. He was a prompt penman, often answering in hot haste letters that excited his feelings, and following his first replies up by others to allay their fervour, or as the Persians have it, 'eating his words.' But the Greek Committee were not to be fobbed off; they resolved to have him on any terms, so they assented to all he suggested. The official style of the documents sent by the committee, the great seal and the prodigality of wax and diplomatic phrases, as well as the importance attached to his name, and the great events predicted from his personal exertions, tickled the Poet's fancy.[57] The negotiation with the committee occupied some months before Byron, perplexed in the extreme, finally committed himself. He might well hesitate. It would have been difficult to find a man more unfit for such an enterprise; but he had a great name, and that was all the committee required. The marvel was that he lent it. Moore, Byron's biographer, suggests that he embarked in this crusade to rekindle his mental light and failing popularity, whereas the chronology of his works proves that his mental powers waxed stronger as he grew older, and that his last poems were his best. That envy, malice, and hatred bedogged his steps, snarling and snapping, is true, but neither his power nor popularity had declined, nor did he think so.

In after years I called on Mr Murray, his late publisher, whom I met coming from his *sanctum*, accompanied by a sallow-visaged young man. As soon as the young man left the shop, Murray said,

'He asked me to read a poem he had with him, and, if I approved, to publish it; said that it was highly commended, &c., &c. I declined, saying I was no judge; that I had refused several popular writers. I had made up my mind, on losing the great poet, not to publish another line of verse.'

'Have you,' I asked, 'found poetry unprofitable?'

He replied,

'This morning I looked over my ledger, and I find £75,000 has passed over that counter from Lord Byron's pen alone. Can any one in the trade say as much? And then look at the time it was done in – ten years. I think that proves he was a great poet.'

I said, 'And yet you declined publishing what he wrote in the last year of his life, intimating that his popularity was declining, and that his writings were becoming immoral, which offended him. Shelley said his "Vision of Judgment" and the last cantos of "Don Juan" were excellent.'

Murray replied,

'His friends were at me from morning till night. They said that the people in good society were shocked at the low tone he had fallen into. They attributed this to the vicious set he had got about him at Pisa (looking knowingly at me, as I was one of them); and they bothered me into remonstrating with him, and I was fool enough to do so in haste, and have repented at leisure of my folly,[58] for Mr Gifford, the ablest scholar of them all, and one who did not throw his words away, as well as a few men of the same stamp, occasionally dropped remarks which satisfied me I had done wrong in alluding to the subject, for it was after reading the latter cantos of "Don Juan" that Mr Gifford said –

' "Upon my soul, I do not know where to place Byron. I think we can't find a niche for him unless we go back and place him after Shakespeare and Milton" – after a pause – "there is no other place for him."

'When I advertised a new poem from his pen, this quiet street was as thronged with carriages and people as Regent Street, and this shop was crowded with lords and ladies and footmen, so that the trade could not get near the counter to be served.* That was

---

*It is related that 14,000 copies of the 'Corsair' were sold in one day.

something like business. That great man with his pen could alone have supported a publishing establishment, and I was bereft of my senses to throw it away. They talked of his immoral writings: there is a whole row from the greatest writers – including sermons – why don't they buy them? I am sick of the sight of them, they have remained there so long they seem glued to the shelf.'

I said, 'That is what Byron tells you is the cant of the age.'[59]

I observed to Murray that Moore had only seen Byron in society; his Life of his brother Bard was a mystification; his comments might be considered very eloquent as a rhapsody, if they had been spoken over the Poet's grave, but they give no idea of the individuality of the man.

'The most valuable parts of Moore's Life are the letters addressed to you,' I continued; 'and as they were designed for publication, you should have printed them with his prose works.'

Murray replied, 'You are quite right. If ever a statute of lunacy is taken out against me, it must be on the plea of my mad agreement with Moore for Byron's Life, by which I lost credit, and a great deal of money; but it is not too late to redeem my error so far as the public is concerned; rather than leave it as it is, I will get Lockhart, or somebody else, to do the thing as it should be done.'

I have been seduced into this digression to show from what a small squad of malignants came the cry of Byron's failing powers and popularity:[60] I am also reminded of a conversation I had with Byron. I found him at Albaro one day counting up his money, and some remark being made about how he and Scott had raised the price of literature, and the large sum Moore was said to have received for 'Lalla Rookh,' he said, 'I have been calculating, and find that I have received £24,000, that is pretty well.'

In December 1822, I laid up the Poet's pleasure-boat, paid off the crew, retaining the first mate in my service as a groom, and early in the following year, 1823, started on horseback – with the aforesaid sailor, mounted, to act as tender, – to take a cruise inland. So during Byron's negotiation with the Greek Committee, and Blaquiere's visit to Albaro, I was absent, but being apprized of what was going on I was not surprised when in Rome at receiving the following note:—

June 15, 1823

My dear T.

You must have heard that I am going to Greece. Why do you not come to me? I want your aid, and am exceedingly anxious to see you. Pray come, for I am at last determined to go to Greece; it is the only place I was ever contented in. I am serious, and did not write before, as I might have given you a journey for nothing; they all say I can be of use in Greece. I do not know how, nor do they; but at all events let us go.

Yours, &c., truly,
N. Byron.

To show Byron's vacillating state of mind, I quote some passages from letters I received at that time.

Captain Roberts, in a letter dated May 26, 1823, Genoa, says, 'Between you and me, I think there is small chance of Byron's going to Greece; so I think from the wavering manner in which he speaks of it; he said the other day, "Well, Captain, if we do not go to Greece, I am determined to go somewhere, and hope we shall all be at sea together by next month, as I am tired of this place, the shore, and all the people on it." '

Ten days after, in a letter dated the 5th June, Roberts writes me:

'Byron has sold the "Bolivar" to Lord Blessington for four hundred guineas, and is determined to go to Greece: he says, whilst he was in doubt, fearing it might prove no reality, he did not like to bring you here; now, he wishes much to see you to have your opinion as to what steps it will be most necessary to take. I have been on board several vessels with him; as yet he has not decided on any of them. I think he would find it answer, now he has sold the schooner, to buy the three-masted clipper we saw at Leghorn, to refit and arm her (as I am much of your way of thinking) for a big gun or two, and legs to run and wings to pursue, as the case may be, for the Greek waters are pestered with pirates. I have written by his desire to Dunn about her; if you come here by way of Leghorn, pray overhaul her, and then you will be able to give him your opinion. I think she will do excellently well, except the accommodation – the cabin is small. He has asked me to be of the party.'

Four days after I had received the above, Mrs Shelley having just seen Byron, wrote me from Genoa, June 9th:

'Lord Byron says, that as he has not heard from Greece, his going there is uncertain: but if he does go, he is extremely desirous that you should join him, and if you will continue to let him know where you may be found, he will inform you as soon as he comes to any decision.'

This was not the last of Byron's counter-messages to me, besides commissions which I was urged instantly to execute; knowing him, I took no heed nor made any preparations until he wrote me that he had chartered a vessel. On the 22nd I received this note from him:

Dear T.

I have engaged a vessel (now on her way to Leghorn to unload), and on her return to Genoa we embark. She is called the 'Hercules;' you can come back in her if you like, it will save you a land journey. I need not say I shall like your company of all things. I want a surgeon, native or foreign, to take charge of medical stores, and be in personal attendance. Salary, a hundred pounds a year, and his treatment at our table, as a companion and a gentleman. He must have recommendations, of course. Could you look out for me? Perhaps you can consult Vaccà, to whom I have written on the same subject; we are, however, pressed for time a little. I expect you with impatience, and am ever yours,

N. B.

Byron's letters to his literary allies were written carefully, expressly to be shown about. He said, on seeing the word *private* on a letter, 'That will insure its becoming public. If I really wish mine to be private, I say things that my correspondents don't wish divulged.' When he wrote on the spur of the moment his letters were often obscure and peevish; if he gave them me to read, and I told him they would offend, he would rewrite them still more offensively. Omitting his more lengthy scrawls, as they would require tedious notes to explain them, I give two or three short samples of his ordinary natural style.

On his hearing that a naval officer of the 'Despatch' sloop of war had boarded his boat at Leghorn, and taken away her pennant, he wrote to me:

Pisa, August 10, 1822

Dear T.

I always foresaw and told you that they would take every opportunity of annoying me in every respect. If you get American papers and permission to sail under their flag, I shall be very glad, and should much prefer it, but I doubt that it will be very difficult.

Yours,
N. B.

Byron had a dispute with Captain Roberts on a very frivolous subject; he sent me a letter to forward to the Captain; I refused to forward it, saying it would not do, on which he wrote me the following.

Genoa, 9ᵇᵉʳ 29ᵗʰ, 1822

My dear T.

I enclose you a letter from, and another to, Captain R., which may be more to your taste, but at any rate it contains all that I have to say on the subject; you will, I presume, write, and enclose it or not according to your own opinion [it was one of his long-winded, offensive epistles, so I did not send it]. I repeat that I have no wish for a quarrel, but if it comes unlooked for, it must be received accordingly. I recognize no right in any man to interfere between me and men in my pay, of whose conduct I have the best right to judge.

Yours, ever and afterwards,
N. B.

9*ber* 21*st*, 1822

My dear T.

Thank you, I was just going to send you down some books, and the compass of the 'Don Juan,' which I believe belongs to Captain Roberts; if there is anything of yours on board the 'Bolivar,' let me know, that I may send it or keep it for you. I don't know how our account stands; you will let me know if there is any balance due to you, that I may pay it. I am willing to make any agreement with a proper person in the arsenal to look after her, and also to have the rigging deposited in a safe place. I have given the boy and one of the men their clothes, and if Mr Beeze had been civil, and Frost honest, I should not have been obliged to go so near the wind with them. But I hate bothering you with these things, I agree with you in your parting sentence, and hope we shall have better luck another time. There is one satisfaction, however, which is, that the displeasures have been rather occasioned by untoward circumstances, and not by the disposition of any party concerned. But such are human things even in little; we would hardly have had more plague with a first-rate. No news of any kind from England, which don't look well.

Yours ever and truly,

N. B.

This referred to a threatened prosecution of his 'Vision of Judgment,' which had been published in Hunt's 'Liberal.'[61]

Leigh Hunt, in his metaphysical gossip about Byron, professes to assign motives for everything he said; but the constitution of their minds was so dissimilar in the whole world you could not find two men more differently constituted. Indeed a man himself cannot assign a motive for all the idle words he speaks, or even for his trifling acts; they are involuntary.

Chapter 16

He passed forth, and new adventure sought;
Long way he travelled before he heard of aught.
Faery Queene.

FORWARDING my traps to Leghorn, I was soon on the road to Genoa. My sailor groom had returned to his family, and I engaged an American born negro to fill his place. In Italy, I invariably travelled on horseback. The distances from one town to another are short, the scenery is varied, and the climate beautiful; besides, Italy is peculiarly adapted to this slow, yet only way of thoroughly seeing a country. Most travellers fly through in a string, like a flock of wild geese, merely alighting at the great cities. As the weather was hot and the days long, we started every morning at four or five o'clock, and jogged along until ten or eleven, then pulled up at town, village, or solitary locanda, or in default of these, looked out for a wood, dell, ruin, or other place that promised shade and water. Then dismounting we fed our horses from nosebags, made up a fire, boiled coffee, breakfasted off such things as we had brought with us, smoked our pipes and fell asleep. Our provender was carried by the black, in old-fashioned saddle-bags. In that fine climate our wants were so few that they provided ample stowage room. I had two excellent Hungarian cavalry horses, bought from an Austrian colonel. Our usual day's travel was from thirty-five to forty-five miles; the best half of the distance we always accomplished before breakfast, so that our day's journey was completed at four or five in the evening, and every day both horses and men improved in condition. If there is any healthier or pleasanter way of life than this, I can only say, I have never enjoyed it.

However long the journey, it was never tedious, and I always regretted its termination. I stopped two days at Florence, and then shaped my course for the sea-board, through Massa and

Rapallo, Sarzana, Lerici and Spezzia, on which coast everything was familiar to me, and associated with the memories of my lost friends Shelley and Williams. My horses stopped at their accustomed locandas, and many familiar faces came out to welcome me.

I arrived early at Lerici, and determined to sleep there, and finish my journey to Genoa on the following day. In the evening, I walked to the Villa Magni, where the Shelleys had last lived, and the ground-floor having neither door nor window, I walked in. Shelley's shattered skiff in which he used to go adventuring, as he termed it, in rivers and canals, was still there: in that little flat-bottomed boat he had written many beautiful things, –

> 'Our boat is asleep on Serchio's stream,
> Its sails are folded like thoughts in a dream,
> The helm sways idly, hither and thither;
> Dominic, the boatman, has brought the mast,
> And the oars and the sails: but 'tis sleeping fast.'

And here it was, sleeping still on the mud floor, with its mast and oars broken. I mounted the stairs or rather ladder into the dining-room they had lived in, for this and four small bedrooms was all the space they had. As I surveyed its splotchy walls, broken floor, cracked ceiling, and poverty-struck appearance, while I noted the loneliness of the situation, and remembered the fury of the waves that in blowing weather lashed its walls, I did not marvel at Mrs Shelley's and Mrs Williams's groans on first entering it; nor that it had required all Ned Williams's persuasive powers to induce them to stop there. We men had only looked at the sea and scenery, and would have been satisfied with a tent. But women look to a house as their empire. Ladies without a drawing-room are like pictures without frames, or birds without feathers; knowing this, they set to work with a will, and transformed it into a very pleasant abode.

One of the customs of the natives of this bay reminded me of the South Sea Islanders. At sunset the whole population of men, women, and children, took to the water, sporting in it for hours like wild ducks; we occasionally did the same, Shelley especially delighting in the sport. His wife looked grave, and said 'it was improper.' Shelley protested vehemently against the arbitrary power of the word, saying, 'Hush, Mary; that insidious word has never been echoed by these woods and rocks: don't teach it them. It was one of the words my fellow serpent whispered into Eve's ear, and when I hear it, I wish I was far away on some lone island, with no other inhabitants than seals, sea-birds and water-rats.' Then turning to his friend, he continued, 'At Pisa, Mary said a jacket was not proper, because others did not wear them, and here it's not proper to bathe, because everybody does. Oh! what shall we do?'

The next day I started at daylight for Genoa, and when I came near Albaro, I sent my horses to the city, and walked to the Casa Saluzzi; of which all the doors and windows were open, as is usual in Italian country houses during summer evenings. I walked in, and as I did not see any of Byron's people, I looked into five or six of the fifty or sixty rooms which the palace contained, before I found the Pilgrim's penetralia: he was so deeply absorbed that he did not hear my steps. There he sat with a pen in his hand and papers before him, with a painfully perplexed expression and heated brow, such as an inspired Pythoness might have had on her tripod. I thought it a sacrilege to profane his sanctuary, and was hesitating whether I should retreat or advance, when his bull-dog Moretto came in from the hall: so I spoke to the dog.

Byron, recognizing my voice, sprang up with his usual alacrity and shook my hand with unusual warmth. After a hasty chat, he hallooed out lustily for his servants, for there were no bells: he was going out of the room, saying, 'You must be hungry, we will see what there is in the house.'

I assured him that I was not, and that I could not stop, as I wished to see Mrs Shelley and the Leigh Hunts.

'Aye, aye,' he observed, 'they are flesh-eaters – you scorn my lenten fare. But come back soon, I will dispatch my salad and sardines, and then we will discuss a bottle of hock, and talk over matters; I have a great deal to tell you, but I must first balance these cursed bills; I have been an hour poring over this one you found me at, and my *tottle* don't square with Lega;[62] in the time thus lost I might have written half a canto of "Don

Juan" – and the amount of the bill is only one hundred and
forty-three lire, which is not six pounds. In cases of lunacy, the
old demon Eldon decided men's sanity by figures; if I had been
up before him (I was very near doing so), and he had given me
the simplest sum in arithmetic, I should have been consigned to
durance vile –

> "For the rule of three it puzzles me,
> And practice drives me mad."

In about an hour and a half, I returned to the Casa Saluzzi,
and found the Poet still hard at work on his weekly bills: he
observed archly, 'I have found out, in another account of the
steward's, that he has cheated himself; that is his affair, not
mine.' This put him in good humour, so he gathered up the
scattered accounts and put them away. He then read me his correspondence with the Greek Committee, or rather the last portion of it, and a letter from Blaquiere, from Greece, and told me
what he thought of doing. Promising to see Byron the following
day, I left him and walked to my locanda at Genoa. He thought
he was in honour bound to go to Zante to meet Blaquiere, – the
rest seemed to depend on blind chance. The Committee suggested no definite plan, nor could he form one.

Mental as well as physical diseases are hereditary. Byron's
arrogant temper he inherited, his penurious habits were instilled
into him by his mother; he was reared in poverty and obscurity
and unexpectedly became a Lord, with a good estate; this was
enough to unsettle the equanimity of such a temperament as his.
But fortune as well as misfortune comes with both hands full,
and when, as he himself said, he awoke one morning and found
himself famous, his brain grew dizzy, and he foolishly entered
the great donkey sweepstakes, and ran in the ruck:[63] galled in
the race, he bolted off the course, and rushed into the ranks of
that great sect that worships golden images. If you come too near
the improvident or the reckless, there is danger of being engulfed
in the vortex they create, whereas with the thrifty, you may do
well enough. Thus ruminating, I reached my inn, the Croce di
Malta.

The next day Byron called, he wished me to go on board the

brig he had chartered – the 'Hercules,' Captain Scott, – to see her equipments and accommodations, and report thereon. I did so, and was very much dissatisfied. She was a collier-built tub of 120 tons, round-bottomed, and bluff-bowed, and of course, a dull sailor, with the bulkheads, the horse-boxes, and other fittings newly put up, ill-contrived, and scamped by the contractor. The Captain, one of the rough old John Bull stamp, was well enough – the mate better, and no fault to be found with the crew, but that they were too few in number. For such an expedition we should have had a well-manned and fast-sailing clipper-built craft, adapted to the light winds and summer seas prevailing in the Greek Archipelago, so that after calling at the Ionian Islands, we could have used her as a yacht, run over to the Morea, touching at several ports not blockaded by the Turks, and ascertained the exact state of the war, its wants, capabilities, and, more especially, the characters of those who conducted it. We might then have exacted conditions before committing ourselves to any specific line of action. Under the English flag, this and much more might have been done. On saying this to Byron, he answered –

'There was no other vessel than the "Hercules" to be had at Genoa.'

'Leghorn is the place for shipping,' said I.

'Why, then, did you not come here sooner? I had no one to help me.'

'You had Captain Roberts, the very man for the occasion; we might as well have built a raft and so chanced it.'

Then smiling, he replied, 'They say I have got her on very easy terms.'

'Aye, but the time she will be on her voyage will make her a bad bargain; she will take a week to drift to Leghorn, and it should be done in twenty hours.'

'We must make the best of it. I will pay her off at the Ionian Islands, and stop there until I see my way, for here we can learn nothing. Blaquiere is to meet me at Zante by appointment, and he is now in the Morea.'

Chapter 17

Awaking with a start,
The waters heave around me: and on high
The winds lift up their voices: I depart,
Whither I know not.

Childe Harold.

ON the 13th of July, 1823, we shipped the horses, four of Byron's, and one of mine, and in the evening, Byron, Gamba, and an unfledged medical student with five or six servants embarked. I and my negro completed the complement. On my observing to Byron the Doctor would be of no use, as he had seen no practice, he answered, 'If he knows little I pay little, and we will find him plenty of work.' The next day it was a dead calm, so we re-landed; on the 15th we weighed anchor at daylight, several American ships, in compliment to Byron, sending their boats to tow us out of the bay, but made very little progress; we lay in the offing all day like a log upon the main under a broiling sun, – the Italians skipping about, gesticulating, and chattering like wild monkeys in a wood. The Pilgrim sat apart, solemn and sad, – he took no notice of anything nor spoke a word. At midnight the sea breeze set in and quickly freshened, so we shortened sail and hauled our wind. As soon as the old tub began to play at pitch and toss, the noisy Italians, with the exception of the Venetian gondolier, Battista, crept into holes and corners in consternation. The horses kicked down their flimsy partitions, and my black groom and I had to secure them, while the sea got up and the wind increased. I told Byron that we must bear up for port, or we should lose our cattle – 'Do as you like,' he said. So we bore up, and after a rough night, re-anchored in our former berth; as the sun rose the wind died away, and one by one the landlubbers crawled on deck. Byron, having remained all night on deck, laughed at the miserable figure they cut; they all went on shore, and I set to work with two or three English carpenters to repair damages.

In the evening we took a fresh departure, and the weather continuing fine, we had no other delay than that which arose from the bad sailing qualities of our vessel. We were five days on our passage to Leghorn, not averaging more than twenty miles a day. We all messed and most of us slept on deck. Byron, unusually silent and serious, was generally during the day reading Scott's 'Life of Swift,' Col. Hippesley's 'Expedition to South America,' Grimm's 'Correspondence,' or Rochefoucauld. This was his usual style of reading on shore. We were two days at Leghorn completing our sea stores. A Mr Hamilton Browne and two Greeks, who had previously applied to Byron for a passage, came on board. One of the Greeks called himself Prince Shilizzi, the other, Vitaili, assumed no higher rank than Captain. The friends who accompanied them on board whispered me to be wary of them, asserting that the Prince was a Russian spy, and the Captain in the interests of the Turks. This was our first sample of the morality of the modern Greeks. On my telling this to Byron, he merely said, 'And a fair sample too of the ancient as well as modern, if Mitford[64] is to be believed.'

Our Scotch passenger, with no other handle to his name than plain Mr Hamilton Browne, was an acquisition; he had been in office in the Ionian Islands, spoke Italian and Romaic, and knew a good deal of the Greeks, as well as the characters of the English residents in command of the Islands. From what we learnt from him we altered our plan, and instead of Zante decided on going to Cephalonia, as Sir J. C. Napier[65] was in command there, and the only man in office favourably disposed to the Greeks and their cause. We remained two days at Leghorn completing our stores. I don't remember that Byron went on shore more than once, and then only to settle his accounts with his agent, Webb. As we were getting under weigh, my friend Grant came on board, and gave Byron the latest English papers, Reviews, and the first volume of Las Cases' 'Memoirs of Napoleon,' just out. On the 23rd of July, 1823, we put to sea in the finest possible weather; drifting leisurely along the Italian coast, we sighted Piombino, a town in the midst of the pestilential lagoons of the

Maremma famous for its wild fowl and fevers; a dark line of jungle fringed the shore for many leagues; we crossed the mouth of the muddy Tiber; saw the Alban Mount, and Mount Soracte, the landmarks which point out the site of Rome. On coming near Lonza, a small islet, converted into one of their many dungeons by the Neapolitan government, I said to Byron,

'There is a sight that would curdle the milky blood of a poet-laureate.'

'If Southey were here,' he answered, 'he would sing hosannas to the Bourbons. Here kings and governors are only the jailers and hangmen of the detestable Austrian barbarians. What dolts and drivellers the people are to submit to such universal despotism. I should like to see, from this our ark, the world submerged, and all the rascals on it drowning like rats.'

I put a pencil and paper in his hand, saying,

'Perpetuate your curses on tyranny, for poets like ladies generally side with the despots.'

He readily took the paper and set to work. I walked the deck and prevented his being disturbed. He looked as crestfallen as a riotous boy, suddenly pounced upon by a master and given an impossible task, scrawling and scratching out, sadly perplexed. After a long spell, he said,

'You think it is as easy to write poetry as smoke a cigar, – look, it's only doggerel. Extemporizing verses is nonsense; poetry is a distinct faculty, – it won't come when called, – you may as well whistle for a wind; a Pythoness was primed when put upon her tripod. I must chew the cud before I write. I have thought over most of my subjects for years before writing a line.'

He did not, however, give up the task, and sat pondering over the paper for nearly an hour; then gnashing his teeth, he tore up what he had written, and threw the fragments overboard.

Seeing I looked disappointed –

'You might as well ask me to describe an earthquake, whilst the ground was trembling under my feet. Give me time, – I can't forget the theme : but for this Greek business I should have been at Naples writing a fifth canto of "Childe Harold," expressly to give vent to my detestation of the Austrian tyranny in Italy.'

Some time after, I suggested he should write a war song for

the Greeks; he did so afterwards. I saw the original amongst his papers at Missolonghi, and made a copy of it, which I have lost. Proceeding on our voyage, it was not until we had been some days fairly at sea, with no land to look back upon, that the Pilgrim regained something of his self-command – he may have felt the truth of the old song –

> 'Now we're in for it, damme what folly, boys,
>   To be downhearted, yo ho.'

A balmy night at sea, almost as light as day, without its glare. Byron, sitting in his usual seat by the taffrail, had been for hours 'chewing the cud of sweet and bitter fancy;' if a tropical night like this can't soothe a lacerated mind nothing but death can; all hands were asleep, but the helmsman and mate keeping watch.[66]

BYRON: If Death comes in the shape of a cannonball and takes off my head, he is welcome. I have no wish to live, but I can't bear pain. Don't repeat the ceremony you went through with Shelley – no one wants my ashes.

TRE.: You will be claimed for Westminster Abbey.

BYRON: No, they don't want me – nor would I have my bones mingled with that motley throng.

TRE.: I should prefer being launched into the sea, to the nonsense of the land ceremonies.

BYRON: There is a rocky islet off Maina – it is the Pirates' Isle; it suggested the 'Corsair.' No one knows it; I'll show it you on the way to the Morea. There is the spot I should like my bones to lie.

TRE.: They won't let me do so without you will it.

BYRON: I will, if you are with me when I die; remind me, and don't let the blundering, blockhead doctors bleed me, or when I am dead maul my carcass – I have an antipathy to letting blood. My Italians have never lost sight of their homes before, they are men to look at, but of no use under any emergency – your negro is worth them all.

TRE.: But you have your ancient page, Fletcher.

Byron said, smiling, 'He is the worst of them, grunting and grumbling all the morning, and fuddled at night. They say the bones harden with age – I am sure my feelings do; nothing now that can happen can vex me for more than twenty-four hours.'

On a similar occasion, all day it had been a dead calm, and it continued so all night – at midnight everything seemed dead or asleep: the sea slept, the sails were asleep, all living things on board slept, except the Poet and myself, for the helmsman dozed. I had eaten nothing since midday. I looked about to find some living thing to get me somewhat, and stumbled on my black fellow – it is no easy thing to arouse a negro, his sleep is akin to death. I lifted him, and set him upright, and shaking him, commissioned him to get me some provender: when it was brought I began my supper – it was one o'clock. The Pilgrim came over: 'Your demon has brought these things to tempt me – I could have resisted any other edibles – but biscuits, cheese, and bottled ale, I can't resist those. Nightmare is sure to follow it.'

TRE.: The Stoics say that all pleasure is pain.

BYRON: It is so to me, the Byrons have no livers; cramps, spasms, convulsions are my heritage.

After supper we resumed our seats.

BYRON: I have no loves, I have only one friend, my sister Augusta, and I have reduced my hates to two – that venomous reptile Brougham, and Southey the apostate. At twenty-five the hair grew too low on my brow, I shaved it, and now at thirty-five I am getting bald and bleached.

His sadness intermitted, and his cold fits alternated with hot ones. Hitherto he had taken very little notice of anything, and when he talked it was with an effort. The lonely and grim-looking island of Stromboli was the first object that riveted his attention; it was shrouded in the smoke from its eternal volcanic fires, and the waves, rolling into the deep canyons at its base, boomed dismally. A poet might have compared it to the bellowings of imprisoned demons.

Our Captain told us a story at night. It was an old tale told by all Levant sailors, and they are not particular as to names and dates.

'That a ship from the port of London was lying off this island loading with sulphur, when her Captain, who was on shore superintending the men, distinctly saw Alderman Curtis—'[67]

'Not Alderman Curtis,' shouted Byron, 'but cut-throat Castlereagh!'

'Whoever it was, my Lord,' continued the skipper, 'he was walking round and round the edge of the burning crater; his mate and crew were witnesses of the same: and when the vessel returned to England they heard that the person they had seen was dead; and the time of his death tallied exactly with the above event, as entered in the ship's log-book.'

Byron, taking up the yarn-spinning said –

'Monk Lewis[68] told me, that he took lodgings at Weimar in Germany, and that every morning he was awakened by a rustling noise, as of quantities of papers being torn open and eagerly handled; the noise came from a closet joining his room; he several times got out of bed and looked into it, but there was no one there. At length he told the servant of the house: the man said, "Don't you know the house is haunted? It belonged formerly to a lady; she had an only son, he left her and went to sea, and the ship was never heard of, – but the mother still believed he would return, and passed all her time in reading foreign newspapers, of which the closet was full; and when she died, at the same hour every morning, in that closet, her spirit is heard frantically tearing open papers."

'Monk Lewis,' added Byron, 'though so fond of a ghost story, was not superstitious, he believed nothing. Once at a dinner party he said to me, across the table, "Byron, what did you mean by calling me Apollo's sexton in your English Bards?"[88] I was so taken aback I could not answer him, nor could I now. Now, Tre,' he said, 'it's your turn to spin a yarn.'

'I will tell you one of presentiment,' I said, 'for you believe in that.'

'Certainly I do,' he rejoined.

'The Captain of Lord Keith's ship, when she was lying at Leghorn, was on a visit to Signor Felleichi, at Pisa; the Captain was of a very gay and talkative turn; suddenly he became silent and sad; his host asked if he was ill? he said "No, I wish I was on board my ship; I feel as if I were going to be hanged." At last he was persuaded to go to bed; but before he got to his room, an express arrived with the news that his ship was on fire. He instantly posted to Leghorn, went on board, and worked his ship out of the harbour to avoid perilling the other vessels lying there, but in spite of great exertion the fire reached the magazine, and every soul perished. A little middy on shore at Leghorn, with a heart as great as his Captain's, gave a boatman a draft on Signor Felleichi for sixty pounds, to put him alongside his ship.'

The Poet had an antipathy to everything scientific; maps and charts offended him; he would not look through a spy-glass, and only knew the cardinal points of the compass; buildings the most ancient or modern he was as indifferent to as he was to painting, sculpture, and music. But all natural objects and changes in the elements he was generally the first to point out and the last to lose sight of. We lay-to all night off Stromboli; Byron sat up watching it. As he went down to his cabin at daylight, he said –

'If I live another year, you will see this scene in a fifth canto of "Childe Harold." '

In the morning we entered the narrow strait of Messina, passed close by the precipitous promontory of Scylla, and at the distance of a mile on the opposite shore, Charybdis; the waters were boiling and lashed into foam and whirlpools by the conflicting currents and set of the sea; in bad weather it is dangerous to approach too near in small craft. The Poet had returned to his usual post by the taffrail; and soon after Messina was spread out before us, with its magnificent harbour, quays, and palaces; it was a gorgeous sight, and the surrounding scenery was so diversified and magnificent, that I exclaimed –

'Nature must have intended this for Paradise.'

'But the devil,' observed the Poet, 'has converted it into Hell.'

After some deliberation, the wind blowing fresh and fair, we reluctantly passed the city, and scudded through the Straits along the grim and rugged shores of Calabria; at 2 P.M. we got into the vortex of another whirlpool, and the conflicting winds, currents, and waves contending for mastery, held us captive. Our vessel was unmanageable, and there we lay oscillating like a pendulum for two hours close to the rocks, seeing vessels half-a-mile from us scudding by under double-reefed topsails. The spell broken, we resumed our course. On passing a fortress called the

Faro, in the narrowest part of the Strait, we had a good view of Mount Etna, with its base wreathed in mists, while the summit stood out in bold relief against the blue sky. To the east we had the savage shores of Calabria, with its grey and jagged rocks; to the west the sunny and fertile coast of Sicily, – gliding close by its smooth hills and sheltered coves, Byron would point to some serene nook, and exclaim, 'There I could be happy!'

Chapter 18

But let it go – it will one day be found
 With other relics of 'a former world,'
When this world shall be *former* underground,
 Thrown topsy-turvy, twisted, crisp'd, and curl'd,
Baked, fried, and burnt, turn'd inside out or drown'd.

Don Juan.

IT was now the 30th of July, twelve days since our departure from Genoa, our ship would do anything but go a-head, she was built on the lines of a baby's cradle, and the least touch of Neptune's foot set her rocking. I was glad of this, for it kept all the land-lubbers in their cribs. Byron was not at all affected by the motion, he improved amazingly in health and spirits, and said, 'On shore, when I awake in the morning, I am always inclined to hang myself, as the day advances, I get better, and at midnight I am all cock-a-whoop. I am better now than I have been for years.' You never know a man's temper until you have been imprisoned in a ship with him, or a woman's until you have married her. Few friendships can stand the ordeal by water; when a yacht from England with a pair of these thus tried friends touches, – say at Malta or Gibraltar, – you may be sure that she will depart with one only. I never was on shipboard with a better companion than Byron, he was generally cheerful, gave no trouble, assumed no authority, uttered no complaints, and did not interfere with the working of the ship; when appealed to he always answered, 'do as you like.' Every day at noon, he and I jumped overboard in defiance of sharks or weather; it was the only exercise he had, for he could not walk the deck. His favourite toys – pistols – were not forgotten; empty bottles and live poultry served as targets; a fowl, duck or goose, was put into a basket, the head and neck only visible, hoisted to the main yard-arm; and we rarely had two shots at the same bird. No boy cornet enjoyed a practical joke more than Byron. On great occasions when our Captain wished to be grand, he wore a bright scarlet waistcoat; as he was very corpulent, Byron wished to see if this vest would not button round us both. The Captain was taking his siesta one day, when Byron persuaded the boy to bring up the waistcoat. In the meantime, as it was nearly calm and very hot, I opened the coops of the geese and ducks, who instinctively took to the water. Neptune, the Newfoundland dog, jumped after them, and Moretto the bull-dog followed.

'Now,' said Byron, standing on the gangway, with one arm in the red waistcoat, 'put your arm in, Tre, we will jump overboard, and take the shine out of it.'

So we did.

The Captain hearing the row on deck, came up, and when he saw the gorgeous garment he was so proud of defiled by seawater, he roared out, 'My Lord, you should know better than to make a mutiny on board ship [the crew were laughing at the fun]. I won't heave to, or lower a boat, I hope you will both be drowned.'

'Then you will lose your *frite*' (for so the Captain always pronounced the word freight), shouted Byron.

As I saw the dogs worrying the ducks and geese, I returned on board with the waistcoat, pacified the skipper, lowered a boat, and with the aid of a boy, sculled after the birds and beasts; the Newfoundland brought them to us unharmed, but Moretto the bull-dog did not mouth them so tenderly. After the glare and oppressive heat of the day, the evenings and nights were delightful: balmy air, no dew, and light enough to distinguish everything near.[70]

Sitting with Byron at the stern – his valet Fletcher and the Captain of the vessel were carousing at the gangway – the Captain, a thorough John Bull, in his blunt manners and burly form, said,

'What is your master going to such a wild country of savages for? My mate was at Corfu, and he says an officer of the garrison crossed over to Albania to shoot, and was shot by the natives; they thought the brass buttons on his jacket were gold.'

'When I was there,' said Fletcher, 'the Turks were masters, and kept them down.'

CAPTAIN: What may the country be like?

FLETCHER: Bless you! there is very little country; it's all rocks and robbers. They live in holes in rocks, and come out like foxes; they have long guns, pistols, and knives. We were obliged to have a guard of soldiers to go from one place to another.

CAPTAIN: How did you live?

FLETCHER: Like dogs, on goat's flesh and rice, sitting on the floor in a hovel, all eating out of one dirty round dish, tearing the flesh to pieces with their fingers; no knives, no forks, and only two or three horn spoons. They drink a stuff they call wine, but it tastes more of turps than grapes, and is carried about in stinking goat-skins, and every one drinks from the same bowl; then they have coffee, which is pounded, and they drink it, dregs and all, without sugar. They are all smoking when not sleeping; they sleep on the floor in their clothes and shoes; they never undress or wash, except the ends of their fingers, and are covered with lice and fleas. The Turks were the only respectable people in the country. If they go, Greece will be like bedlam broke loose. It's a land of lies, and lice, and fleas, and thieves. What my lord is going there for the Lord only knows, I don't.' Then seeing his master was looking, he said, 'And my master can't deny what I have said is true.'

'No,' said Byron, 'to those who look at things with hog's eyes, and can see nothing else. What Fletcher says may be true, but I didn't note it. The Greeks are returned to barbarism; Mitford says the people never were anything better. Nor do I know what I am going for. I was tired of Italy, and liked Greece, and the London Committee told me I should be of use, but of what use they did not say nor do I see.

TRE.: We shall have excitement; the greatest of all – fighting.

BYRON: By all accounts the Greeks have no field artillery, no cavalry, no bayonets or discipline; they are led on by old brigands and shepherds who know the country thoroughly. The Turks are all cavalry, without order; they are brave horsemen, but they have lost the art of war. Cavalry is no use in a rugged, roadless country like Greece without being flanked by infantry. The Turkish horse go blindly through the ravines like a drove of buffaloes, and the Greeks, hidden amongst the rocky heights, rush down on them like wolves, and fusilade them under cover of the rocks. Their sole object is plunder. This is not war, but carnage. Wordsworth calls carnage God's daughter.

I followed Fletcher's example in regard to the supper, and the Poet, saying he could not resist temptation, joined me. We discussed the pleasures and independence of sea-life as contrasted with the eternal restraint and botheration on shore. 'Here,' I observed, 'we have only the elements to contend with, and a safe port under our lee, whereas on shore we never know what mischief is brewing; a letter, or the idle gossip of a good-natured friend, stops our digestion. How smoothly the time glides on, now we are out of the reach of men and mischief-makers.'

'Women, you should say,' exclaimed Byron; 'if we had a womankind on board, she would set us all at loggerheads, and make a mutiny, would she not, Captain?'

'I wish my old woman was here,' replied the skipper, 'she would make you as comfortable in my cabin at sea, as your own wife could in her parlour on shore.'

Byron started and looked savage – the Captain went on, as unconscious of offending as a cart-horse would be after crushing your toes with his hoof. 'My wife,' he continued, 'on my last voyage from Rio, saved my ship. We had touched there for water, homeward bound : she waked me up at night, – her weather eye was always open, – the men were *desarting* in a crimp's shore-boat. In the morning it came on to blow like blazes.'

'If we are to have a yarn, Captain, we must have strong waters.'

'I have no objection to a glass of grog,' said the Captain; 'I am not a temperance man, but I can't *abide* drunkenness at sea. I like to have my allowance.'

'How much is that?' asked Byron.

'No more than will do me good.'

'How much is that?'

'Why, a bottle of good old Jamaica rum sarves me from 11 A.M. till 10 P.M., and I know that can't hurt any man.'

Byron read a critique on O'Meara's 'Napoleon at St Helena,' in the 'Quarterly.' He remarked, 'If all they assert is true, it only affects the character of the author. They do not disprove a single statement in the book : this is their way. If they crush an author, it must be in the shell, as they tried to do with me : if the book has life enough to out-live the year, it defies their malice – for who reads a last year's review? Whilst our literature is domineered over by a knot of virulent bigots and rancorous partisans, we shall have no great or original works. When did parsons patronize genius? If one of their black band dares to think for himself, he is drummed out, or cast aside, like Sterne and Swift. Where are the great poets and writers the Reviewers predicted were to be the leviathans of our literature? Extinct : their bones hereafter may be grubbed up in a fossil state with those of the reptiles that puffed them into life. If this age has produced anything good or great, it has been under every possible discouragement.

'People say that I have told my own story in my writings : I defy them to point out a single act of my life by my poems, or of my thoughts, for I seldom write what I think. All that has been published about me is sheer nonsense, as will be seen at my death, when my real Life is published : everything in that is true. When I first left England I was gloomy. I said so in my first canto of "Childe Harold." I was then really in love with a cousin [Thirza, he was very chary of her name], and she was in a decline. On my last leaving England I was savage; there was enough to make me so. There is some truth as to detail in the "Dream," and in some of my shorter poems. As to my marriage, which people made such ridiculous stories about, it was managed by Lady Jersey and others. I was perfectly indifferent on the subject; thought I could not do better, and so did they. It was an experiment, and proved a failure. Everything is told in my memoirs exactly as it happened. I told Murray Lady Byron was to read the MS. if she wished it, and requested she would add, omit, or make any comments she pleased, now, or when it was going through the press.'

It is strange that Byron, though professing to distrust everybody, should have had no misgiving as to the fate of his memoirs; he was glad Moore sold them to Murray, as he thought that ensured publication. He considered it indispensable to his honour that the truths he could not divulge during his life should be known at his death. He knew that Moore prided himself on his intimacy with lords and ladies, for he was always talking of them, and that the chief aim and object of that Poet's whole life was pleasure at any price. Had he fulfilled his trust by giving Byron's memoirs to the world, he would have compromised himself with society, as they contained many a reminiscence which would have cast a shadow on the fashionable circles which Tom Moore delighted to honour. When the question was raised after Byron's death of the publication or suppression of his memoirs, his friend Tom Moore acted as if he was quite indifferent on the subject; so he must have been, for although he permitted others to read them, he never found time to do so himself. He consulted the most fashionable man he knew on the subject, Lutterell, who, as Rogers says, 'cared nothing about the matter, and readily voted they should be put in the fire.' Byron said, 'some few scenes and names in his memoirs it might be necessary to omit, as he had written the whole truth. Moore and Murray were to exercise their own discretion on that subject.' He added, 'that the truth would be known and believed when he was dead, and the lies forgotten.' So there is nothing to extenuate the great wrong done to Byron by Tom Moore.[71]

Byron's autobiography contained a narrative of the principal events of his life, with running comments on those he came in contact with, or who crossed his path. It was written in a straightforward, manly manner, and in a vigorous, fearless style, and was apparently truthful as regarded himself; – if it was not the whole truth, it contained much more of that commodity than other writers have generally left us in their memoirs. Autobiography was the kind of reading he preferred to all others.

Chapter 19

His life was one long war with self-taught foes,
Or friends by him self-banished, for his mind
Had grown Suspicion's sanctuary.

Childe Harold.

BYRON formed his opinion of the inhabitants of this planet from books; personally he knew as little about them as if he belonged to some other. From reading Rochefoucauld, Machiavelli, and others, he learnt to distrust people in general; so, as he could do nothing without them and did not know how to manage them, he would complain of being overreached, and never getting what he wanted. I don't think he ever knew what he did want : few there are that do.

To resume my log on board the good ship 'Hercules.' On the 2nd of August, the islands of Cephalonia and Zante were in sight, and shortly after Byron pointing out the Morea, said, 'I don't know why it is, but I feel as if the eleven long years of bitterness I have passed through since I was here were taken off my shoulders, and I was scudding through the Greek Archipelago with old Bathurst, in his frigate.' That night we anchored in the roadstead; the next morning we worked into Argostoli, the harbour of Cephalonia, and anchored near the town. An officer from the Health Office having examined our papers and log, gave us pratique. The secretary of the Resident, Captain Kennedy, came on board; he told us Colonel Napier was absent, but that we might depend on the Colonel's readiness to aid us in anything that his orders to observe strict neutrality permitted. The captain gave us the latest news from the seat of war, and said Blaquiere had gone to England, at which Byron was sorely vexed. The truth flashed across his mind, that he had been merely used as a decoy by the committee. 'Now they have got me thus far they think I must go on, and they care nothing as to the result. They are deceived, I won't budge a foot farther until

I see my way; we will stay here; if that is objected to, I will buy an island from the Greeks or Turks; there must be plenty of them in the market.' The instinct that enables the vulture to detect carrion afar off, is surpassed by the marvellous acuteness of the Greeks in scenting money. The morning after our arrival a flock of ravenous Zuliote refugees alighted on our decks, attracted by Byron's dollars. Legà, the steward, a thorough miser, coiled himself on the money-chest like a viper. Our sturdy skipper was for driving them overboard with hand-spikes. Byron came on deck in exuberant spirits, pleased with their savage aspect and wild attire, and, as was his wont, promised a great deal more than he should have done; day and night they clung to his heels like a pack of jackals, till he stood at bay like a hunted lion, and was glad to buy them off, by shipping them to the Morea. On Colonel Napier's return to the island, he warmly urged Byron, and indeed all of us, to take up our quarters at his house; from first to last, all the English on the island, the military as well as the civilians, vied with each other in friendly and hospitable acts. Byron preferred staying on board; every afternoon he and I crossed the harbour in a boat, and landed on a rock to bathe; on one of these occasions he held out his right leg to me, saying,

'I hope this accursed limb will be knocked off in the war.'

'It won't improve your swimming,' I answered; 'I will exchange legs if you will give me a portion of your brains.'

'You would repent your bargain,' he said; 'at times I feel my brains boiling, as Shelley's did whilst you were grilling him.'

After bathing, we landed in an olive grove, eating our frugal supper under the trees. Our Greek passengers during the voyage said that the Greeks generally were in favour of a monarchical government; the Greeks on the island confirmed this, saying it was the only way of getting rid of the robber chiefs who now tyrannized and kept the country in a state of anarchy; and as they must have a foreigner for a king, they could not do better than elect Byron. The Poet treated this suggestion lightly, saying, 'If they make me the offer, I may not refuse it. I shall take care of my own "sma' peculiar;" for if it don't suit my humour, I shall, like Sancho, abdicate.' Byron several times alluded to this in a bantering vein; it left an impression on his mind. Had he lived to reach the congress of Salona as commissioner of the loan, the dispenser of a million silver crowns would have been offered a golden one.

Our party made an excursion to the neighbouring island of Ithaca; contrasted with the arid wastes and barren red hills of Cephalonia, the verdant valleys, sparkling streams, and high land, clothed in evergreen shrubs, were strikingly beautiful. After landing, it was proposed to Byron to visit some of the localities that antiquaries have dubbed with the titles of Homer's school, – Ulysses' stronghold, &c.: he turned peevishly away, saying to me, 'Do I look like one of those emasculated fogies? Let's have a swim. I detest antiquarian twaddle. Do people think I have no lucid intervals, that I came to Greece to scribble more nonsense? I will show them I can do something better : I wish I had never written a line, to have it cast in my teeth at every turn.' Browne and Gamba went to look for some place where we might pass the night, as we could not get mules to go on until the next day.

After a long swim, Byron clambered up the rocks, and, exhausted by his day's work, fell asleep under the shade of a wild fig-tree at the mouth of a cavern. Gamba, having nothing to do, hunted him out, and awakened him from a pleasant dream, for which the Poet cursed him. We fed off figs and olives, and passed our night at a goatherd's cottage.

In the morning we rode through the pleasant little island to Vathy, the capital. The Resident, Captain Knox, his lady, and everyone else who had a house, opened their doors to welcome us, and the Pilgrim was received as if he had been a prince. On the summit of a high mountain in the island there is an ancient monastery, from which there is a magnificent view of the Ionian Sea, Greece, and many islands. The day after our arrival we ascended it, our party amounting to ten or twelve, including servants and muleteers. As usual, it was late when we started; there was not a breath of air, and the heat was intense. Following a narrow zigzag path between rocks and precipices in single file, as our mules crept upwards our difficulty increased, until the path became merely stone steps, worn by time and travel in the solid limestone. We all dismounted but Byron; he was jaded and irritable, as he generally was when deprived of his accustomed midday siesta: it was dusk before we reached the summit of the mountain. The Abbot had been apprized by the Resident of our visit; and when we neared the monastery, files of men stood on each side of our path, bearing pine torches. On coming up to the walls we saw the monks in their grey gowns, ranged along the terrace; they chanted a hymn of glorification and welcome to the great lord, saying, 'Christ has risen to elevate the cross and trample on the crescent in our beloved Greece.' The Abbot, clad in his sacerdotal robes, received Byron in the porch, and conducted him into the great hall, illuminated for the occasion; the monks and others clustered round the honoured guest; boys swung censers with frankincense under the Poet's nose. The Abbot, after performing a variety of ceremonies in a very dignified manner, took from the folds of his ample garments a roll of paper, and commenced intoning through his nasal organ a turgid and interminable eulogium on my 'Lordo Inglese,' in a polyglot of divers tongues; while the eyes of the silent monks, anxious to observe the effect of the holy father's eloquence, glanced from the Abbot to the Lord.

Byron had not spoken a word from the time we entered the monkery; I thought he was resolved to set us an example of proper behaviour. No one was more surprised than I was, when suddenly he burst into a paroxysm of rage, and vented his ire in a torrent of Italian execrations on the holy Abbot and all his brotherhood. Then turning to us with flashing eyes, he vehemently exclaimed.

'Will no one release me from the presence of these pestilential idiots? they drive me mad!' Seizing a lamp, he left the room.

The consternation of the monks at this explosion of wrath may be imagined. The amazed Abbot remained for some time motionless, his eyes and mouth wide open; holding the paper he had been reading in the same position, he looked at the vacant place left by Byron, and then at the door through which he had disappeared. At last he thought he had solved the mystery, and in a low tremulous voice said, – significantly putting his finger to his forehead: –

'Eccolo, è matto poveretto!' (Poor fellow, he is mad.)

Leaving Hamilton Browne to pacify the monks, I followed Byron. He was still fretting and fuming, cursing the 'whining dotard,' as he called the Abbot, who had tormented him. Byron's servant brought him bread, wine, and olives. I left him and joined the mess of the monks in their refectory. We had the best of everything the island produced for supper. Our host broached several flasks of his choicest vintages: but although he partook largely of these good things, they failed to cheer him. We were all glad to retire early to our cells.

In the morning, Byron came forth refreshed, and acted as if he had forgotten the occurrences of the evening. The Abbot had not, and he took care not to remind him of them. A handsome donation was deposited in the alms-box, and we mounted our mules and departed, without any other ceremony than a hasty benediction from the holy father and his monks. However we might have doubted the sincerity of their ovation on receiving us, we did not question the relief they felt and expressed by their looks on our departure.

The next day we retraced our steps through the flowery ravines and tranquil glades of this lovely islet, our road winding along the foot of the mountains. The grey olive-trees, bright green fig, and rampant vine, that grew above our heads, screened us from the sun; the fresh breeze from the sea, with the springs of purest water gushing out of the rocks, soothed the Poet's temper. He turned out of the path to look at a natural grotto, in a grove of forest trees, and said, 'You will find nothing in Greece or its islands so pleasant as this. If this isle were mine, – "I would break my staff and bury my book." – What fools we all are!'

On reaching our former landing-place, we had to wait a long time for a boat to ferry us across the strait to Cephalonia. As usual, he and I took to the water; in the evening we crossed, and it was night when we regained our old quarters on board the 'Hercules.'[72] At two o'clock Byron went to his cabin, I slept on deck.

The only thing in sight at sunset was an Austrian bark, eight or ten miles distant. A little after sunrise I was aroused by a great commotion – the bark was close alongside of us. It was and had been a dead calm. Old salts say that ships are like living creatures. If left to themselves and the wind don't interfere, they will if they sight each other draw close together. It is so; but why I don't know. I have often observed it. We were bound in opposite directions. This phenomenon is a puzzle to all sailors.

It was near noon of the next day, when I had occasion to speak to Byron on pressing business. I descended to his cabin, – he was fast asleep. I repeatedly called him by name; at first in a low voice, – then louder and louder; at last he started up in terror, staring at me wildly. With a convulsive sigh he said, 'I have had such a dream! I am trembling with fear. I am not fit to go to Greece. If you had come to strangle me I could have done nothing.'

I said, 'Who could against a nightmare? the hag don't mind your pistols or your bible' (he always had these on a chair close to the side of his bed). I then talked on other subjects until he was tolerably composed, and so left him.

The conflicting accounts that came day by day from the Morea distracted us; to ascertain the real state of things, I proposed to go there. Byron urged me to stay until he went, so I remained for some time; but when he talked of leaving the ship and taking a house, I determined to be off.

Chapter 20

Where Athens, Rome, and Sparta stood,
 There is a moral desert now;
The mean and miserable huts,
Contrasted with those ancient fanes,
The long and lonely colonnades,
Through which the ghost of Freedom stalks.
                                        Queen Mab.

I WELL knew that once on shore Byron would fall back on his old routine of dawdling habits, plotting – planning – shilly-shallying – and doing nothing. It was a maxim of his, 'If I am stopped for six days at any place, I cannot be made to move for six months.'

Hamilton Browne agreed to go with me; he was a most valuable ally. In my hasty preparations for going, I was tearing up and throwing overboard papers and letters. Byron stopped me, saying, 'Some day you will be sorry for this; they are parts of your life. I have every scrap of paper that was ever written to me, – letters, notes, – even cards of invitation to parties. There are chestfuls at Hansom's, Douglas Kinnaird's, and Barry's at Genoa.[73] They will edify my executors.'

'Is this quite fair to your correspondents?' I asked.

'Yes; for they have mine and might use them against me. Whilst I live they dare not, – I can keep them all in order; when I die and my memoirs are published, – my executors can verify them by my letters if their truth is questioned.'

I told Byron that two Frenchmen, just landed, wished to see him; I thought they were officers. He said, 'Ask Hamilton Browne to see what they want. I can't express myself like a gentleman in French. I never could learn it, – or anything else according to rule.' He even read translations of French books in preference to the originals. His ignorance of the language was the reason why he avoided Frenchmen and was never in France.

In our voyage from Italy, Byron persuaded me to let him have my black servant, as, in the East, it is a mark of dignity to have a negro in your establishment. He likewise coveted a green embroidered military jacket of mine; which, as it was too small for me, I gave him; so I added considerably to his dignity.[74] I engaged one of the refugee Zuliotes (or Zodiacs, as old Scott, our Captain, called them) to go with me. He was a vain, lazy, swaggering braggart, – sullen and stupid as are most of his tribe.

Byron gave us letters addressed to the Greek government, if we could find any such constituted authorities, – expressing his readiness to serve them when they had satisfied him how he could do so, &c., &c., &c. As I took leave of him, his last words were, 'Let me hear from you often, – come back soon. If things are farcical, they will do for "Don Juan;" if heroical, you have another canto of "Childe Harold." '

Hamilton Browne and I went on board a light boat of the country, called a caique, crossed over with a fair wind in the night, and landed early the next morning on a sandy beach, at a solitary ruined tower near Pyrgos. A dirty squad of Moorish mercenaries, quartered at the tower, received us; some of them accompanied us to the village of Pyrgos; where, as we could not procure horses or mules, we slept.

In the morning we commenced our journey to Tripolitza, the capital of the Peloponnesus, visiting the military stations on our way. We slept at the ruined villages, and were generally well received when our mission was known. The country is so poor and barren, that but for its genial climate it would be barely habitable. In the best of times there would not be plenty; but now that war had passed over the land with fire and slaughter there was scarcely a vestige of habitation or cultivation.

The only people we met, besides soldiers, looked like tribes of half-starved gipsies; over our heads, on some towering rock, occasionally we saw a shepherd with his long gun, watching us, and keeping guard over small flocks of goats and sheep, whilst they fed off the scanty shrubs that grew in the crevices under them; they were attended, too, by packs of the most savage dogs I ever saw. Except in considerable force, the Greek soldiers dared not meddle with these warlike shepherds and their flocks. Many of the most distinguished leaders in the war, and the bravest of their followers, had been shepherds.

To compensate for the hard fare and bodily privations to be endured, there was ample food for the minds of any who love the haunts of genius. Every object we saw was associated with some great name, or deeds of arts or arms, that still live in the memory of all mankind. We stopped two or three days at Tripolitza, and then passed on to Argos and Napoli di Romania; every step of our way was marked by the ravages of the war. On our way to Corinth, we passed through the defiles of Dervenakia; our road was a mere mule-path for about two leagues, winding along in the bed of a brook, flanked by rugged precipices. In this gorge, and a more rugged path above it, a large Ottoman force, principally cavalry, had been stopped, in the previous autumn, by barricades of rocks and trees, and slaughtered like droves of cattle by the wild and exasperated Greeks. It was a perfect picture of the war, and told its own story; the sagacity of the nimble-footed Greeks, and the hopeless stupidity of the Turkish commanders, were palpable : detached from the heaps of dead, we saw the skeletons of some bold riders who had attempted to scale the acclivities, still astride the skeletons of their horses, and in the rear, as if in the attempt to back out of the fray, the bleached bones of the negroes' hands still holding the hair ropes attached to the skulls of their camels – death like sleep is a strange posture-master. There were grouped in a narrow space five thousand or more skeletons of men, horses, camels, and mules; vultures had eaten their flesh, and the sun had bleached their bones. In this picture the Turks looked like a herd of bisons trapped and butchered in the gorges of the rocky mountains. The rest of their battles, amidst scenery generally of the same rugged character, only differed in their magnitude. The Asiatic Turks are lazy, brave, and stupid. The Greeks, too crafty to fight if they could run, were only formidable in their fastnesses. It is a marvel that Greece and Greeks should be again resuscitated after so many ages of death-like slavery. No people, if they retain their name and language, need despair :

'Naught may endure but Mutability!'

We arrived at Corinth a short time after the Acrocorinthus

had, for the second time, fallen into the hands of the insurgents; and there saw Colocotroni and other predatory chiefs. Thence we crossed to the Isle of Salamis, and found the legislative and executive bodies of the provisional government accusing each other of embezzling the public money. Here, too, we saw the most potent leaders of the chief Greek military factions, – Primates, Hydriotes, Mainotes, Moreotes, Ipsareotes, Candiotes, and many others, each and all intent on their own immediate interests. There, too, I saw the first specimens of the super-subtle Phanariotes, pre-eminent in all evil, reared at Constantinople, and trained in the arts of deception by the most adroit professors in the world. These pliant and dexterous intriguers glided stealthily from tent to tent and from chief to chief, impregnating their brains with wily suggestions, thus envenoming their feuds and causing universal anarchy. Confounded at this exhibition of rank selfishness, we backed out of these civil broils, and sailed for Hydra; one of our commissions being to send deputies from that island to England to negotiate a loan. We speedily accomplished this, and Hamilton Browne went to London with the deputies.

I relanded in Greece and went to Athens. Odysseus [75] held undisputed sway there and in Eastern Greece, the frontiers of the war, and had played an important part in the insurrection. Descended from the most renowned race of Klephtes, he was a master of the art of mountain warfare, and a thorough Greek in cunning; strong-bodied, nimble-footed, and nimble-witted. I bought horses, hired soldiers, and accompanied him on an expedition to Eubœa, then in the hands of the Turks; and under his auspices became familiar with many of the most interesting localities, – Attica, Marathon, Thebes, Thermopylæ, Cheronea, Livadia, Talanta, Mount Parnes, Pindus and Cythæron. Our head-quarters were on Parnassus. Our ambuscades, onslaughts, rock-fighting, forays, stalking Turkish cavalry, successes and failures, intermingled with conferences, treaties, squabbles, intrigues, and constant change, were exciting at the time : so is deer-stalking; so was the Caffre war to those engaged in it; but as they are neither edifying nor amusing to write nor to read about, I shall not record them.[76]

In January 1824, I heard that Byron was at Missolonghi; that a loan was about being negotiated in London, and that Colonel Stanhope and other English had arrived in Athens. I pressed upon Odysseus the necessity of our instantly returning thither, which we did. Shortly after, Stanhope proposed, and Odysseus agreed, to hold a congress at Salona, and that I should go to Missolonghi to invite Byron and the chiefs of Western Greece to attend it. I started on my mission with a band of followers; and we had been two days winding through the mountain passes, – for nothing can induce the Greeks to cross level ground, if there are Turks or the rumour of enemies near, – when a messenger from Missolonghi on his way to Salona, conveying the startling news of Byron's death, crossed our path, as we were fording the river Evvenus. Thus, by a stroke of fate, my hopes of being of use in Greece were extinguished : Byron and Stanhope, as commissioners of the loan, would have expended it on the war; and the sordid and selfish primates, Machiavelian Phanariotes, and lawless Captanria would have been held in check. Byron thought all men rogues, and put no trust in any. As applied to Greeks, his scepticism was perfect wisdom. Stanhope was of a frank and hopeful nature; he had carefully examined the state of things, and would have been an able coadjutor, for he possessed those inestimable qualities, – energy, temper, and order – which Byron lacked. The first thing Stanhope did was to establish a free press : many opposed this as premature, if not dangerous, but it was of eminent service, and the only institution founded at that time which struck root deep into the soil.

Colonel Stanhope gave me the following note to Byron, but the Colonel's prophetic warning was too late : –

Salona, 17 April, 1824

My dear Lord Byron,

We are all assembled here with the exception of your Lordship and Monsieur Mavrocordato. I hope you will both join us; indeed, after the strong pledges given, the President ought to attend. As for you, you are a sort of Wilberforce, a saint whom all parties are endeavouring to seduce; it's a pity that you are not divisible, that every prefecture might have a fraction of your person. For my own part, I wish to see you fairly out of Missolonghi, because your health will not stand the climate and the constant anxiety to which you are there subjected.

I shall remain here till we receive your and the President's answer; I mean then to go to Egina, Zante, and England. If I can be of any service, you may command my zealous services.

Once more, I implore you to quit Missolonghi, and not to sacrifice your health and perhaps your life in that Bog.

I am ever your most devoted

Leicester Stanhope.

Chapter 21

Do you – dare you
To taunt me with my born deformity?
Deformed Transformed.

WITH desponding thoughts I entered Missolonghi on the third
day from my leaving Salona. Any spot on the surface of the
earth, or in its bowels, that holds out a prospect of gain, you will
find inhabited; a morass that will produce rice, the crust of a
volcano in which the vine will grow, lagunes in which fish
abound, are temptations which overcome the terror of pestilence
or death. So I was not surprised at seeing Missolonghi, situated
as it is on the verge of the most dismal swamp I had ever seen.
The marvel was that Byron, prone to fevers, should have been
induced to land on this mudbank, and stick there for three
months shut in by a circle of stagnant pools which might be
called the belt of death. Although it was now the early spring,
I found most of the strangers suffering from gastric fevers. It was
the 24th or 25th of April when I arrived; Byron had died on the
19th. I waded through the streets, between wind and water, to
the house he had lived in; it was detached, and on the margin
of the shallow slimy sea-waters. For three months this house had
been besieged, day and night, like a bank that has a run upon it.
Now that death had closed the door, it was as silent as a cemetery.
No one was within the house but Fletcher, of which I was glad.
As if he knew my wishes, he led me up a narrow stair into a
small room, with nothing in it but a coffin standing on trestles.
No word was spoken by either of us; he withdrew the black pall
and the white shroud, and there lay the embalmed body of the
Pilgrim – more beautiful in death than in life. The contraction of
the muscles and skin had effaced every line that time or passion
had ever traced on it; few marble busts could have matched its
stainless white, the harmony of its proportions, and perfect finish;
yet he had been dissatisfied with that body, and longed to cast

its slough. How often I had heard him curse it! He was jealous of the genius of Shakespeare – that might well be – but where had he seen the face or form worthy to excite his envy? I asked Fletcher to bring me a glass of water. On his leaving the room, to confirm or remove my doubts as to the exact cause of his lameness, I uncovered the Pilgrim's feet, and was answered [77] – it was caused by the contraction of the back sinews, which the doctors call 'Tendon Achilles,' that prevented his heels resting on the ground, and compelled him to walk on the fore part of his feet; except this defect, his feet were perfect. This was a curse, chaining a proud and soaring spirit like his to the dull earth. In the drama of 'The Deformed Transformed,' I knew that he had expressed all he could express of what a man of highly-wrought mind might feel when brooding over a deformity of body; but when he said,

> 'I have done the best which spirit may to make
> Its way with all deformity's dull deadly
> Discouraging weight upon me,'

I thought it exaggerated as applied to himself; now I saw it was not so. His deformity was always uppermost in his thoughts, and influenced every act of his life, spurred him on to poetry, as that was one of the few paths to fame open to him, – and as if to be revenged on Nature for sending him into the world 'scarce half made up,' he scoffed at her works and traditions with the pride of Lucifer; this morbid feeling ultimately goaded him on to his last Quixotic crusade in Greece.

No other man, afflicted as he was, could have been better justified than Byron in saying,

> 'I ask not
> For valour, since deformity is daring;
> It is its essence to o'ertake mankind
> By heart and soul, and make itself the equal –
> Ay, the superior of the rest. There is
> A spur in its halt movements, to become
> All that the others cannot, in such things
> As still are free to both, to compensate
> For step-dame Nature's avarice at first;
> They woo with fearless deeds the smiles of fortune,
> And oft, like Timour the lame Tartar, win them.'

Knowing and sympathizing with Byron's sensitiveness, his associates avoided prying into the cause of his lameness; so did strangers, from good breeding or common humanity. It was generally thought his halting gait originated in some defect of the right foot or ankle – the right foot was the most distorted, and it had been made worse in his boyhood by vain efforts to set it right. He told me that for several years he wore steel splints, which so wrenched the sinews and tendons of his leg, that they increased his lameness; the foot was twisted inwards, only the edge touched the ground, and that leg was shorter than the other. His shoes were peculiar – very high heeled, with the soles uncommonly thick on the inside and pared thin on the outside – the toes were stuffed with cotton-wool, and his trousers were very large below the knee and strapped down so as to cover his feet. The peculiarity of his gait was now accounted for; he entered a room with a sort of run, as if he could not stop, then planted his best leg well forward, throwing back his body to keep his balance. In early life whilst his frame was light and elastic, with the aid of a stick, he might have tottered along for a mile or two; but after he had waxed heavier, he seldom attempted to walk more than a few hundred yards, without squatting down or leaning against the first wall, bank, rock, or tree at hand, never sitting on the ground, as it would have been difficult for him to get up again. In the company of strangers, occasionally, he would make desperate efforts to conceal his infirmity, but the hectic flush on his face, his swelling veins, and quivering nerves betrayed him, and he suffered for many days after such exertions. Disposed to fatten, incapable of taking exercise to check the tendency, what could he do? If he added to his weight, his feet would not have supported him; in this dilemma he was compelled to exist in a state of semi-starvation; he was less than eleven stone when at Genoa, and said he had been fourteen at Venice. The pangs of hunger which travellers and shipwrecked mariners have described were nothing to what he suffered; their privations were temporary, his were for life, and more unendurable, as he was in the midst of abundance. I was exclaiming, 'Poor fellow, if your errors were greater than those of ordinary men, so were your temptations and provocations,' when Fletcher returned with a bottle and glass, saying, 'There is nothing but slimy salt water in this horrid place, so I have been half over the town to beg this clear water,' and, answering my ejaculation of 'Poor fellow,' he said,

'You may well say so, sir – these savages are worse than any highwaymen; they have robbed my Lord of all his money and his life too,[78] and those' – pointing to his feet – 'were the cause of all my Lord's misfortunes.'

Fletcher gave me a sheet of paper, and from his dictation I wrote on Byron's coffin the following particulars of his last illness and death :–[79]

'Particulars of Lord Byron's death, as related by his servant, William Fletcher. Written on his coffin, at the house of the Primate of Argostoli, by Edward Trelawny. – April 10th, 1824: Lord Byron, taking his usual ride and being warm, was caught in a shower of rain. He had but very recently recovered from a violent epileptic fit, which had left him weak. In the course of the eve he complained of being unwell, and there were slight symptoms of fever. On the 11th he got up as usual, but complained of his head. Only his usual medicine – fever and pain in his head augmenting – good spirits – to bed early. 12th : Got up late – his usual medicine, with magnesia. He ate nothing during his illness but a few spoonfuls of very weak broth. A very bad night; complained of an obstruction in his stomach. 13th : His usual purgatives, with pain in his stomach; got up late and shaved. On the 14th he got up and took his usual medicine, pills and magnesia. Much worse; his head dizzy and his nerves shaken. As soon as his bed was made he returned to it. Much fever, slow, and sleepless night. He was advised to be bled, but had a natural or acquired antipathy to bleeding. On the night of the 14th Fletcher advised a doctor being sent for from Zante. Fletcher thought him at this time confused in his ideas. Byron said, "Where are my shoes? I can only see three, and have been looking this hour." Fletcher said, "There are four." Byron said, "I am in the hands of assassins, they will murder me." This was in the morning of the 15th. Fletcher told him he was in danger. Byron said, "That be damned; it's all a plot." He sent for the doctors to ask what they would do; his fever slowly augmenting.

16th: Much in the same way. He ate nothing – getting very weak – continual pain in his stomach – bad night – sleepless. On being asked to let blood, he said, "Damn you all! my blood will be on you." Parry was frequently with him for hours, and all people turned out of the room, but merely to amuse him. Parry always told him he was getting better. On the 17th worse; still getting worse. A boat sent to Zante to get medical advice. Lord Byron asked if he were thought in danger. They said "Yes." He said, "Well, let them do as they like. I care not a damn. Only this I know, man can but live a certain time without sleep, and then he must die or go mad; but I will make short work with that whilst I have a pistol;" consequently the arms were taken from his bedside. He said he would leave Missolonghi for the islands if he got better – that his disease was not known. He sent Dr P. out of the chamber, and on the doctor saying he could not leave him thus, he said, "I order you out. What! has it come to this? Can I not change my shirt without a set of blackguard doctors in the room?" Continued his medicine; took strong purges, salts and magnesia. "These doctors," he said, "know nothing of my complaint. I want to know what is my disease. These people know nothing about my sickness." He had no confidence in his doctors. He went on in his usual careless Don Juan style of rattling away on trifles with Parry. That night worse; took pills, salts and magnesia – violent pains in his stomach. This evening at about seven P.M. he consented to be bled, and a few minutes after he fainted. They took about a pound. Very weak and debilitated, the pain in his head during the night, and he spoke confusedly of Fleming, Hobhouse, and Douglas Kinnaird. This was on the 18th. He had been again copiously bled. He took bark at about two; drank a glass of wine and water. He was worse after this, and became delirious and violent; began to talk and give directions; took hold of one of Fletcher's and one of Tita's hands. Fletcher said, "Shall I write?" Byron muttered to him for half an hour, his lips moving, but indistinct. He said, "Now I have told you everything: 4,000 dollars for the — and —; but 'tis too late. I have said all; do you understand me? If you don't obey me I will haunt you if I can." "I have not understood a word," said Fletcher. "That's a pity,"

Byron replied, "for 'tis now too late. You will go to Mrs Leigh — and tell her and say — and everything, and her children," &c. "And tell Lady Byron" – heavily sighing, but only muttered – "these are dying words." Fletcher said again he did not understand. "Good God!" he said and tried to repeat it, but his lips only moved. He understood Fletcher, and seemed to strain hard to make himself understood, and to feel his inability. After six o'clock this evening he said, "I want to sleep." They had given him opiates, and from that time he never more spoke word, nor moved hand or foot, nor showed the least appearance of life except by difficulty in swallowing, and stiffness. They had put blisters on his thighs and mustard on his feet. He objected to it at first; at last he let Fletcher do it, having ordered everyone out of the room. "Oh, my child, my child! Oh, Ada! that I had seen thee, my child!" He fancied he had told Fletcher everything about his friends. Very angry with the doctors, who, he said, had assassinated him. "There is you – Tita and Luke – I will." From six o'clock in the evening of the 18th to six in the evening of the 19th he remained speechless, senseless, and inanimate; only sign of life was at wide periods a little difficulty in breathing, which was very quick just before he expired. They bathed him and tried every effort to make him move, but in vain. Just before he died he opened his eyes, gave two or three low moans, and without the slightest appearance of pain or sensibility he died. Once he said, "Give me – but – no – that is – weakness, weakness." A few hours before he became insensible he said (on reading a letter in which Loriotti says to the Prince, "you must consult and attend to the advice of Lord Byron, Stanhope, and Napier, for they enjoy great reputation here"), "This is their damned Greek policy; they are all rascals; but when Napier comes I will work them all." In his delirium he often muttered broken passages of Scripture, with replies such as he was used to with Kennedy at Cephalonia. He swore, however, much, particularly against pain. Seems never to have known death had got hold of him till a few hours before he became insensible, and then he found he had trifled too long – that it was too late. He had much to have done and said, but his voice refused to be the organ of his mind.'

This account differs in many particulars from the one already published; in the same way that the fresh rough notes of an eye-witness, taken on the spot, differ on passing through the hands of the editor of a review to be served out to the public as an article to further a cause or strengthen a faction – so let it be, I shall not question it.

A letter from his half-sister, Augusta Leigh, was on his writing-table. This lady was the only relation Byron had, or at least acknowledged; and he always spoke of her in the most affectionate terms. He was in the act of writing to her when he was taken ill. This unfinished letter I copied, – as the original would run many risks of being lost before it reached its destination. It is interesting as the last of Byron's writings – as an index, too, of his real and inward feelings; those letters that have been published were written, as I have already observed, under an assumed character and for effect.

His sister's letter contained a long transcript of one from Lady Byron; with a minute mental and physical account of their child, Ada, as follows :–

Hastings, December 1823

My dearest Augusta,

I will now answer those passages from Lord Byron's letter of December 8th, which required information from me.

Ada's prevailing characteristic is cheerfulness, a disposition to enjoyment; this happy disposition was only partially interrupted when at the most oppressive period of her illness, under which she was patient and tractable.

The impression she generally makes upon strangers is that of a lively child. Of her intellectual powers observation is the most developed. The pertinency of her remarks and the accuracy of her descriptions are sometimes beyond her years; she is by no means devoid of imagination, but it is at present chiefly exercised in connection with her mechanical ingenuity, her self-invented occupation being the manufacture of ships and boats, or whatever else may attract her attention. Hitherto she has preferred prose to verse because she is puzzled by the poetical diction; she is particularly fond of reading since she has resumed those pursuits which depend upon sight. Previous to the suspension of them she had made some proficiency in music and began to like it. She had also opportunities of learning a little French : these with writing and the reading suited to her age formed her acquirements. She is not very persevering, and with the tendency which her constitution has manifested it is not advisable to stimulate her exertion (all excitement being injurious), though it is desirable to regulate their objects. She is at present very desirous to draw, and shows a singular aptitude for that art, as far as she is permitted to use her pencil. With respect to her temper, it is open and ingenuous – at an earlier age it threatened to be impetuous but is now sufficiently under control. She is very fond of society and talking, yet not dull when alone. Her person is tall and robust, and her features not regular, but countenance animated. The miniature is still life; she would be known by the enclosed profile.

She is now in really good health under the present system laid down by Warren and Mayo. It consists of mild medicine and sparing régime. There is great justice in Lord Byron's *medical* conjecture, but I am informed that the tendency to local congestion is not always relieved at *that period*, as the depletion may not be more than adequate to the increased supply of blood, and for some other reasons. I hope I have not omitted to notice any point expressed by Lord Byron.

> I am yours affectionately,
> A. N. B.

Lady Byron's letter mentions a profile of the child. I found it, with other tokens that the Pilgrim had most treasured, scattered on the floor, – as rubbish of no marketable value, and trampled on. I rescued from destruction a cambric handkerchief stained with his blood, and marked with a lady's name in hair; a ringlet; a ribbon; and a small glove. These relics I folded with some of his own hair that I had shorn from his head.

This unfinished letter was the last of Byron's writings; it is to his half-sister, Augusta Leigh.

Missolonghi, Feb. 23, 1824

My dearest Augusta,

I received a few days ago your and Lady B.'s report of Ada's health, with other letters from England; for which I ought to be, and am (I hope) sufficiently thankful, as they are of great comfort, and I wanted some, having been recently unwell – but am now much better, so that you must not be alarmed.

You will have heard of our journeys and escapes, and so forth, – perhaps with some exaggeration; but it is all very well now, and I have been some time in Greece, which is in as good a state as could be expected considering circumstances. But I will not plague you with politics – wars – or earthquakes, though we have had a rather smart one three nights ago, which produced a scene ridiculous enough, as no damage was done except to those who stuck fast in the scuffle to get first out of the doors or windows; amongst whom some recent importations from England, who had been used to quieter elements, were rather squeezed in the press for precedence.

I have been obtaining the release of about nine-and-twenty Turkish prisoners, – men, women, and children, and have sent them, at my own expense, home to their friends; but one pretty little girl of nine years of age, named Hato or Hatagée, has expressed a strong wish to remain with me or under my care; – and I have nearly determined to adopt her, if I thought that Lady B. would let her come to England as a companion to Ada (they are about the same age), and we could easily provide for her, – if not, I can send her to Italy for education. She is very lively and quick, and with great black Oriental eyes and Asiatic features. All her brothers were killed in the revolution. Her mother wishes to return to her husband, who is at Previsa; but says that she would rather entrust the child to me in the present state of the country. Her extreme youth and sex have hitherto saved her life, but there is no saying what might happen in the course of the war (and of such a war). I shall probably commit her to the care of some English lady in the islands for the present. The child herself has the same wish, and seems to have a decided character for her age. You can mention this matter, if you think it worth while.

I merely wish her to be respectably educated and treated; and if my years and all things be considered, I presume it would be difficult to conceive me to have any other views.

With regard to Ada's health, I am glad to hear that she is so much better; but I think it right that Lady B. should be informed (and guard against it accordingly) that her description of much of her disposition and tendencies very nearly resembles that of my own at a similar age, – except that I was much more impetuous. Her preference of *prose* (strange as it may now seem) *was*, and indeed *is*, mine (for I hate reading verse – and always did); and I never invented anything but 'boats, – ships,' and generally something relative to the ocean. I showed the report to Colonel Stanhope, who was struck with the resemblance of parts of it to the paternal line, – even now.

But it is also fit, though unpleasant, that I should mention that my recent attack, and a very severe one, had a strong appearance of epilepsy; – why, I know not – for it is late in life, its first appearance at thirty-six, and, so far as I *know*, it is *not* hereditary; – and it is that it may not *become* so, that you should tell Lady B. to take some precautions in the case of Ada.

My attack has not returned, – and I am fighting it off with abstinence and exercise, and thus far with success; – if merely casual, it is all very well'—

Gordon, in his 'History of the Greek Revolution,' speaking of Byron just before his death, says: 'His health declined, and we cannot be surprised, considering what he had suffered, and was daily suffering, from the deceptions practised upon him, and importunate solicitations for money. Parry talked a great deal and did little; Mavrocordato promised everything, and performed nothing, and the primates, who engaged to furnish 1,500 dollars towards the expenses of the fortifications, could not produce a farthing, and in lieu thereof presented him with the freedom of the town. The streets and country were a bed of mire, so he could not take any exercise out of doors.'

To return to what passed in Byron's house. On hearing a noise below, I went down into the public room, and found Parry with a comrade carousing. This man (Parry) had been a clerk in the civil department of the Ordnance at Woolwich, and was sent out by the committee with the munitions of war, as head fire-master. In revolutions, however severely the body may suffer for want of pay and rations, your vanity is pampered to satiety by the assumption of whatever rank or title you may have a fancy for. Mavrocordato dubbed himself Prince; Byron, Commander-in-Chief; Parry, the ordnance clerk, Major.

I said, 'Well, Major, what do you think was the cause of Lord Byron's death?'

'Think? I don't think anything about it; I am a practical man, not a humbugging thinker; he would have been alive now if he had followed my advice. He lived too low; I told him so a thousand times. Two or three days before he slipped his wind, he said: "Parry, what do you think is the matter with me? The doctors don't know my complaint." "No," I said, "nor nothing else, my lord; let me throw them out of the window." "What will do me good, Parry?" "Brandy, my lord; nothing but brandy will save you; you have only got a chill on an empty stomach; let me mix you a stiff glass of grog, and you will be all right to-morrow," but he shook his head, so I gave him up as a lost man. My father,' he continued, 'lived to a great age on brandy, and then he would not have died, but the doctor stopped his drink, and the death-rattle choked his scuppers.'

'What did the doctors do, Parry, with Lord Byron?'

'Do! why, they physicked and bled him to death. My lord called them assassins to their faces, and so they are. A pair of more conceited ignorant scamps I never saw; they are only fit to stand at the corners of alleys to distribute Doctor Eady's hand-bills.'

The doctors were Bruno, an Italian, and Millingen,[80] an English student from Germany. The great Poet was in the hands of these novices – their first patient – and they practised on him as they had been taught. The fashion at that time was bleeding, blistering, and killing people with aperients; and this treatment, to a patient so sensitive, attenuated, and feeble as Byron, was certain death.

The fire-master was a rough burly fellow, never quite sober, but he was no fool, and had a fund of pot-house stories which he told in appropriately slang language; he was a mimic, and amused Byron by burlesquing Jeremy Bentham and other members of the Greek Committee. Besides these accomplishments, he professed a thorough knowledge of the art of fortification, and said he was the inventor of shells and fire-balls that would destroy the Ottoman fleet and the garrison of Lepanto. All he did, however, was to talk and drink. He was three months in Greece, returned to England, talked the committee out of £400 for his services, and drank himself into a mad-house.[81] When he could get no more brandy to keep down the death-rattle, he died as he said his father had done. Six artificers whom he brought to Greece with him, stayed there only a fortnight, and cost the committee £340.

Out of the first loan of £800,000, negotiated in England, the Greeks got £240,000. The money Byron advanced by way of loan was repaid by the Greeks; but I believe it was invested in the Greek loan, and so lost.[82] The other portion was paid in materials for war.

All my readers know Byron's lines ('Childe Harold,' Canto iii) to his daughter: –

> 'Is thy face like thy mother's, my fair child,
> 　Ada, sole daughter of my house and heart?
> When last I saw thy young blue eyes, they smiled,
> 　And then we parted: not as now we part,
> 　But with a hope ...'

It will be interesting to know how Ada's mind developed, as shown in the following letter from her mother: –

London, Nov. 9, 1839

To Rev. Dr T.
　Boston.

I feel very grateful to your daughter, dear Dr T., for giving me so many details of your illness; they give me a little more hope than I felt before. I wish I could send you a letter which I received lately from Ada, containing her views of death. It has been much in her thoughts lately, though not from any instance of mortality in her own circle, nor from any apprehensions for herself, and I rejoice that she has reasoned herself into such happy conclusions before the hour of trial arrives. I think you will be interested in some passages which I will copy:—

'I have long conceived life here to be only a particular mode of action (a peculiar mode of vibration, perhaps, in some subtle fluid akin to the electrical ether, if not identical with it), and that death is nothing but a change in this *mode of action*, in consequence of which it ceases to remain *connected with the brain*; ceases to be concentrated, if I may so speak, and consciousness becomes marvellously extended. I wish I could truly express all I mean and feel: so vivid and peculiar is the impression at times that I could almost fancy I *had* died already. I have a glorious conception of death. I am strongly inclined to *material* views of the intelligent principle. I think there is a *kind* and mode of existence of matter so very different from anything here in *evidence* around us, that by comparison it may be called spiritual. But in the strictly spiritual I do not believe. I think there is a mode of action which when once given birth to by our Creator (or rather under His laws), can never, never cease. This is immortality. I call our life here a *concentrated life*, and until our intelligence and conscience have acquired a certain practice, it is probably necessary that there should be this concentration of the sphere of action. I much question if any of the bad principles (by which I mean those which abuse has rendered bad) *can exist*, except in a highly concentrated form, and therefore I should imagine that the bad have to go through some state or states much more akin to the present than the good have. No wonder Christ wished to save us from this! My metaphysical doctrines are not *founded* on Scripture, but I am delighted to find that all Scripture confirms them, in some parts very strikingly, I find.'

Surely these are very curious speculations to *originate* in the mind of a young woman not twenty-five.

An enthusiastic simpleton asked me once, 'Do you consider that Shelley was a perfect man?' I replied, 'What do *you* regard as a perfect man?' Different people entertain different opinions as to manly perfection. Here, in a letter from Lady Byron, dated in 1835, is an indication of the sort of character that she viewed with predilection :–

'I can give you not my own impressions merely, but the concurrent testimonies of the wise and good. He is thirty years of age, has travelled in various parts of the world. He has thus gained considerable knowledge of men and affairs, but he has not lost the love of home, nor of those pursuits which form the duties of an English land-owner and magistrate. He is much occupied with improving the condition of his tenantry and of the poor. He goes to church every Sunday with the people of his parish, and returns for that purpose when staying in town. He reads family prayers every morning to his servants. These habits would not, however, assure me of his having the Christian *spirit*. It is from his conduct in his private relationships that I have inferred it. In his own family he has been singularly tried, having been in a manner set aside, owing to the excessive partiality felt by both his parents for the second brother, to whom all the unentailed property has been left. But he has been dutiful and affectionate to *every* member of his family – to the mother who almost disowns him, and to the brother who was preferred to him. He has superior abilities and information, with some of those accomplishments which are graceful in society. It is, however, of much more importance that he is singularly right-minded and evenly tempered; that he values the intrinsic more than the external; that he feels the inseparable connection of virtue and happiness; that he substitutes a rigid self-control for the indulgences which are often considered venial in young men of his rank, and appears to have adopted as the rule of life, "Do unto others," &c. He is interested, I am happy to say, in prison discipline and juvenile reformation.'

Chapter 22

When a man hath no freedom to fight for at home,
  Let him combat for that of his neighbours;
  Let him think of the glories of Greece and of Rome,
  And get knock'd on the head for his labours.
                                          Don Juan.

EARLY in the morning Gamba and I looked over Byron's papers; there were several journals and note-books; they contained memorandums of his thoughts, not of his actions – violent invectives on the Zuliotes and others – Italian and English letters, fifteen stanzas of the seventeenth canto of 'Don Juan,' dated 8th May, several songs finished, and sundry beginnings of poems, his opinions of Napoleon's banishment, continuations of 'Childe Harold' and the 'Deformed Transformed,' and other fragments. Mavrocordato came in; finally we sealed up everything. The 30,000 or 40,000 dollars which Byron had brought with him to Missolonghi were reduced to 5,000 or 6,000. Mavrocordato urged that this sum should be left with him as a loan, and that he would be responsible for its repayment. I objected to this as illegal, and insisted on the money being shipped to the Ionian Islands. The prince was exceedingly put out at this; he evidently thought my scruple arose from no other motive than personal enmity to him. The congress at Salona he considered a scheme of mine to get Byron out of his hands, and to deliver him, Mavrocordato, into the clutches of Odysseus, and he was in great terror of that chief. These things I could see engendered in his mind a deadly hatred of me. After the consummate art which this prince of Phanariotes had displayed in inveigling Byron and his dollars into Missolonghi, he looked upon him as a lawful prize, and on my efforts to rescue his victim as the height of audacity. I had no enmity to the prince, but I had a strong feeling of goodwill towards Byron; and never lost sight of his interest. To be brief, my plan had been simply this – to get Byron to Athens. Odysseus, whose confidence I had won, engaged to deliver up the Acropolis of that city, to put the said fortress into my hands the instant Byron promised to come there, and to allow me to garrison it with my own people and hold it; with no other condition than that of not giving it up to the Greek government as at the time constituted. There the poet would have been in his glory; he loved Athens. In that fortress with a Frank garrison he would have been thoroughly independent; he would have been safe from fevers, for it is the healthiest site in the world, as well as the most beautiful. If the Greeks succeeded in raising a loan, and he was appointed to control its expenditure, at Athens he would have been in a commanding position: aloof from the sordid civil and military factions, he might have controlled them. Byron was no soldier,

> 'Nor the division of a battle knew
> More than a spinster.'

To carry on the war a disciplined army and an able general were indispensable. Sir C. J. Napier was the man exactly fitted for such an emergency: skilful, fearless, prompt, and decided as fate. The deep interest that great soldier felt in the cause of the Greeks was such, that he would have undertaken the war, although it would have cost him his commission in the British service, if solicited by the proper authorities, and furnished with sufficient means and power. When Byron was on his death-bed, and wandering in his mind, Napier was uppermost in his thoughts; he cursed the mercenary and turbulent Zuliotes, exclaiming: 'When Napier comes, I will have them all flayed alive.'

In one of my visits to Cephalonia, expressly to inform Napier of the state of anarchy in Greece, I told him the first duty he would have to perform would be that of shooting and imprisoning half-a-dozen of the most refractory of the leaders of factions, as well as of the Captanria.

'No,' he said, 'you shall do that; you shall be Provost Marshal. If I go there, we will raise the price of hemp; and I won't go without two European regiments, money in hand to pay them, and a portable gallows.'

'I will accept the office, and do my duty,' I answered.

To resume my story. After I had seen Byron's effects despatched to Zante, I left Missolonghi to return to Salona. Many of the foreign soldiers who had been in Byron's pay, now that pay was stopped, volunteered to join me. I engaged as many as I could afford to keep. I had likewise five brass guns, with ammunition, and some other things sent out by the English committee, which I was authorized to take to Eastern Greece. Mavrocordato opposed this order, – but I enforced it; so that I had now a cavalcade of fifty or sixty horses and mules, and about a hundred men, including the Roumeliotes whom I had brought with me. In all my motley squad there was only one who spoke English, and he was a Scot. It would have been better had I omitted that one. When I arrived at Salona, I found Stanhope and a host of others, who had come to meet Byron. Stanhope had received a letter from the Horse Guards ordering him home.[83]

Several people have asked, and one has written to me to know if Byron was addicted to the noxious weed – tobacco; and this is my answer : –

'Age thinketh many things, youth is full of imaginings. Our chief pleasures spring from our imaginations; when they have furnished you with one keep it to yourself, don't analyse or seek evidence to ascertain its reality, for it is volatile and may fly off; dry facts, like dry bones, are displeasing to the sight and feelings. The tale of the meerschaum pipe you ask me about is simply this. When I went to Greece in 1823 with Byron, I left my impediments to the care of an old friend, Captain Roberts, of the Navy. Byron died; I was dangerously wounded, and soon after reported dead; Roberts had deposited my things with Dunn, a shopkeeper at Leghorn; he was in debt to Dunn, and Dunn advised him to sell the things I had left with him. Byron had had dealings with Dunn whilst he was living at Pisa, and travellers, hearing this, often applied to him for autographs or other things that had belonged to Byron as memorials. This suggested to the crafty shopkeeper that it would be a grand speculation to dispose of some of the best things as Byron's, and that as we were both gone, and no claimants in my case, there would be no evidence to the contrary. The fact is, Byron had nothing whatever to do with the pipe you mention, never had it in his hand, much less smoked it – in truth, Byron never smoked either pipe or cigar. Poets are addicted to stimulants, but not sedatives; tobacco dulls the senses, wines excite them. Not liking to dissipate your illusion I have left your letter unanswered till now.'

The greatest man, although not the greatest poet, is said always to have smoked a pipe before he went to bed – John Milton. This I did not know until after I had written the above letter. In consequence of that sale by Dunn, many things belonging to me are treasured in museums as records of the great Poet.

I had now no motive for remaining in Greece. The Greeks were jealous of foreigners; those who had not money wandered about in rags and wretchedness, although many of them were very able soldiers and had greatly distinguished themselves. But I did not like deserting Odysseus; he was very anxious I should stay. He said: 'The Greeks are naturally treacherous, artful, sordid, and fickle; and that history and tradition proved they had always been so.'[84]

Jeremy Bentham wrote a Constitution for the Greeks: Colonel Leicester Stanhope gave me a copy of it – it was founded on the Swiss Federal Government, being clear, and I thought admirably constructed for the then state of Greece. The population of Greece at the time of the revolution was only a million and a quarter. The leaders of the soldiers who drove the Turks from their provinces considered the provinces as theirs, and this is the origin of all governments; but the civilians in the towns, seeing that they would have no power, were stirred up by some intriguing Phanariotes to dispute these claims, and some of the most energetic conspired to form a self-constituted government. Mavrocordato, Tricoupi, and Colette took the lead. The military chiefs in the first place took little heed of the movements of the civilians, and when the rumour of a loan of money reached the chiefs they ridiculed it, not believing it possible that anyone could lend money without security, and Greece had none to offer.

The congress dispersed. I returned with Odysseus into Livadia, and we revisited Athens and Euboea, – carrying on the war in the same inefficient and desultory way as before, unaided by the government and abandoned to our own resources. Hitherto the military chiefs held all the real power in Greece; the territory they wrested from the Turks they considered as lawful prize : in short, they acted on

> 'The good old rule, the simple plan,
>   That they should take who have the power,
>   And they should keep who can.'

As to the government, it was a mere farce, but its members knew it might one day become a reality. Their chief occupation consisted in raising money from those few spots not previously ravaged by the ruthless soldiers. The insignificant revenue thus raised they appropriated to their own uses.[85]

This self-constituted government, however, did get a loan from England, and with that they made their power felt; they raised soldiers and gathered the small chiefs about them. The more powerful chiefs held aloof, but from mutual jealousy they were all at enmity with each other.

The government were now assembled at Nauplia. An English vessel arrived in that port with £40,000 assigned to them, – this being the first instalment of the Greek loan. The rush to the diggings in California and Australia, on the first discovery of gold in those regions, was partial, if not orderly, as compared with the wild and universal rush of the Greeks on Nauplia. That town was beleaguered by armed legions of robbers, frantically clamouring for their share of the spoil. Their military leaders soon found, not only that they should get no money, but that they were in imminent peril of losing their heads.

The government determined to rule with a strong hand, and to crush their military rivals. They commenced organizing a force and inveigling the men from their chiefs; they attempted to assassinate Odysseus, and were plotting to seize the great Moreote chieftain, Colocotroni, – so the great captains fled to their mountain strongholds. The government ultimately arrested Colocotroni and many others.[86]

Odysseus, who commanded in Eastern Greece before the revolution, had been given the command of that province by Ali Pasha of Yanina, for the express purpose of exterminating the brigands, who at that time numbered a thousand men, and had controlled that part of Greece for centuries. This object Odysseus effected completely. Those who submitted he took into his service; and at the outbreak of the revolution with those men he fought the first important battles against the Turks.

I remained with a hundred men between Livadia and Mount Parnes. Odysseus joined me there, and gave me an account of the state of things at Nauplia. He was the ablest soldier in Greece, and the Turks could only get to the Morea through his province. His acuteness and power made him the most formidable enemy to the Greek government; they could neither buy nor intimidate him.

He said: 'By stratagem and force, with my own small means, I have kept the Turks out of the Morea for three years without aid from the government. The territory we captains have dispossessed the Sultan of, our self-elected government have sold to the Russians; and with the money they are to get rid of us, to make way for a foreign king and foreign soldiers.'

I asked, 'What king?'

He said, they were 'divided on that subject, but the Russian party was the strongest, for they had the priests, the Phanariotes and Moreotes, with them,[87] backed by the people of the towns and strengthened by Russian agents, who were always for arbitrary and military government like their own.'

The different chiefs as well as Odysseus, to whom I had explained Bentham's Constitution, were eager for it, as they would have retained their power.

Odysseus added: 'What puzzles me is, that England should advance money to make Greece a hospodariot of Russia. I never met any Greek who could understand the reason why so shrewd a nation of traffickers as the English should lend them such large sums of money, since everyone must know, they said, that they neither could nor would repay any portion of it.'

I urged Odysseus to resign his command, and with a few followers retire to the mountains – adding that 'borrowed money in the hands of a knavish government would soon vanish.'

Odysseus said: 'This part of the country, Livadia, my father inherited from his father, who won it by his valour, and when it was lost through the treachery of the Venetians, who sold my father to the Sultan, I regained it by my wits, and have kept it with my sword.'

'And so you may again, if you are dispossessed now,' I answered, 'if you bide your time.'[88]

He then told me that the Greek government would not allow him money or soldiers to defend the Greek passes into the Morea, and that it was impossible for him to oppose the Turks' entry into his territory, as he had only two or three hundred men in his pay, and that if they did not assist him he should make a treaty with the Turkish pasha at Negropont not to oppose their march into the Morea if they would pass through his territory (Livadia and Attica) with a flag of truce; but that if the government furnished him with the means, he would prevent the Turks from entering into his territory.

How can a soldier, with nothing but his sword, defend himself against infernal machinations devised by a Prince of Hell, armed with a chest of gold? Phanariotes, like devils, work in the dark!

In one of the precipices of Mount Parnassus, in Livadia, the highest mountain in Greece, there is a cavern, at an elevation of a thousand feet above the plain. This cavern Odysseus had, with great ingenuity, managed to ascend, and convert into a place of safety for his family and effects during the war. The only access to it was by ladders, bolted to the rock. The first ladder, forty-five or fifty feet in length, was placed against the face of the rock, and steadied by braces; a second, resting on a projecting crag, crossed the first; and a third, lighter and shorter, stood on its heel on a natural shelf in the fractured stone. This third ladder led to a trap-door, the bolts and bars of which being removed, you entered a vaulted guard-room, pierced with lancet-holes for musketry. This opened on a broad terrace, eighty feet in length, screened by a substantial parapet-wall, breast high, with embrasures mounted with cannon. The height of the natural arch spanning the cave is thirty feet above this lower terrace, so that it is particularly light, airy, and cheerful, commanding extensive and magnificent views. Ascending by steps to a yet higher terrace of solid rock, the breadth and height of the cave diminish, until the end is reached. On the right of the great cave there is a smaller one; besides which there are many small grottoes, the size of chambers, connected by galleries. They are perfectly dry, and were used for store-rooms and magazines. One of them I converted into a chapel for an old priest, covering the rugged walls with gaudy hangings, flaming paintings, and holy relics of saints, saved from the desecrated churches in the neighbourhood.

The interior of this magnificent cavern often reminded me, with its grottoes, galleries, and vaulted roof, of a cathedral, particularly when the softened light of the evening obscured its ruggedness, or by moonlight. The towering mass of rock above the cave projected boldly over its base. To make it perfect, there was a never-failing supply of the purest water, which found its way through subterranean channels from the regions of perpetual snow, filtering through fractures in the rock above into a capacious cistern built on the upper terrace.

This cavern was our citadel, and by removing the upper ladder became impregnable without the aid of a garrison. We built boarded houses within it, and stored it with all the necessaries and many of the luxuries of life, besides immense supplies of arms and ammunition.

I urged Odysseus to abide in this stronghold, saying that the borrowed money was sure to be embezzled by a government composed of arrant sharpers; and that but a small part of it would be applied to the purpose it was contracted for. Besides, Ibrahim Pasha was on his way to Greece with an immense force. Civil wars were already rife in the Morea. 'The Greeks,' I continued, 'and their country are so admirably adapted for guerilla warfare, that those chiefs who had carried on the insurrection successfully, and had shown that they alone had capacity to continue it, must be recalled from banishment to defend their country. Then you can retaliate on the government by demanding an account of their stewardship.'

'I did expose their frauds to their faces,' exclaimed the chief, 'in the National Assembly at Nauplia, and on the same night two shots were fired at me from a window opposite to the one I was sitting at. My guards seized the miscreants, and I gave them up to the police, but they were not punished. If I stay here, we shall be beleaguered by assassins, and prevented from communicating with my lieutenants and followers. Ghouras still holds the Acropolis of Athens. I cannot stay here; a stag at bay is more to be feared than a lion blockaded in his den.'

It was decided that I should remain, and he go forth. I had shared in his prosperity, and would not leave him in his adversity. As a garrison was superfluous, I reduced mine to half-a-dozen. To guard against treachery, I chose men of different countries, who were not likely to conspire together: a Greek, Turk, Hungarian, and Italian, a venerable priest, and two Greek boys as servants.

Our other inmates were the chief's son, an infant, his wife, mother, and two or three other women.[89] I entrusted the keys of the entrance to the Albanian Turk, a resolute determined fellow.

In the mountains of Pindus and Agrafa, in Thessalia, they have the noblest breed of dogs in the world. In size and strength they are not much inferior to the king of beasts, and in courage and sagacity they are superior. When thoroughbred and well trained they are held in such estimation by their owners, that money will not buy them. We had one of these. He did the duty of a guard of soldiers, patrolling the lower terrace at night, and keeping watch at the guard-room door by day. He would not enter a room. He was best pleased in the winter snow-storms, when the icicles hung on his long brindled hair and shaggy mane. It was impossible to elude his vigilance or corrupt his fidelity; he would not take food from any other hands than mine or the Albanian's, and could not be bribed. This is more than I could say of any Greek that I had dealings with, during the three years that I lived amongst them.

In addition to the small number within the cave, I had a much larger force at the foot of the ladders. They were hutted within a stone breast-work. I gave the command of them to the Scotchman whom I had brought from Missolonghi. Their duty was to patrol the passes of the mountain, to collect the tithes or tribute from the neighbouring villages (these were paid in kind), to learn the news, and to keep up my correspondence with the chief and others.

The name of the Scotchman was Fenton. Thomas was, I think, his Christian name. He introduced himself to me, as I have before narrated, on my visit to Western Greece, saying he had come out expressly to join Lord Byron's regiment; that he had served in the civil wars in Spain, was skilled in guerilla warfare, that his funds were exhausted, and, as I was proceeding to the war, he begged me to take him with me.

I pointed out the deplorable condition of foreigners in Greece generally, and the peculiar state of things in that part of the country I was going to in particular, and offered to advance him money to return home. As he persisted in his wish to go with me, I reluctantly yielded to his importunity.

He was a tall, bony man, with prominent eyes and features, dark hair, and long face, in the prime of life, thirty-one or thirty-two years of age. His dress, accoutrements, and arms were all well chosen. He was restless, energetic, enterprising, and a famous walker. During the time he was with me I sent him on many missions to the Ionian Islands for money, to the seat of government to see what they were doing, and with letters to friendly chiefs, so that he was not much at the cave; and when he was, he lived in a hut below it. I supplied him with all he wanted – my purse was his. He was not squeamish on these points, but sensual, and denied himself nothing within his reach. When in my neighbourhood, he passed most of his time with me. No querulous word or angry glance ever ruffled our friendly intercourse. I thought him honest, and his staying with me a proof of his goodwill, if not personal friendship, and never omitted an occasion of doing him a service.

When Odysseus had been absent three or four months, rumours reached me in January, 1825, that the government were resolved to deprive the chief of his command in Eastern Greece.

To do this effectually, they were endeavouring to detach his lieutenant, Ghouras, who held Attica, from him. I despatched Fenton to Athens and Nauplia, to ascertain the truth of these reports.

Chapter 23

Another proudly clad
In golden arms, spurs a Tartarian barb
Into the gap, and with his iron mace
Directs the torrent of that tide of men.

Hellas. – SHELLEY.

I WAS told some time after this that Odysseus was corresponding with Omer Pasha of Negropont, and fearing that he might resort to some desperate measures in his present difficulties, I left the cave one night in a snowstorm, and with a trusty follower who knew the country, we descended to the plain, threading our way through the rocks and pine-trees. We mounted two swift Arab horses, galloped along a hollow valley, crossed a deep stream, the Sperchius, and proceeded towards the town of Livadia, where we arrived the next day. I was surprised to see Turkish Delhi cavalry, known at a great distance by the immense height of their head-gear, careering on the plain. On meeting Odysseus, he told me he had made a truce for three months with Omer Pasha. The only stipulation between them was that, for that period, Eastern Greece was to be a neutral territory – he said, 'It is the only way in which I could save the people from being massacred. I have written to the Athenians to say that, as the government have not only refused to give me rations or money for my troops, but are doing their utmost to induce them to desert me, I cannot longer defend the passes which lead to Athens.'

I knew it was a common practice of the military leaders in Greece to make treaties with the enemy in the provinces they governed, for especial objects, on their own responsibility – yet I saw at once the chief had made a fatal error in doing so on the present occasion. I told him that, although his family had ruled in Livadia for three generations, the Turks in the Morea had been dispossessed after four centuries of possession; that now the Greek government were strong, and would direct all their forces to crush him. If he took refuge with the Turks, they would betray him, and send him or his head to Constantinople. 'I know that,' he answered, 'I shall take care of that; they are in my power; what I have done is only to bring the Greek government to terms.' I saw that he was anxious and perplexed, and that he repented of the step he had taken, and had been plotting to extricate himself before I arrived at Livadia. The next day we went to Thebes, and on the one succeeding followed the line of the Eubœan Strait to Talanta.

The hollowness of this armistice was apparent – Odysseus and the Ottoman bey, suspecting each other of treachery, used every precaution to avoid being ensnared. The Turkish horse stuck to the level ground, the Greeks clung to the hills; Odysseus skirted them, his best men and swiftest runners dogging his steps, and keeping him from being cut off from his guerillas.

The Delhi Colonel was selected from the Turkish host at Eubœa, as the only soldier capable of contending in arts or arms with the wily and able Greek chief : he was the best specimen of an Eastern warrior I had seen – calm, vigilant, and dexterous in the disposition of his troopers. Our chief knew the country better than any man in it. I urged him to give the enemy the slip, and to come to the cavern. His answer was, 'Stay, not yet !'

It was early in February we stopped at Talanta on a wet stormy night : in selecting his quarters, our chief with his usual sagacity fixed upon the ruins of a Greek church, situated, as the Greek churches, chapels, and monasteries usually are, on an elevated and defensible site – the town was abandoned and in ruins. After we had supped and were smoking our pipes, some of the Greek patrols came in, saying they had captured two Franks. They were ordered to bring them in. I told the chief to make no allusion to me, but to question them through his secretary.

As they entered, one of them observed to his comrade in English, 'What a set of cut-throats ! Are they Greeks or Turks ?'

'Mind what you say.'

'Oh ! they only want our money,' answered the other. 'I hope they will give us something to eat before they cut our throats. I am famished.'

Certainly appearances were against us. At one end of the building, Odysseus, the Greek chief, the Turkish bey, and I sat smoking our pipes. At the other end, within the church, stood our horses saddled, ready for mounting, the soldiers lying down in clusters along the sides, with all their gear on, for neither Greeks nor Turks divest themselves of a single article of dress or arms during the night. Their hands still grasped their weapons, and they slept so lightly that if in talking a voice was raised their eager wolfish eyes were instantly upon the speaker. On the strangers entering, some of the soldiers sprang up, others leant on their elbows to listen or rather to look on, for they could not understand a word. The travellers told their story,—stating that they were last from Smyrna, and had landed that morning from an English brig, at a small port in the Gulf of Eubœa, with no other object than to see the country. Neither of the chiefs believed them, nor did I; nevertheless, they were treated hospitably, had supper, coffee, and pipes, and their baggage placed beside them. They sat together in a spare corner close to us, with no arms but fowling-pieces. One of them was very ill at his ease, the other, who I learnt from their discourse was a Major,[90] took things as coolly as if he had been at an inn, said the cold lamb (it was goat) was the best he had ever tasted, and asked the Greek attendant if he had no rackie (spirit), the only Romaic word he had learnt. Odysseus understanding what he wanted, told the boy to give him wine.

'If they are robbers,' exclaimed the Major, 'they are damned good fellows, so I drink success to their next foray.' Soon after one of them lay down in a dark corner. Turks, Greeks, and all Orientals consider it the greatest possible insult, as well as an outrage on decency, for any one in public to change his garments or expose any part of his person below the waist. The Major was a remarkably tall, gaunt, bony man : after finishing his wine, he set to work to make up a comfortable bed with horse-cloths, slips of carpet, a bag for a pillow, &c.; when he had done this to his satisfaction, we supposed he would lie down, as his companion had done. On the contrary, he deliberately, as if in his own barrack-room, utterly regardless of our presence, took off his boots, socks, coat, waistcoat, trousers, and shirt, folding each article carefully up and placing it by his bedside. Thus exhibiting himself in all possible attitudes stark naked, he leisurely filled the bowl of his Turkish pipe, and advanced towards us to light it at the fire.

The two chiefs at first looked on the Major's novel proceedings with curiosity, as visitors in the Zoological Gardens do at the hippopotamus; but as the process of stripping advanced, they looked serious; the shirt scene took away their breath; their pipes went out when the Major advanced towards them. The Turk started up in horror with his hand on his sword. The Major, supposing he was making way for him from civility, and unconscious of giving any offence, made a very polite bow to us generally; and, in a gentle and conciliatory tone, said, in his own language, 'Pray, gentlemen, keep your seats, don't let me disturb you;' he then bent his body into a sharp angle, so as to draw a light from the burning embers. The position he stood in was so ludicrous, that Odysseus and I could not resist laughing. The Major, considering this a token of good fellowship, insisted on shaking hands with us, saying, 'I am sure you are both good fellows – Good night!'

I now saw by the light of the fire that he was not absolutely naked, for he had a leather waistcoat and drawers on, but they fitted as tight as his skin, and were exactly of the same colour. The Major lay down and smoked himself to sleep. Odysseus went out and brought back the Turkish bey.

Expecting to be surprised by Turks or Greeks, and distrusting those with us, we could not sleep; so our chief, to conceal his own anxiety, and to while away the time, recounted to the Turk the marvellous things he had seen done at Yanina by the Franks whilst he was serving with Ali Pasha. Odysseus then questioned the Osmanlee about Paradise and Mahomet, very profanely. The Albanian Turks are by no means bigots; our bey had evidently very little faith in anything but his sword. At length we dozed as we sat.

Before daylight the Major got up and went out; I followed him, accosting him in his native tongue.

'How well you speak English, my good fellow,' he said.

The frank and cordial manner of the Major so impressed me

with his honesty, that I hurriedly explained who I was, the critical state of things with us, and my anxiety to extricate Odysseus from the peril that encompassed him.

The Major instantly and earnestly entered into my views, saying, 'The vessel we came in will remain two or three days in the port; it will take but a few hours to reach her. I will return and stop by her for Odysseus, detain her as long as I can, and go on with him to the Ionian Islands.'

I told the chief our plan, he eagerly accepted the offer, – I pledged myself to keep possession of his mountain home, and to protect his family until altered circumstances permitted him to return to Greece. Hastily making the needful arrangements, the good-hearted Major departed on his mission. The chief having much to say to me, and thinking it probable I might be in danger on my return to the cave, convoyed me with his whole force. On our parting, he called some of his principal followers, and said, 'I call you to witness, I give this Englishman the cavern and everything of mine in it.' Then turning to me he said, 'Do what you think best without referring to me.' As we sat on the turf by a broken fountain, he placed his rough hairy hand on my bosom, saying, 'You have a strong heart in a strong body: you find fault with me for distrusting my countrymen, – I never doubted you. I trusted you from the first day as I do now on the last we may ever be together; though I cannot understand why you give money and risk life to serve those who would shoot you for money, as they will me if they can.'

Either from the vigilance of the Ottomans at Eubœa, or of those with him, or from some other impediment, the chief did not reach the port he was to have embarked from until after the vessel had sailed with the Major, although he had detained her as long as possible. I then expected the chief would make for the cave; we kept a sharp look-out, and posted men at the several passes; he wrote to me from time to time, but nothing definitively; and we passed months in this state of suspense.

I sent Fenton to Argos in the Morea, where the government was to give them the conditions proposed by Odysseus, and get what information he could of their designs. I gave Fenton a horse, guide, some soldiers, and what money he wanted. When

he arrived he sent me small brief notices by couriers of conferences he had had with the Secretary of War, one of the most
acute and unprincipled of the hangers-on of the government,
who was confident every man had his price, instinctively discovered that Fenton was one of his own type, and after many
conferences they devised a plan to entrap Odysseus and assassinate me. To effect this it was necessary to get Odysseus out of the
cavern, and to assassinate me in it. The stronghold was supposed
to be crammed like an argosy with wealth derived from plunder
of the Turks in many battles. If Fenton were successful he was
to have half of everything that was in the cavern. To be brief,
Fenton returned to me with a budget of special lies. The cavern
was so secure that in quiet times I despatched the few soldiers I
had in it on different errands.

I was in the daily habit of sallying forth to gather news,
though warned against it. Early in April, when I was some distance from my den, I was startled by a shot; the red-capped
Greeks were dogging me behind the rocks and pine-trees; I
hastened up the steep ascent, gained the lower ladder, mounted
slowly until I recovered my wind, then faster, the musket-balls
whistling by me right and left – above and below. I should have
come down faster than I went up, but from the great advantage
my men above had, and the sharp cross-fire they kept up to cover
my retreat. On my entering the trap-door my assailants retreated
across the mountains.

Shortly after this occurrence a large body of Greeks came to
Velitza, a village at the foot of our mountain, a detachment
ascended towards us; on coming near, one of them advanced,
holding a green bough as a flag of truce: he said Odysseus was
with the troops below, and that he had brought a letter from him
to me. It was to this effect, that he – Odysseus – was now with
his friend Ghouras; he entreated me to come to him to confer
on matters of great importance; saying that hostages would be
given for my safe return, &c.

I merely answered, 'If what you say is true, why don't you
come here? you may bring Ghouras or half-a-dozen others with
you.'

Several notes of this sort were exchanged. In the last, our chief urged me to capitulate as the only means of saving his life; telling me that I might now do so on my own terms, for those with him were Roumeliotes favourably disposed to him and to me; and that if I lost this opportunity, I should be blockaded by his enemies, the Moreotes, who would give us no quarter. Of course I declined, for I knew the chief was writing under compulsion: the messenger tried what he could do by tampering with my men, individually proffering large bribes; so I told one of the men to shoot him if he spoke another word. During this parley the most nimble-footed of the enemy scaled the cliffs to see if it was possible to get at us by the aid of ropes from above, or by blasting the rocks, or with shot or shell. I sent several of my people to mingle with the foe, offering five thousand dollars to those who would aid the escape of Odysseus.[91] On the fourth of fifth day they departed – leaving spies to watch us, as I knew they would. I then sent all the men I could trust to follow on the trail of our chief, and wrote to all his friends. That I might not be made a target of a second time, I did not venture forth alone.

Chapter 24

Spare me! oh spare! – I will confess.
                    They
Tempted me with a thousand crowns, and I
And my companion forthwith murdered him.
                         Cenci.

In the latter end of May, 1825, Fenton had brought with him from Racora, in Bœotia, a light-headed, but apparently simple-minded English Philhellene named Whitcombe; he said he had been in the East Indian Army, and that he came to Greece to seek adventures.[92] At all times glad to see my countrymen, I was particularly so at that time; Fenton was especially pleased with him. They both dined and passed their evenings with me, but slept below in Fenton's hut. On the fourth day after our noonday meal we sat smoking and drinking under the verandah of my house, on the lower terrace, longer than usual.[93] I had then no one in the cavern but the Albanian, who watched the entrance, a Hungarian, and the Italian unarmed secretary and interpreter.

It was intensely hot; all my people had retreated into one of the upper grottoes, where it was always cool, to enjoy their usual siesta. Fenton said, he had made a bet with Whitcombe about their shooting, and that I was to decide it. My Italian servant, Everett, then put up a board for a target at the extremity of the terrace. After they had fired several shots, at Fenton's suggestion I sent the Italian to his comrades above. Fenton then said to me, after some more shots had been fired wide of the mark, 'You can beat him with your pistol, he has no chance with us veterans.'

I took a pistol from my belt and fired; they were standing close together on a flat rock, two yards behind me; the instant I had fired I heard another report, and felt that I was shot in the back. They both exclaimed, 'What a horrid accident!' As one of their flint guns had just before hung fire, and I had seen Fenton doing something to the lock of his, I thought it was an accident. I said, 'Fenton, this must have been accidental!' He assured me it was so, and expressed the deepest sorrow. No thought of their treachery crossed my mind. I did not fall, but sat down on a rock with the pistol in my hand, and in perfect possession of all my faculties. Fenton said, 'Shall I shoot Whitcombe?' I answered, 'No.' I took my other pistol from my belt, when Fenton said, 'I will call your servant,' and hastily left me, following Whitcombe to the entrance porch. The dog, growling fiercely, first stopped their flight; he had the voice of a lion, and never gave a false alarm. The Hungarian, always prompt, was quickly at his post on the upper terrace.[94] Fenton, who had run away, called to him, 'A dreadful accident! will you come down and help!' The Hungarian said, 'No accident, but treachery! If you don't put your carbine down I shall shoot you.' Fenton as a last resort was raising his carbine, when the Hungarian shot him and he fell dead.

The Albanian came from the guard-room, and understanding no language but his own, was quite bewildered. Whitcombe, Fenton's dupe and confederate, attempted to escape by the trap-door leading to the ladder; the dog threw him on his back, and held him as if he had been a rat. Achmett, the Turk, seized him, bound his arms, dragged him to a crane used for hoisting things from below, put a slip-knot in the rope, and placed it round his ankles to hang him. His convulsive shrieks and the frantic struggles he made as his executioners were hoisting him over the precipice, calling on God to witness that he was innocent, thrilled through my shattered nerves; he besought me to let him live till the morning, or for one hour, that he might write home, or even for five minutes until he had told me everything.[95] Everett informed me what they were at; I sent him to the Hungarian, desiring him to defer what he was doing until I had ascertained from Whitcombe the facts which constitute my present narrative. I could not conceive it possible that an English gentleman, my guest, on the most cordial terms with me, should after four days' acquaintance, conspire with Fenton to assassinate me – there had been no provocation, and I could see no motive for the act. Fenton had never seen Whitcombe before, nor had I. If there was foul play, Fenton must have been the traitor : I had very great difficulty in staying the execution, everyone in the cave clamouring for vengeance. His life now hung on mine, and everybody thought that I was mortally wounded. They all swore, if I died, they would roast him by a slow fire: this was no idle threat, for it had been done on more than one occasion during that sanguinary war.

When I was shot, I sat down on the rock I had been standing on; bending down my head to let the blood flow from my mouth, a musket-ball and several broken teeth came with it – the socket of the teeth was broken, and my right arm paralysed. I walked without assistance into the small grotto I had boarded up and floored and called my house; it was divided into two small rooms, and there was a broad verandah in front. Squatting in a corner, my servant cut open my dress behind, and told me I had been shot with two balls between my shoulders, near together, on the right side of my spine, and one of them close to it. One of the balls, as I have said, its force expended on my bones, dropped from my mouth without wounding my face; the other broke my collar-bone, and remained in my breast – it is still there. No blood issued from the places they had entered at. We had no surgeon or medicines in the cave; the air was so dry and pure, our living so simple, that this was the first visit sickness or sorrow paid us. Nature makes no mistakes, doctors do; probably I owe my life to a sound constitution and having had no doctor.

The morning after I had respited Whitcombe, my servant brought me the following letter from him, which he read to me, though he could not speak English:

'For God's sake, sir, permit me to see you, if it is but for five minutes' conversation; it will save my life. In the fulness of contrition I yesterday told Favourite (Everett) my crime, and through misconstruction, or some other cause, he has interpreted it to Camerone, so as to cause my death. They all declare to me they will kill me and burn me. Camerone knocked me down and has thrown me in irons. For the mercy of Almighty God, let me see you; instead of augmenting, my explanation will palliate my offence. I wish not that it should be done alone. I wish also that Camerone and Everett should be by, to question me before you, and to endeavour to implicate me if they can. I wish only to tell you all the circumstances which I told Everett.

Camerone declares that I have plotted all the evil for Ulysses (Odysseus). For God's sake let me explain myself immediately, and do not let me be murdered without a word of explanation. O God! my misery is already too great; they care not for what you tell them; they want to tie me up by my irons to the beam of the room, and cut my head off.'

I refused to see him: he then wrote an incoherent account of what took place between him and Fenton – the latter accusing me of having usurped his place, as Odysseus wished him to have the command during his absence; saying that Odysseus had sent a messenger to him at Athens to that effect, and that on his return he should take possession of the cave; that there were beautiful women in it, and stores of gold; he would man it with English, clothe his followers with rich dresses and jewels: there would be a row first, a scene of blood, but that all he wanted was a friend to stand by him. By Whitcombe's account – too rambling and absurd to transcribe – his feeble brain was worked up to a state of homicidal insanity; he used the gentle term infatuation. He persisted in his asseveration than Fenton shot me, and his only crime was not warning me of my danger. The only thing his writing proved was that he had a very feeble intellect, and that Fenton had taken advantage of his weakness. He was now mad with terror, he screamed and shrieked if anyone came near him, he was in irons and chained to the wall, with no other food than bread and water. I resolved on the twentieth day of his imprisonment to set him free, which I did. When restored to life and liberty he wrote me the following letter: –

Much-injured Sir,

I cannot express to you what I feel for your unmerited kindness to me for your releasing me from an untimely death; other release it is not in the power of man to procure for me, my internal misery and shame being complete. May you never feel the half that I do. May you never be like me, reduced by an acquaintance of four days with a villain from the smiling circles who loved me, and had pleasure in my society, to the solitary wretched outcast which I am now become. I have now no home, no family, no friends – and all I regret is that I have still the gnawings of a conscience which makes me prefer life a little longer, with all my former enjoyments cut off, to an ignominious and untimely end. I can say no more, perhaps now I have troubled you too much.

That God may send you a speedy recovery, and turn every curse which falls upon my head into a blessing on yours, is the prayer of the wretched

W. G. Whitcombe.

He subsequently addressed one of his friends as follows: –

Camp, August 11, 1825

My dear Sir,

You will, perhaps, be astonished at my addressing you, when, from the unhappy circumstances into which my fatality has immersed me, I ought only to calculate on your discarding all converse with a being whose sin has placed between him and society a gulf fitter to be removed by any hands but his. But I cannot, cannot bear so sudden a transition into exquisite misery and shame without a line which may give palliatives to my offence. Scan it with a dispassionate eye; my only motive for begging this last favour of you is, that you may rather hold me the weak, unsuspecting tool, than the practised, unprincipled villain. Others played that part; others saw my easy nature, and thought me a fit instrument for the furthering of their grand speculations and enterprises. They discerned rightly – they have entailed the curse upon me; they have made the villain of me that they wished; but yet shall that curse be retaliated upon them. One is dead : the other still lives, and has left behind him many little interesting traits of character which will tend well to the blazonment of his fame, and conscience, if not warped by constant meannesses, shall by its sweet recollections requite him for the rest.

Charmed by Mr Humphreys'[96] account of the excessive intrepidity, honour, romantic situation, &c. &c. of his friend Fenton, added to his good-nature and *bonhomie*, I was induced by the repeated, by the urgent entreaties of that Mr Humphreys, added to a letter (expressing the most pressing invitation from

Fenton addressed to Humphreys, with many dark mystic expressions, known only, I presume, to himself) – I was induced, I say, to pay that visit to the cave. On my arrival I was beset by Fenton's utmost talents of duplicity (in which never mortal man has excelled him). Touched by his mournful tales of wrongs, rejection, deprivation of right, viewing him only as the romantic, the injured, the generous hero he had been represented by Humphreys, I swore to stand by him on his resolution to recover his rights or die. He worshipped me for it, and being too good a discerner of character to disclose further the nature of his designs, at the idea of which he knew I would revolt, he nailed me to the spot and moment of action, and by not giving a minute's time to recover from my infatuation, he precipitated me into that hell of guilt and shame which had long yawned for the wretched adventurer as his meed, but which, without arraigning Providence, might still, methinks, have been withheld from me. But where misfortune ever exists, there am I sure to get acquainted with it. And because such a villain survived in the same land, I, without holding with him a shadow of previous connection, without one thought, in the whole association of our ideas, which brought with it the slightest similitude whereby to enable me to account, by a harsh destiny, for my being coupled with the memory of such a villain's fate, am nevertheless doomed, solely because such an one exists, to connect myself, and all my happiness and honour, irretrievably with his fate. I am now a wandering outcast, a being whose very claim on society is departed, and would not now wish to renew those claims, from the recollections of dependence which would necessarily hang on that renewal.

But it is not for myself that I am wretched. No; I can roam to far distant regions, and amidst other scenes and other inhabitants, commence a new career, unembittered by the past. It is for my family, a family who had boasted that, through all their branches and connections, it had never had a spot to sully it. That that family should, through my faults, be disgraced, is more than I can bear. My mother is a parent who loves me to distraction. I received a letter a few days ago from that quarter. She has been dangerously ill, and the only reflection that contributes to her recovery is that of seeing me return crowned with laurels. They will be laurels!

Now view the reverse. It has been reported that I was dead. That report, with aggravated causes, will reach the ears of my family; my mother, I know, will not survive it. And all this for me.

I only regret that being too great a coward to put an end to my existence, I cannot cut off the miseries of anticipation.

But I have troubled you too long with subjects about which you can feel but little interest. Only one word more. Should an opportunity present itself, for God's sake let not accounts reach England that I am killed.

With hopes that you will excuse my long and selfish letter, and with many kindest remembrances to Mrs Alison and all your family,

> I remain
> Your sincere though unfortunate friend,
> (Signed)   W. G. Whitcombe.

P.S. – I sincerely regret that, by the most untoward circumstances, both the letters which you have been good enough at different times to send me, have been lost before they reached my hands; the one by the lies of that rascal Charlilopulo, the other by Dr Tindal,[97] amongst his other things.

Chapter 25

> 'Tis thus
> Men cast the blame of their unprosperous acts
> Upon the abettors of their own resolve,
> Or anything, but their weak, guilty selves.
>
> SHELLEY.

FOUL plots have been devised, and fit instruments found to execute them in less than four days. I was much more astonished and humiliated at the retrospection of my idiotic infatuation when, by Fenton's papers and other evidence, I discovered that I had been his dupe from the first – a blind man led by a fiendish cur, no more. He was foisted on me at Missolonghi, to act as a spy on Odysseus, and had done so for a whole year.[98]

My credulity in trusting Fenton on so short an acquaintance, without any previous knowledge, was unpardonable; but as Iago says of Othello, –

> 'He thinks men honest
> That do but seem to be so.'

And several small things concurred to deceive me. On landing in Greece, Fenton had nothing but his arms and his knapsack; in that small space he had Shakespeare's and Burns's works, and often read and quoted them. I afterwards found that the Hungarian had suspicions of Fenton's honesty, from talking to the soldiers who had accompanied him to Argos. Had he been less prompt in action Fenton would have been successful, for he had government soldiers screened in the woods, who on a given signal would have appeared. It was on the same day that this happened that Odysseus was trapped, captured some distance from the cavern; was taken to the Acropolis of Athens, imprisoned in a tower, and put to the most excruciating tortures, to extort from him a confession of where he had hid his treasures. He was afterwards hamstrung, and thrown from the tower in which he was confined. Ghouras was killed as he was walking his rounds on the Acropolis by a Turkish shell at night.

To cut short this disagreeable subject, I extract from Gordon's always fearless and generally accurate 'History of the Greek Revolution,' his brief notice of the affair :—

'On taking the field, Odysseus deposited his family in his den on Mount Parnassus, which he confided to the guard of Trelawny (who had lately married his youngest sister), with a handful of men, for that singular cavern is impregnable, and when the ladders that gave access to it were removed, neither armies nor artillery could make any impression. It is a perpendicular height of one hundred and fifty feet from the bottom of a precipice, and sheltered above by a lofty arch. In front were natural and artificial bulwarks, concealing the interior, and a portal cut in the rock, to which the flights of ladders gave access; within were houses, magazines stored for the consumption of years, and a fine spring of water.

'An attempt was made to murder Trelawny by two of his own countrymen, one of whom, Fenton, a determined villain, having accepted a bribe from the Government, seduced the other, a crack-brained young man, into complicity by extravagant tales, and the perpetual excitement of potent liquors. Although pierced through the back with two carbine balls, fracturing his arm and his jaw, the wonderful vigour of his constitution enabled Trelawny to recover. In the midst of his agony, he had the magnanimity to dismiss, unhurt, the unhappy youth who fired at him; as for Fenton, the prime assassin, he was instantly shot by a Hungarian soldier.

'In the same month on the 17th of June, the rising sun disclosed the lifeless body of Odysseus, stretched at the foot of the tower that had been his prison; it was said, that a rope by which he was lowering himself had broken, and that he was killed by the fall; however, no one gave credit to this story; it was supposed that he had been strangled, and then thrown from the top. Ghouras subsequently felt remorse for the death of his former patron; heard with pain the mention of his name, and occasionally murmured, "In that business I was misled." There can be no doubt that Mavrocordato was at the bottom of these tragical

events, instigated fully as much by private revenge as care of
the public weal. Odysseus was undoubtedly a tyrant and a traitor;
Trelawny in open rebellion, and suspected of tampering with
the Turks, who were very anxious to get possession of the cave;
but all this might have been forgiven, had they not previously
been the personal foes of the Director-General of Western
Greece.' [99]

For the first twenty days after being wounded I remained in
the same place and posture, sitting and leaning against the rock,
determined to leave everything to nature. I did not change or
remove any portion of my dress, nor use any extra covering. I
would not be bandaged, plastered, poulticed, or even washed;
nor would I move, or allow anyone to look at my wound. I was
kept alive by yolks of eggs and water for twenty days. It was
forty days before there was any sensible diminution of pain; I
then submitted to have my body sponged with spirit and water,
and my dress partly changed. I was reduced in weight from
thirteen stone to less than ten, and looked like a galvanized
mummy. I was first tempted to try and eat by seeing my Italian
eating raw ham of a wild hog which I had shot and cured; by
great effort I opened my mouth sufficiently to introduce a piece
of the size of a shilling, notwithstanding the agony of moving
my fractured jaw, and by degrees managed to devour it, and
from that time gathered strength. Excepting coffee, I refused all
wishy-washy or spoon-food and stuck to wild boar, which in
turn stuck to me; it spliced my bones and healed my flesh, excepting my right arm, which was shrivelled up and paralysed.

In three months after I had been wounded, my hurts were
healing, and my health returning, but my right arm was painful,
withered, and paralysed: my only hope of regaining the use of
it was to get the ball extracted; and for that purpose a surgeon
was indispensable.

Ghouras had been nominated to the command of Eastern
Greece, as the stipulated payment for his treachery to his former
chief, but the Turks held all the plains. So we were environed with
foes and closely watched, but my trusty and zealous friends the
Klephtes were always on the alert; nestling with the eagles
amongst the most inaccessible crags by day, and coming down

with the wolves at night, they supplied us with fresh provisions and kept us informed of everything that took place around. They even brought me a Klephte surgeon, stipulating to kill him if he did not cure me; he made an incision with a razor under my breast-bone, and poked about with his finger to find the ball, but in vain; the Klephtes then proposed to escort me to any place I chose to go for a Frank doctor, or to kidnap one at Athens, and bring him to me, and to leave their families as hostages. I had perfect faith in their probity, but lingered on hoping for a change. Soon after this, Zepare, one of their leaders, brought me news at night that his men were on the trail of a Frank, and they would bring him to me : he said a medico, for they believe all the Franks are more or less so, from their habit of carrying and giving medicines. The next morning a party of soldiers arrived escorting the Major who so astonished Odysseus and the Turkish Bey at Talanta, by his eccentricity. I was even more surprised now than then at meeting him. It appeared he had never lost sight of me. When he heard I was in peril, he made several unsuccessful attempts to come to me; he then took a cruise in search of the Commodore on the station, Hamilton, and stated my case. Hamilton, always prompt in acts of humanity, insisted not only on the Government's permitting the Major to have free access to me, but that I should have liberty to embark in one of his ships, if I chose to do so. After some days of deliberation and consultation with Odysseus' widow, and the inmates of the cave, I reluctantly agreed to take advantage of this favourable occasion; my trusty crew promised to remain at their posts until my return, or until the enemies of their former chief, then in power, were ousted, and then to be guided by circumstances.

No sooner had I left than Ghouras closely invested the place. The eagerness of both the Greeks and Turks to possess the cave arose from the stories current in that land of lies of the fabulous treasures it contained. The cupidity of the Greeks was lashed up to frenzy; every stratagem their subtle wits could devise was tried; crouching behind every rock and tree, they kept up a continual fusillade; they might as well have fired at the man in the moon as at the men in the mountain – if they came too near, the Hungarian stopped them with a shower of grape from the cannon. Some months after, when men and things were changed, the inmates of the cavern came to terms with some of the old friends of the late chief, who had always used their influence to protect the cave, as well they might, since much of the plunder they had accumulated during the war was deposited within it.

If the Hungarian Camerone had served in any other country than Greece, in a time of war he would have ranked high, for he was a well-trained warrior, skilful, resolute, and modest; he had been nearly two years in Greece when I fell in with him at Missolonghi, serving without pay or promotion: noted he certainly was, for his valour had been conspicuous in many battles.

Chapter 26

Victory! Victory. Austria, Russia, England,
And that tame serpent, that poor shadow, France,
Cry peace, and that means death, when monarchs speak.

SHELLEY.

WHEN the Muses deserted Parnassus, the Klephtes, *i.e.*, outlaws, took possession of their haunts, and kept alive the love of freedom and the use of arms. They were the only Greeks I found with any sense of honour; they kept their words and fulfilled their engagements; I protected and fed their families, and they escorted me in all my expeditions; I was continually in their power, yet they never attempted to betray me. The Klephtes were the only efficient soldiers at the commencement of the insurrection; and their leaders maintained the war for three years so successfully that the Greek Government were enabled to borrow money. The Government then resolved to divide the forces of the Klephtes, to appoint their own partisans as leaders, and to conduct the war themselves; they raised forces and imprisoned the former military leaders, wasted time in disputing about their plans of campaigns, and the nomination of the commissioners to see that they were carried out. In two scientific campaigns carried on by civilians, the Greeks lost all the territory the former arbitrary chiefs had won; and of the foreign loan, £2,800,000, there remained only five shillings in bad money at the close of those campaigns. If there had been any place of refuge, the insurrection would have ended by the flight of the leaders and submission of the people. The members of the Government sent away the money they had embezzled, and the primates and other rich rascals attempted to escape with their families, but they were stopped by the populace.

Greece was reconquered; the vanquished Christians sat in sullen groups round the walls of their only remaining fortress in the Morea; death, or to resume the Moslem's chains, their only alternative. At this critical period a messenger arrived from Navarino, proclaiming, in the words of our great poet,

'News, friends; our wars are done, the Turks are drowned.'

The people now sprang up frantic with joy.[100]

For six years all the Christian States had been standing looking on at the bloodiest insurrection on record, sympathizing with the unbelieving Ottomans. At the twelfth hour, the three great maritime Leviathans turned round, and falling unexpectedly upon their ancient allies, annihilated them.

The policy of the crafty Muscovite is intelligible. He wanted to possess Greece and cripple his natural enemy, the Turk. He did both at little cost; the Ottoman fleet was destroyed, and Greece converted from a Turkish into a Russian Hospodariat. The policy of France and England is inexplicable; it is one of those inscrutable diplomatic mysteries devised by heaven-born ministers, which men of women born cannot comprehend.

From the beginning to the end of the insurrection in Greece, Commodore Rowan Hamilton and Colonel C. J. Napier were the only English officers in command who acted justly and generously to the Greeks. Sir Thomas Maitland, and his successor, Sir Frederick Adams, High Commissioners of the Ionian Islands, from their natural sympathy with tyranny, favoured the Turks on all occasions. Napier was high-minded and independent in his opinions, which is always a disqualification in the eyes of officials. His general popularity and superior influence with the Ionians mortified Sir Frederick Adams excessively; he did all he could in his official capacity to thwart Napier; he gave vent to his rancour in the most trivial matters; he even sent an official letter to Napier on the impropriety of his wearing moustachios. The Colonel was very much amused at this despatch; he instantly obeyed the mandate by cutting them off and enclosing them in his reply to the Lord High Commissioner, who, no doubt, forwarded this important correspondence, with the enclosure, to the Commander-in-Chief. If these emblems of war are preserved amongst the trophies at the Horse Guards, the hair may be used as the lion's beard is by the Indians – they burn it, and swallow the ashes, believing it will give them the strength and courage of the lion.

It was particularly revolting to the mind as well as feelings of Napier to witness the war as waged in Greece – without a plan, combination, system, or leader; every man frantic with excitement to kill and plunder on his own account. Napier, as I have before said, would have undertaken the war when he was solicited by the Greeks to do so, if they had complied with the terms he considered indispensable to their success, which were that he should have uncontrolled power over the army. Whilst the Greek Government were treating with Napier, a distinguished French officer, Colonel Fabvier, volunteered his services without any stipulations, and was accepted. Napier, having no other object than the success of a just cause, pointed out to me on the map the strategy and tactics he should have used at that juncture had he commanded the Greek forces in the Morea. I asked him to write his plan, as the art of war is so little studied by our military men. I transcribe a campaign on scientific principles, as improvised on the exigency of the moment, by the great master of the art; the general principles laid down by so skilful a commander are applicable to any other locality in all times, especially in defensive warfare, and it requires no prophet to foretell there will be many such wars ere the lamb lies down with the lion.

Napier's letters not only exemplify the skill of the soldier, but show the frank, generous, manly character of the man. Byron, in a letter to the Greek committee from Cephalonia, in 1823, speaking of Colonel Napier, says, 'Of his military character it is superfluous to speak; of his personal, I can say, from my own knowledge as well as from all rumour or private report, that it is as excellent as his military; in short, a better or a braver man is not easily to be found; he is our man, to lead a regular force, or to organize a national one for the Greeks. Ask the army – ask anyone.'

The following letters are addressed to me by this great General :–

26th May, 1826

Circumstances must decide in war, speaking generally, but

frequently they may be commanded by able arrangements; instead of waiting to see what an enemy will do, he may be often forced to do that which we want him to do. I think this may be now accomplished by the Greek troops, should Ibrahim Pacha besiege Napoli di Romania.[101] In this event, I conclude he will have about 15,000 men, and that he will draw his supplies from Navarin or Mordon, a distance of about eighty miles, and have an intermediate depôt at Tripolitza, which is about twenty-five from Napoli. These roads pass through the mountains, and great difficulties will arise in marching his convoys, both from the nature of the country itself, and the exposure to constant attacks.

I also conclude that the Greek forces will amount to about 6,000 regulars and 10,000 irregulars, exclusive of the garrison of Napoli, in which I would leave only irregulars, the best to be had; taking the worst, with the whole regular force, to Monemvasia, into which place I would throw in as much provision as possible; and leaving this fortress with the smallest possible garrison picked from the irregulars, but (as well as Napoli di Romania) with the most *resolute governor and engineers*, I would issue forth and throw the whole regular and remaining irregular force on the communications of the besieging army.

The point at which I would cut them must be *determined* by local circumstances, viz., the force of the enemy; the distribution of that force; the nature of the country; and the exact knowledge of distances, or rather *times of march*. By this, the Greek army would oblige the Egyptian army to *raise the siege*, or to *send a force able to clear the road of the Greek army*, or he must go without provisions; if he raises the siege, such a failure, besides its actual cost, would have an immense moral effect to his prejudice, and enable the Greeks to take more bold measures; in short, it would be, what they have yet not seen, a victory produced by sound principles of war.

If he prefers the second way, viz., to send a force which he thinks capable of clearing the road, and reopening his communications, what is the consequence? His army must be so weakened that the siege cannot be continued with vigour; and the detached force will either be fought and defeated by the Greeks, or they would retire before this force into Maina, and even to Monemvasia. The moment this was done, this detached force would again march to join Ibrahim before Napoli; and would be followed up by the Greek army, which would again occupy its old position on the communication. This might be repeated twice or three times; but it is impossible that Ibrahim could continue this game long, and the moment he ceased to play it, he would be obliged to raise the siege. It seems difficult to say how this plan could fail, unless the Greek commander allowed the force detached against him to cut him off from Monemvasia, or from wherever he drew his subsistence.

As to the third choice, it is evident that he could not adopt it, as, although his Egyptians may live upon little, yet that little they must have; he would therefore try to receive his supplies from Patras; and although there would, perhaps, be more difficulty still, the Greek general might play the same game on that line of operation, as he would on the line with Navarin. He might occupy the *last* with his regulars, and detach his irregulars on the first. A Turkish force could hardly venture against the Greek irregulars, having their left flank exposed to the regular army of Greeks. I do not know whether I have clearly explained my meaning; but I am sure that if the Greek Government will do what they ought, viz., give Colonel Fabvier the full and uncontrolled direction of the war, or do this with Colonel Gordon, both these gentlemen will see what I mean, and that this plan is formed on sound strategical principles.

It is impossible to believe that any force which Ibrahim could detach would be able to force six thousand regular Greek soldiers through the passes of the Mainiote country back upon Monemvasia. I have only supposed the *worst* in supposing that they would do this, but in point of fact I imagine the Greek regular force could occupy some strong position in which it would force the troops detached against it to give battle under every disadvantage; and should the Greeks be defeated, that they might rally at and defend a multitude of defiles in the strong country between Tripolitza and Monemvasia – all these things are details of the execution, which depend on the talents of the commanders.

If this commander is Colonel Fabvier with Colonel Gordon supporting him, there is no doubt in my mind of its success; if the Greek force, on the contrary, is commanded by the Greek General-in-Chief, Colocotroni, it must inevitably fail, as he is incapable of even comprehending, much less of executing such a campaign.

In regard to the number of forces that I have supposed on each side, it is not very material that I should be exact, because the principle will hold good as long as the disproportion between the opposed armies is not *so great* as to put an end to all opposition, and this is a disproportion so vast that in such a country as Greece I can hardly conceive possible. Supposing that the Turkish forces receive their provision by sea, then they would not perhaps detach a force against the Greek army coming from Monemvasia, which might attack Tripolitza at its leisure: this, I suspect, would quickly produce the desired results. And last, though not least important, one has everything to expect from Lord Cochrane, who will not allow this provision to arrive by sea so easily. Are we to suppose that one of the greatest men of the age, for such he decidedly is, will be unable to effect anything against the enemy? Lord Cochrane's whole life has been a series of proofs that he possesses all the qualities of a great commander.[102]

Dear Trelawny,

When I returned from my ride, I wrote down what I said; – if you think it would be of any use, send it to Gordon. Not but that both he and Fabvier could form this plan as well or better than I, but my own opinion may have some weight with the Greeks, in support of those held by these two officers. For my own part, I would try this plan had I but *one* thousand men and *one* cannon! so convinced am I that it is a sound one; and that if executed with skill, activity, and courage it would make Ibrahim lose his game.

Yours,
C. Napier.

I dare say this is full of errors, for I wrote as fast as I could scribble. Keep it, for I have no copy; I wish you to give me one.

Cephalonia, 20th June, 1826

Dear Trelawny,

   Many thanks for your note dated 12th, which I have only this morning received. I hear Hastings has reached Napoli, which I hope will help Gordon to make arrangements. I hear that Ibrahim Pacha has taken and fortified Sparta. – If he can occupy Leondari and Sparta with strong detachments, he may render the execution of my plan difficult; but if he divides his forces with such numerous garrisons, the question arises, whether or not he can keep the field? However, he would greatly embarrass all operations by fortifying Leondari and Mistra (Sparta). These posts are, at this moment, the real points of 'strategy' for the defence of Napoli; and his seizure of them denotes a good military head. Were I in Gordon's place, supposing him master of his movements, I would make them keep their *vigils* in Sparta. That garrison should have no sinecure; but my fear is, that at Napoli they are all in such a state of confusion and ignorance, that he will not be able to make any movements at all. However, all I can say is, that the loss of any strong post demands that the Greeks should act upon the same principle against those posts that would have been acted upon against the original positions of the Turks. The general principle remains the same, but is applied to a different locality. For example (take your map). – When Mistra is held by the Turks, the Greeks can no longer throw themselves on the line of communication between Tripolitza and Navarin. They must then change their *object*, and throw themselves on the line between Mistra; and from wherever the garrison draws its provisions, Mistra becomes the object instead of Tripolitza. How this is to be accomplished, God knows. The war is, in this instance, on too small a scale to judge by a map, as I could in a large movement acting against Tripolitza; but military talent in a country like the Morea, finds ways to do what it wants. The grand secret in *mountain* countries is to *isolate* the enemy, which obliges him to abandon *his strong* position, and attack you in *yours*. It is not to one so well acquainted with the country as you are, that I need say what it would be to attack a good position in Greece, even without fortifications, much more with them.

It is in the art of forcing an enemy to fight you on your own chosen ground that military genius consists, and few things are more difficult in practice – it unites so much theory and so much practice with great fearlessness of character: no timid man will throw himself into those decisive positions which produce great results.

Yours truly,
C. Napier.

24 July 1826, Cephalonia

Dear Trelawny,

A Mr Ruppenthal[103] called upon me and begged of me to give him a written opinion on Greek matters. I have done so, but whether in the way he wishes I neither know or care; only I beg of you in giving them to him to receive from him a promise in writing not to publish them. He may be a *true man* or *not*, for I know nothing more of him than that he wrote to tell Canning I was at Missolonghi arranging plans with Mavrocordato. This was an error of his, but still a queer one enough, and I can trace, in his officiousness, much inconvenience which arose to me from an opinion formed by Mr Canning (I believe) of my conduct and feelings about the Greeks: be this as it may I forgive him, because he told the thing himself. As he thinks my opinion may be of use, I give it to him – I see nothing improper in so doing. As to my going, it is quite out of the question; a man always sets so high a price on himself, that *no one will buy!* Joking apart, though, it is quite impossible for me to go without my price. I am not such a damned fool as to let go one hand without having good hold with the other. I have seen too much of war to go to work without equivalent means, and I will add that, even with the force I have mentioned, a man must do his business *well*, or he would fail. I think it might be done with 500 men, but the other 1,500 are necessary to meet adverse circumstances which no man can calculate or foresee, and which daily arise in war. For example, an epidemic fever might arise which, out of 2,000 men, would not leave you 200 fit to fight or make a sharp march.

Calculations for war need wide margins for corrections; however, I honestly think with 2,000 men a fellow who knew his business well might give some stiff work to Ibrahim Pacha, and put the blessed rulers of Greece into some order. There is a sad want of [here follows a sketch of a man hanged on a gallows] among our friends.

Yours,

C. N.

Dear Trelawny,

I send you Cobbett. Muir behaved devilish ill to me; he left me in my utmost need. I always admired your magnanimity till six o'clock yesterday: then my opinion changed, and at ten o'clock hell had no hole half hot enough for you. Chs. Sheridan sets up for a wit and a philosopher; nature repents her extravagancy towards his father, and is bringing up her leeway. I'll give you no leisure to shoot; the game is not worthy the sportsman. Come and dine with me to-morrow if you have nothing better to do; we will get Muir, and have a jaw.

Yours,

C. J. Napier.

Cephalonia, 1st August, 1826

My dear Trelawny,

Pray do not let Mr Ruppenthal say that I made proposals to him, without contradicting him, because I did no such thing. I think I know what he is; but be he what he may, he can make nothing of my letters that can do me any harm, supposing he should be a bad one. When one has *no secrets* it is hard to discover them!

I hope Gordon has made port. I do not understand Fabvier's movements. I dare say they are not voluntary. I give no man credit for doing what he likes – what is wise – in Greece, until I hear that he has 2,000 good European drilled soldiers at his back, and 100,000 in his pockets, and a gallows with his advanced guard. I think were I there with the only power that would tempt me to go, I should raise the price of hemp 50 per cent. in ten days. What has become of Lord Cochrane? all hands say *he comes* – but he comes not! With kind regards to Gordon if he is with you, believe me

Yours hastily,
C. J. Napier.

I wish to God something may be done for the Greeks, for our orders are positive not to admit fugitives, and really though I think the rules laid down by the Government are just, it is very distressing to execute them – at least to me it is so.[104]

Extract from a Letter of Col C. J. Napier.

2 August, Cephalonia

Some poor Cephaloniote Greeks here have made up sixty dollars to ransom three women, or rather two and a child, who were taken at Missolonghi, and are now at Patras. I send you their names, and pray you to speak to Mr Green, our Consul at Patras, to endeavour to get these poor females ransomed; and tell him rather than he should fail, I will add forty dollars, and so make up the 100; but I know they are sold at about ten or twenty dollars a-piece generally. I fear if he interests himself in a *direct* manner they will raise the price. Pray lose no time, or they may be killed, and their family here is in great distress. They are poor people: they were, we hear, in the midst of the column that cut its way out; but they were taken, probably from terror.

Yours,
C. J. N.

Appendix

As this re-edition is passing through the press, it occurs to me to add a few particulars, all relating more or less to Shelley, which I can now only introduce by way of Appendix.[105] The sole item which appeared in my former edition is the one now numbered 4.

1 – *Mrs Shelley, Dr Nott, Queen Mab, &c.*

Mrs Shelley was of a soft, lymphatic temperament, the exact opposite to Shelley in everything; she was moping and miserable when alone, and yearning for society. Her capacity can be judged by the novels she wrote after Shelley's death, more than ordinarily commonplace and conventional. Whilst overshadowed by Shelley's greatness her faculties expanded; but when she had lost him they shrank into their natural littleness. We never know the value of anything till we have lost it, and can't replace it. The memory of how often she had irritated and vexed him tormented her after existence, and she endeavoured by rhapsodies of panegyric to compensate for the past. But Dr Johnson says, 'Lapidary inscriptions must not be judged literally.' They are influenced by our own short-comings to the object when living. It would be difficult to find minds more opposite than Shelley's and his wife's; but the tragical end of his first wife was ever present in his mind, and he was prepared to endure the utmost malice of fortune.

Mrs Shelley seldom omitted to avail herself of any opportunities (which were rare) to attend Church service, partly to show that she did not participate in her husband's views of atheism; and she was present when Dr Nott preached in a private room in the basement story of the house in Pisa she and Shelley were living in. Godwin her father had no means of providing for her; and he educated her for a teacher or governess in a perfectly orthodox manner, which he knew was indispensable; and carefully withheld his own particular views and her mother's, as he knew they would be a bar to her success. Mrs Shelley was a firm believer, and had little or no sympathy with any of her husband's theories; she could not but admire the great capacity and learning of her husband, but she had no faith in his views, and she grieved that he was so stubborn and inflexible. Fighting with the world was 'Quixotic.' Her mother, father, and Shelley were martyrs to their opinions, and their great abilities resulted in failures and unhappiness. Mrs Shelley did not worry herself with things established that could not be altered, but went with the stream. She was weak, and had no strength to go against it, and even the strong were swept away.

I said to Shelley, 'I have never found any religion more intolerant than the Christian. Dr Nott, who preached here the other day, could not resist attacking the "Satanic School," of which you are the founder. Byron is writing a satire on him, to the tune of the "Vicar of Bray." He repeated the first verse of it to me this morning :–

> "Do you know Dr Nott,
> With a crook in his lot,
> Who lately tried to dish up
> A neat codicil in the princess's will,
> Which made Dr Nott not a bishop?" '

SHELLEY: Religion itself means intolerance. The various sects tolerate nothing but their own dogmas. The priests call themselves shepherds. The passive they drive into their folds. When they have folded you, then they are satisfied, they know you fear them; but, if you stand aloof, *they* fear *you*. Those who resist they consider as wolves, and, where they have the power, stone them to death.

I said, 'You are one of the wolves.'

SHELLEY: I am not in sheep's clothing.

I continued: 'There is a young student here, a Catholic, who speaks English very well; he is one of the pupils at the University of Pisa. He says he can read Byron's poems very well, but you are difficult for him. What he likes best is "Queen Mab." '

SHELLEY: I'm glad it does some good; it is the worst of my compositions. The matter is good, but the treatment is not equal. I could treat the subject much better now; but, when we have emptied our mind of a theme, it's an odious task to go over it again, the mind turns to something new.

This was a sample of our common talk. The conversation took place within a month of Shelley's death, and therefore there could have been no wavering in his antipathy to all religion.

2. – *Dialogue between Trelawny and Shelley.*

TRE.: Byron said to me the other morning: 'I was reminded by a letter from my sister that I was thirty-four; but I felt at that time that I was twice that age. I must have lived fast.'

SHELLEY: The mind of man, his brain, and nerves, are a truer index of his age than the calendar, and that may make him seventy.

When Shelley at a later date said he was ninety, he was no doubt thinking of the wear and tear of his own mind.

3. – *Burning of Shelley.**

Via Reggio, August 15, 1822

At ten on the following morning Capt. S. and myself, accompanied by several officers of the town, proceeded in our boat down the small river which runs through Via Reggio (and forms its harbour for coasting vessels) to the sea. Keeping along the beach towards Massa we landed at about a mile from Via Reggio, at the foot of the grave; the place was noted by three wand-like reeds stuck in the sand in a parallel line from high to low water mark. Doubting the authenticity of such pyramids, we moved the sand in the line indicated to ascertain their truth, but without success. I then got five or six men with spades to dig transverse lines. In the meanwhile Lord Byron's carriage with Mr Leigh Hunt arrived, accompanied by a party of dragoons and the chief officers of the town. In about an hour, and when almost in

*See p. 171. These are the particulars as written down by me at the time.

despair, I was paralysed with the sharp and thrilling noise a spade made in coming in direct contact with the skull. We now carefully removed the sand. This grave was even nearer the sea than the other, and although not more than two feet deep, a quantity of the salt water had oozed in. This body, having been interred with lime six weeks previously, we had anticipated would have been almost destroyed. But whether owing to the water or other cause it had not further decomposed, but was precisely in the same state as when interred – the dress and linen were black and in shreds, and Corruption had begun his work. The legs had both separated at the knee-joints, the bones of the thigh projecting; the hands were likewise parted at the wrists; the skull, for the scalp was off, was of a dingy hue, and the face entirely destroyed and fleshless; the remains of the body were entire, having been protected by the dress. These devastations on the uncovered part of the body were supposed to have been caused partly by fish, and partly by the peculiar rapidity with which the sea dissolves the human frame. I was now obliged to apply to our guard to clear the ground, as many boats had arrived from the town, filled with parties of well dressed people, particularly women, who seemed particularly anxious to see so novel a ceremony, their curiosity being excited by the preparations to the utmost.

We had built a much larger pile to-day, having previously been deceived as to the immense quantity of wood necessary to consume a body in the unconfined atmosphere. Mr Shelley had been reading the poems of 'Lamia' and 'Isabella,' by Keats, as the volume was found turned back open in his pocket; so sudden was the squall. The fragments, being now collected and placed in the furnace, were fired, and the flames ascended to the height of the lofty pines near us. We again gathered round, and repeated, as far as we could remember, the ancient rites and ceremonies used on similar occasions. Lord B. wished to have preserved the skull, which was strikingly beautiful in its form; it was small and very thin, and fell to pieces on attempting to remove it. Notwithstanding the enormous fire, we had ample time ere it was consumed to contemplate the singular beauty and romantic wildness of the scenery and objects around us.

Via Reggio, the only sea-port of the Duchy of Lucca, built on and encompassed by an almost boundless expanse of deep, dark sand, is situated in the centre of a broad belt of firs, cedars, pines, and evergreen oaks, which cover a considerable extent of country extending along the shore from Pisa to Massa. The Bay of Spezzia was on our right, and Leghorn on our left, at almost equal distances, with their headlands projecting far into the sea and forming this whole space of interval into a deep and dangerous gulf. A current setting strong in with a N.W. gale, a vessel embayed here was in a most perilous situation, and consequently wrecks were numerous; the water is likewise very shoal, and the breakers extend a long way from the shore. In the centre of this bay my friends were wrecked and their bodies tossed about – Capt. Williams seven, and Mr Shelley nine days ere they were found. Before us was a most extensive view of the Mediterranean with the Isles of Gorgona, Caprera, Elba, and Corsica, in sight. All around us was a wilderness of barren soil, with stunted trees, moulded into grotesque and fantastic forms by the cutting S.W. gales. At short and equal distances along the coast stood high, square, antique-looking towers, with flag-staffs on the turrets, used to keep a look-out at sea, and enforce the quarantine laws. In the background was a long broken line of the Italian Alps.

4. – *Further Details of the Cremation, &c.*

TRANSLATION FROM THE ITALIAN.

This Sixteenth day of August, 1822, at 4 o'clock P.M.

We, Domenico Simoncini, captain and official of the maritime quarantine of the city of Via Reggio. In consequence of orders communicated by his Excellency the governor of the said city, President of the Quarantine Commission, in paper No. 90 (together with which is sent a copy of the despatch of his Excellency the Minister of State of the 27th of last month, No. 384, whereby the Quarantine Office is informed that our august Sovereign has granted the request made by the British Legation to be allowed to remove the mortal remains of Mr Shelley, brought to land by the waves of the sea on the 18th day of July, where they were buried according to the quarantine rules in force), E. J. Trelawny, commanding the schooner 'Bolivar,' with the English flag, presented himself to us, authorized by the Consul of Her Britannic Majesty with a paper from the same, dated 13th of this present month, which he produced. Attended by this gentleman, by the Major commanding the place, and the Royal Marine of the Duchy, and by his Excellency Lord Noel Byron, an English peer, we proceeded to the eastern shore, and arrived at the spot where the above-mentioned corpse had been buried. After recognition made, according to the legal forms of the tribunal, we caused the ground to be opened and found the remains of the above-mentioned corpse. The said remains were placed in an iron furnace, there burnt and reduced to ashes. After which, always in the presence of those above-mentioned, the said ashes were placed in a box lined with black velvet, which was fastened with screws; this was left in the possession of the said E. J. Trelawny to be taken to Leghorn.

The present report is made, in double original, of the whole of the above proceedings, and is signed by us, and the above-mentioned gentlemen,

> E. J. Trelawny.
> Dco. Simoncini.
> Noel Byron.

Commissione Sanitaria Marittima, Via Reggio,
Duchy of Lucca.

The body mentioned in the following letter as found near Massa was that of Charles Vivian.

TRANSLATION.

Via Reggio, August 29, 1822

Respected Sir,

I return infinite thanks for the excellent telescope which you have had the kindness to send me, and assure you that I shall ever bear in mind the attention I have received from you. I hope that some favourable occasion may occur when I may be called upon to attend to your honoured commands, and request you freely to dispose of me in anything in which I can be of service in these parts. I have delayed some days before answering your esteemed letter of the 22nd of this month, in respect of receiving from Massa the information you desired, which is as follows :

The same day, the 18th July, when the sea cast on shore the body of Signore Shelley, there was thrown up on the shores of Massa another corpse which could not be recognized, from its having been eaten about the head by fish. It had on a cotton waistcoat, and white and blue striped trowsers; a cambric shirt; and was without shoes. This body was burnt on the shore, and the ashes interred in the sand. At Montignoso the sea threw up a water-barrel; at Cinguale, an empty demijohn and two bottles; and at Motrone, a small boat painted red and black.

This is the news I have been able to obtain, with reference to the misfortune which has happened, and to my own knowledge. If I should meet with any further information, I shall consider it my duty to communicate it forthwith.

Accept the expression of my distinguished esteem and respect.
Your most humble and obedient servant,
Dco. Simoncini.

5. – *Remarks on Mr Barnett Smith's volume, 'Shelley, a Critical Biography.'*

Minute particulars regarding the death of Shelley are sought for and narrated by different writers in different ways. I see the latest by Mr Barnett Smith has many errors. Details can only be interesting from their authenticity, and everything that was done from first to last was done by me alone.

Mr Barnett Smith gives a different version of the details from that which I have published; and he can have no authority for so doing. Amongst other things he says that, when Shelley's body was washed on shore he had firmly grasped in his hand a volume of Æschylus. I have stated in my former account of the poet's death that Shelley's body had been eight days in the water, and his comrade Williams the same, and that all parts of the body not protected by clothes were torn off by dogfish and other sea-vermin, even to their scalps; the hands were torn off at the wrists. That disposes of the Æschylus story. When I parted from Shelley on his embarking on his last voyage, he had a black single-breasted jacket on, with an outside pocket as usual on each side of his jacket. When his body was washed on shore, Æschylus was in his left pocket, and Keats's last poem was in his right, doubled back, as thrust away in the exigency of the moment. Shelley knew that Keats was ripening into a true poet, and was very anxious to read this his last poem; Leigh Hunt had lent it to him. When reading a Greek poet, he would carry the book about with him for months, as he said there were often passages in it that perplexed him. That Greek volume, after I had had it in my possession for twenty or thirty years, I gave to his son Sir Percy. Excepting their wives, no one could have identified the bodies of Shelley and Williams except myself, and no one but I saw them. If I had not been there, probably they would never have been identified, and I could do this only by familiarity with their dress.

Then Mr Barnett Smith says, the Shelley family were never satisfied with the account of the wreck, as being the right one. Except Shelley's wife, and his son, who was under three years old, there were no Shelleys that were in any degree interested, or knew anything about it, except from the papers. Neither Mrs Shelley, Byron, nor Leigh Hunt, knew anything but what I told them.

When I burnt the bodies, Shelley's heart was not consumed when other portions of the body were. In drowning, the blood rushes to the heart; and the heart of Shelley was gorged with blood, so it was no miracle that it would not burn. Ultimately I gave the heart to his wife, and she inconsiderately gave it to Leigh Hunt, and some years ago it was given to Sir Percy Shelley by the Hunts. Mr Barnett Smith says the heart was buried in Rome. It never was in Rome, and it is now at Boscombe, and, for anything I know to the contrary, in an ornamental urn on the mantel-shelf. I purchased ground in the burying-ground of the Protestants at Rome, and there I myself buried not Shelley's heart but his ashes; not near Keats's grave, but isolated; from which place (so I am told, but I cannot affirm it of my own knowledge) the ashes have been surreptitiously taken, and are now in the possession of Lady Shelley.

Mr Barnett Smith also says – The fishermen who ran down Shelley's boat intended keeping Byron till they got a large ransom for him. This is nonsense; there was no brigandage in Tuscany. Their real game was that which they executed. They knew there would be a squall; in that squall they would run down the 'Don Juan,' drown the three people on board, and get the bag of dollars which they had seen taken on board. That was what tempted them. They succeeded in all but the last part; the boat's sinking so suddenly defeated their getting the money. If they had saved any of the lives they would have been subjected to fourteen days' quarantine, besides the investigation which would have followed.

There are many other inaccuracies in Mr Smith's book.

The principal fault I have to find is that the Shelleyan writers, being Christians themselves, seem to think that a man of genius cannot be an Atheist, and so they strain their own faculties to disprove what Shelley asserted from the earliest stage of his career to the last day of his life. He ignored all religions as superstitions. Some years ago, one of the most learned of English Bishops questioned me regarding Shelley; he expressed both admiration and astonishment at his learning and writings. I said to the Bishop, 'You know he was an Atheist.' He said, 'Yes.' I answered: 'It is the key and the distinguishing quality of all he wrote. Now that people are beginning to distinguish men by their works, and not creeds, the critics, to bring him into vogue, are trying to make out that Shelley was not an Atheist, that he was rather a religious man. Would it be right in me, or anyone who knew him, to aid or sanction such a fraud?' The Bishop said: 'Certainly not, there is nothing righteous but truth.' And there our conversation ended.

Certainly there were men of genius before the Christian era: there were men and nations not equalled even at the present day.

A clergyman wrote in the visitors' book at the Mer de Glace, Chamouni, something to the following effect: 'No one can view this sublime scene, and deny the existence of God.' Under which Shelley, using a Greek phrase, wrote, 'P. B. Shelley, Atheist,' thereby proclaiming his opinion to all the world.[106] And he never regretted having done this.

Notes

1. (p. 60) Wordsworth was on his way home from his continental tour of 1820. Mary Wordsworth, writing to her sister, Sara Hutchinson, from Geneva on 22 September, remarks: 'We have met many English, but none we know anything about ... The Public room overflows with English gentlemen.'

2. (p. 61) Edward Elleker Williams (1791–1822) was at Eton at the same time as Shelley. To begin with he had joined the Navy. but in 1811 got a commission with the 8th Dragoons and went to India where he served with Medwin. He returned in 1819 with Jane Cleveland, sister of General John Wheeler Cleveland of the Madras army, whose husband had deserted her. She had two children by Williams, who was drowned with Shelley in the wreck of the *Don Juan*.

Thomas Medwin (1788–1869) was a second cousin of Shelley's. He served in India as a lieutenant in the 24th Dragoons. In 1825 he published his *Journals of the Conversations of Lord Byron* and in 1847 *The Life of Percy Bysshe Shelley*. He married a Swedish baroness, spent all her money, then deserted her. Medwin's reminiscences of Byron and Shelley are often garbled and inaccurate, but he does not deserve Trelawny's trenchant verdict: 'Medwin is a measureless and unprincipled liar.'

3. (p. 64) John Taaffe (1787?–1862), son of an Irish distiller, educated at Stonyhurst and Edinburgh University, contracted a disastrous 'Scotch marriage', to escape the consequences of which he fled abroad, reaching Italy in 1815. He was a would-be poet, and was summed up thus by Shelley: 'Mr Taaffe rides, writes, indites, complains, bows and apologizes; he would be a mortal bore if he came often.'

4. (p. 67) The next three paragraphs were added in 1878.

5. (p. 74) The text from this point to the end of the chapter was added in 1878.

6. (p. 78) The text of the *Recollections* of 1858 continues:

He was never in France, for when he left England, Paris was in the hands of the Allies, and he said he could not endure to witness a country associated in his mind with so many glorious deeds of arts and arms, bullied by 'certain rascal officers, slaves in authority, the knaves of justice!'

Trelawny incorporates this among his new material on pp. 84–5.

7. (p. 79) The next two sentences were added in 1878.

8. (p. 81) In the *Recollections* this sentence ends with a jibe at Byron: 'But he was neither just nor generous, and never drew his weapon to redress any wrongs but his own.' The remainder of the chapter was added in 1878.

9. (p. 83) William Gifford (1756–1826), a redoubted literary critic and editor of the *Quarterly Review*.

10. (p. 86) Samuel Rogers (1763–1855), the banker-poet and patron of the arts. His best-known poem was *The Pleasures of Memory* (1792).

11. (p. 87) Thomas Moore (1779–1852), the Irish poet and song-writer, author of *Lalla Rookh*. His *Life of Byron* (1830) was the first, and remains one of the best, biographies of the poet. Trelawny was jealous of Moore's book, though he drew on it. For Moore and the destruction of Byron's memoirs see Note 70.

12. (p. 91) Probably Lady Hardy, wife of Vice-Admiral Sir Thomas Hardy, captain of Nelson's flagship at the Battle of Trafalgar. She was a cousin of Byron's half-sister, Augusta Leigh.

13. (p. 92) Initials of Richard Edgcumbe. He wrote a biographical sketch of Trelawny and a book on Byron (*Byron, The Last Phase*, 1909).

14. (p. 96) The next five paragraphs, including the dialogue with Byron, were inserted in 1878.

15. (p. 99) The remainder of this chapter was added in 1878.

16. (p. 102) In the 1858 *Recollections* Trelawny quotes stanza 31 of Adonais as Shelley's own self-portrait:

> 'one frail Form,
> A phantom amongst men . . .'

17. (p. 103) A phrase from the 1858 *Recollections* is omitted here: 'Byron was the real snake – a dangerous mischiefmaker.'

18. (p. 104) *The Promise; or a Year, A Month, and A Day*. Three sets of the unpublished MSS are preserved in the Bodleian Library.

19. (p. 106) The dialogue that follows – up to 'What would Mrs Shelley have said to me if I had gone back with your empty cage?' – was added in 1878.

20. (p. 113) Here the 1858 *Recollections* reads 'Sophocles' instead of 'Aeschylus'. See note 38 and the description on p. 160 of finding Shelley's body, where the same alteration occurs. The Aeschylus is also brought in on p. 149. This carefulness proves Trelawny changed the name of the book deliberately (see Introduction, p. 17).

21. (p. 115) The rest of this chapter was added in 1878.

22. (p. 121) The text of Chapter 9 up to this point was added in 1878. In the *Recollections* Chapter 9 begins here, opening with a sentence omitted in 1878 : 'One day I drove the poet to Leghorn.'

23. (p. 122) The next five paragraphs were inserted in 1878.

24. (p. 123) The next six paragraphs were added in 1878.

25. (p. 129) The rest of the chapter was added in 1878.

26. (p. 131) Thomas Jefferson Hogg (1792–1862), an early and life-long friend of Shelley. He began a lively and valuable biography of the poet, which Trelawny commended, but which the Shelley family stopped him from completing. Hogg had a knack for involving himself with Shelley's women – he tried to seduce his first wife, Harriet Westbrook, nearly succeeded in having an affair with Mary Shelley, and after Shelley's death set up house with Jane Williams, to whom Shelley had addressed his last love-poems.

27. (p. 134) For Rogers, see Note 10. John Cam Hobhouse (1786–1869) was Byron's companion to Greece in 1809, and one of the executors of Byron's will. He became a very respectable Liberal politician and was raised to the peerage as Lord Broughton in 1851. For Thomas Moore, see Note 11. 'Scott – not Sir Walter' refers to the editor of the *London Magazine*, John Scott (1783–1821). One of the most brilliant journalists of the day, he was killed in a duel by one of Lockhart's henchmen in a quarrel arising from Lockhart's notorious attack on Keats's poetry in *Blackwood's Magazine*.

28. (p. 136) But it was Trelawny, not Williams, who designed the boat in which Shelley was drowned. Edward Williams's journal for 15 January 1822 reads : 'Trelawny called, and brought with him the model of an American schooner, on which it is settled with S. and myself to build a boat 30 feet long, and T. writes to Roberts at Genoa to commence on it directly.' Soon after the wreck of the *Don Juan* Trelawny wrote a letter to Claire Clairmont saying, 'I induced Shelley to reside here – and I designed the treacherous bark which proved his Coffin.' (26 September 1822.)

29. (p. 138) The *Recollections* of 1858 has a sentence in brackets, here omitted : '(She had been unwell for some time; her afflictions mainly mental.)'

30. (p. 140) The next nine pages, up to the paragraph beginning, 'When I took my departure to Leghorn', on p. 150, consist of new material added in 1878.

31. (p. 145) Doubt has been thrown on the truth of this anecdote, but Newman Ivey White in his biography of Shelley says that he was told the same story by Jane Williams's grandson, Mr R. Wheeler Williams, as family tradition heard from his father. Jane Williams

died in 1884, three years after the death of Trelawny and six years after the publication of the *Records*, and could have contradicted it if it were not true. In his last years Trelawny saw her often – vide his letter to Claire Clairmont, 2 June 1874: 'Jane has called here several times' – though he adds, 'and except for her memory is all right.'

32. (p. 150) Leigh Hunt (1784–1859), essayist and poet, was editor of *The Examiner*, a radical weekly. For describing the Prince Regent as 'a fat Adonis of fifty' he was fined £500 and sentenced to two years in jail. This made him a hero to the young and liberal, though his confinement was not onerous, as he was allowed his own furniture, books, a piano, and daily visits from friends and admirers. Hunt was chronically insolvent, but an able sponger. Shelley paid for the Hunt family's passage to Italy; Byron provided them with lodgings in his own house, and after Shelley's death gave Hunt substantial sums of money, though not with good grace. He once remarked that trying to do something for Hunt was 'like pulling a man out of a river who directly throws himself in again'. In return Hunt pilloried Byron for meanness and snobbery in his vitriolic and self-justifying *Lord Byron and Some of his Contemporaries* (1828). In later years Mary Shelley often came to Hunt's assistance, to be rewarded at the end of it by Hunt turning up at her door accompanied by a lawyer to demand immediate payment, in the form of a capital sum, of an annuity left him by Shelley. Charles Dickens drew a scarifying portrait of Hunt in the character of Skimpole in *Bleak House*.

33. (p. 151) The remainder of this chapter was added in 1878.

34. (p. 154) Though ready to help Hunt because he had lent him moral support at the time of his marriage-scandal in 1816, Byron was not at all keen to have his whole family at the Palazzo Lanfranchi. Shelley had pressed the arrangement on him. The six Hunt children got on Byron's nerves; he described them as 'dirtier and more mischievous than Yahoos. What they can't destroy with their filth they will with their fingers ... Was there ever such a kraal outside the Hottentot country?' For her part Hunt's wife commented in her *Diary*: 'Can anything be more absurd than a peer of the realm and a *poet* making such a fuss about three or four children disfiguring the walls of a few rooms. The very children would blush for him – fye, Lord B., fye!'

35. (p. 155) This was John Taaffe (see Note 3).

36. (p. 156) 'Madame G.' was the Countess Teresa Guiccoli (1799–1873), née Gamba, at that time Byron's mistress. Taaffe's conduct was so craven that Mary Shelley thereafter nicknamed him 'False Taaffe'. One of Byron's servants, his gondolier Tita, and another belonging to

Teresa Guiccoli's father, Count Gamba, were arrested. Byron's servant was acquitted but the other was held in prison for some months. The government used the incident as a pretext to expel the Gamba family from Pisa.

37. (p. 156) Jane Williams's letter to Shelley does not appear in the *Recollections* of 1858.

38 (p. 160) The *Recollections* of 1858 reads 'a volume of Sophocles'. See Introduction, p. 17.

39. (p. 163) The remainder of this chapter was added in 1878. See Introduction, p. 16.

40. (p. 163) Laetitia Trelawny, his daughter by Lady Augusta Goring.

41. (p. 166) Trelawny could be romancing. The substratum of truth in all this may be found in the postscript of Mary Shelley's letter to Maria Gisborne, dated 15 August 1822:

I have left out a material circumstance. – A Fishing boat saw them go down – It was about 4 in the afternoon – they saw the boy at mast head, when baffling winds struck the sails they had looked away a moment & looking again the boat was gone – This is their story but there is little doubt that these men might have saved them, at least Edward [Williams] who could swim. They cd not they said get near her – but 3 quarters of an hour after passed over the spot where they had seen her – they protested no wreck of her was visible, but Roberts going on board their boat found several spars belonging to her – perhaps they let them perish to obtain these. Trelawny thinks he can get her up, since another fisherman thinks that he has found the spot where she lies, having drifted near shore. T does this to know perhaps the cause of her wreck – but I care little about it.

42. (p. 170) It is interesting to compare this description of the exhumation of Williams's body with the contemporary account that Trelawny wrote almost immediately after the event – it is dated 13 August 1822 and can be found in H. Buxton Forman's edition of the *Letters of Edward John Trelawny*:

As a foreground to this romantic scene was an extraordinary group – Lord Byron and Hunt seated in the carriage, the horses jaded and overpowered by the intensity of heat reflected from the deep loose sand, which was so hot that Lord B. could not stand on it. Captain Shenley and myself with the officer and sergeant commanding the nearest look-out tower stood round the grave; four soldiers were employed uncovering the grave, and I was intently gazing to see the first appearance of the body. The sergeant with a boat-hook first pulled out a black handkerchief, then a piece of shirt – I instantly examined these, and by the collar of the last being very peculiarly formed knew it to be Williams – presently we came to some loose wood which had been thrown between the body and the sand; on this being removed the head – or rather skull for it was almost fleshless – appeared – with a spade I bared the whole of it – as Lord B. had always asserted he should know him instantly by his teeth. The body, dreadfully mutilated, was now wholly palpable – both the hands were wanting and one sleeve too separated in its being moved. Having placed the iron in which it was to be burnt near the grave, I went and collected wood on the lee of the little hut at about twelve yards distance to prevent the wind blowing away the ashes. We then with instruments made for the purpose of dragging wrecked seamen out of the sea – for you are on no account allowed to touch a body – (a long pole with a round iron in the form of a sickle) with two of these we dragged the remains out of the grave, and then with poles shoved under lifted him into the furnace. I now called Lord B. – who came to try and identify him. The moment he saw the teeth he exclaimed 'that is him' and his boot being found and compared with one brought for that purpose identified him without a doubt. It was a humbling and loathsome sight – deprived of hands, one leg, and the remaining leg deprived of the foot – the scalp was torn from the head and the flesh separated from the face, the eyes out, and all this mutilation not by time the destroyer – but fish-eaten – it was in the worst state of putrefaction – a livid mass of shapeless flesh. Lord B. looking at it said – 'Are we all to resemble that? – why it might be the carcase of a sheep for all I can see' – and pointing to the black handker-chief – said 'an old rag retains its form longer than a dead body – what a nauseous and degrading sight!'

It will be seen that Byron's few words as noted in 1822 have by 1858 been blown up into a rather sententious speech à la Hamlet. This may serve as a yardstick for the many other dialogues and conver-sations in *oratio recta* scattered through the *Records*, most of them additions to the original text of the *Recollections*. Only a fool would suppose them to be exact transcripts of what was actually said more than fifty years before. They are conflations of whatever Trelawny could remember, eked out on occasion by the published reminiscences of others.

43. (p. 172) An unpublished scrap by Trelawny, dated 1832, now at John Murray's in Albemarle Street, gives this further detail:

Whilst I was burning the body of Shelley – Byron swam off to his schooner with one of his seamen, a remarkable strong Genoese fisherman and his gigantic valet – Baptista – it was a scorching hot day not a breath of air & the sun at his zenith – when alongside – he called to the Genoese to lay to – by treading water – but not to touch the vessel – he then ordered the steward to give him a bottle of wine & glasses – which he filled and they drank & returned on shore & then drank and feasted and grew wild with revelry – I never saw any one but a Malay so phrensied – he was more than two hours & a half in the water – & suffered for months afterward.

See Keats-Shelley Memorial Bulletin, No. IV, 1952: *Trelawny on the Death of Shelley*, by Leslie A. Marchand.

44. (p. 172) Shelley's heart became the object of a squabble. Leigh Hunt got hold of it from Trelawny, and later refused to surrender it to Mary Shelley. When Byron intervened ('What does Hunt want with the heart? He'll only put it in a glass case and make sonnets to it') Hunt wrote to Mary: 'Lord Byron has no right to the heart and I am sure he pretends to none. If he told you that you should have it, it could only have been from his thinking I could more easily part with it than I can.' Jane Williams eventually managed to induce Hunt to restore the heart. When Mary Shelley died it was found in her desk wrapped up in a copy of *Adonais*. In 1889 the heart was buried with the body of Shelley's son, Sir Percy Shelley, in the family vault at Bournemouth.

45. (p. 172) Leigh Hunt in his Autobiography has this to say:

On returning from one of our visits to the seashore, we dined and drank; I mean, Lord Byron and myself dined little, and drank too much. Lord Byron had not shone that day, even in his cups, which usually brought out his best qualities . . . The barouche drove rapidly through the forest of Pisa. We sang, we laughed, we shouted. I even felt a gaiety the more shocking, because it was real and a relief.

46. (p. 179) Trelawny was to be buried here almost sixty years later. In preparing Shelley's grave he was helped by Keats's friend, the painter Joseph Severn, who seems not to have had much time for 'Lord Byron's jackal', as he called Trelawny. Severn says of him in a letter to Charles Armitage Brown written in April 1823:

There is a mad chap come here whose name is Trelawny. I do not know what to make of him, further than his queer, and I was near saying, his shabby behaviour to me. He comes as the friend of Shelley, great, glowing and rich in romance. Of course I showed all my paint-pot politeness to him . . . assisted him to remove the ashes of Shelley to a spot where he himself (when the world has done with his body) will lie.

47. (p. 180) The preceding two paragraphs are a greatly expanded version of a short description of Shelley in the 1858 *Recollections*. The next 9 pages were added to the Records in 1878.

48. (p. 184) Trelawny got much of his information about Harriet Westbrook from T. L. Peacock (1785–1866), a friend of Shelley and Byron. Peacock had wittily caricatured Byron in his satiric novel *Nightmare Abbey*. He knew Harriet well and was her lifelong champion.

49. (p. 189) From this point the text is that of the *Recollections* of 1858.

50. (p. 190) Sydney Smith (1771–1845), the famous wit, pamphleteer, essayist and divine, one of the founders of the *Edinburgh Review*.

51. (p. 191) The remainder of this chapter was added in 1878.

52. (p. 202) Lady Hester Stanhope (1776–1854), a niece of William Pitt. She kept house for him and acted as his secretary, but after his death in 1806 left England and settled among the Druses on Mount Lebanon, where she lived for the rest of her life. Byron had met her on his first visit to Greece.

53. (p. 204) The text of the 1858 *Recollections* continues:

Shelley's solidity had checked Byron's flippancy, and induced him occasionally to act justly, and talk seriously; now he seemed more sordid and selfish than ever. He behaved shabbily to Mrs Shelley; I might use a harsher epithet. In all the transactions between Shelley and Byron in which expenses had occurred, and they were many, the former, as was his custom, paid all, the latter promising to repay; but as no one ever repaid Shelley, Byron did not see the necessity of his setting the example; and now that Mrs Shelley was left destitute by her husband's death, Byron did nothing for her. He regretted this when too late, for in our voyage to Greece he alluded to Shelley, saying, 'Tre, you did what I should have done, let us square accounts tomorrow; I must pay my debts.' I merely observed, 'Money is of no use at sea, and when you get on shore you will find you have none to spare'; he probably thought so too, for he said nothing more on the subject.

I was not surprised at Byron's niggardly ways, he had been taught them in boyhood by his mother. In early manhood he was a good fellow and did generous things; until bad company, called good society, spoilt and ruined him. To recover his fortune and sustain his pride, he relapsed into the penurious habits drilled into him in his youth.

Trelawny must have come to realize that this was too harsh on Byron, so omitted it from the *Records* in 1878. Mary Shelley and others of the Pisan circle were convinced that Byron was a miser, not only because he ironically claimed to have become one, but because they believed he had an income of £12,000 or £15,000. In fact Byron's income at that date was not more than £4,000, and heavily burdened with old debts. After Shelley's death Byron intended to assist Mary Shelley financially, but the negotiations were conducted by Hunt in such a way that both parties felt insulted. In the end Mary Shelley declined Byron's money and borrowed from Trelawny instead. This left Hunt free to press his own claims on Byron. See Doris Langley Moore's

The Late Lord Byron, pp. 406–16, for an account of this involved affair.

54. (p. 205) The text of the 1858 *Recollections* reads: 'Byron, in common with actors and other public characters . . .'

55. (p. 205) This paragraph was added in 1878.

56. (p. 206) The remainder of this paragraph was rewritten and expanded in 1878.

57. (p. 207) In the 1858 *Recollections* the sentence continues: 'and moreover they lauded and my-lorded him to his heart's content. "With as little a web as this I will ensnare as great a fly as Cassio." '

58. (p. 208) The preceding three paragraphs are an expansion of the text of the 1858 *Recollections*, which reads:

In after years, on my talking with the late Mr Murray, his publisher, on the subject, he said, 'I observed no falling off in his Lordship's powers or popularity during the latter period of his life, quite the reverse; but I heard such general censures on him from literary and other people who frequented my shop, and they spoke in such a depreciating tone of his later writings, that I became greatly alarmed as his publisher; and as I entertained a warm personal regard for his Lordship, I lightly touched on the subject in my letters to him. I was a great fool for so doing, for Mr Gifford . . .'

59. (p. 209) The preceding two paragraphs were added in 1878.

60. (p. 209) The remainder of this paragraph was added in 1878.

61. (p. 213) The remainder of this chapter was added in 1878.

62. (p. 216) Byron's steward, Lega Zambelli.

63. (p. 217) The *Recollections* of 1858 continues: 'with his long-eared compeers'.

64. (p. 220) William Mitford (1784–1878), author of *History of Greece*.

65. (p. 220) Sir Charles James Napier (1782–1853), a Peninsular veteran, at that time military resident of Cephalonia. He was later offered, but declined, the command of the Greek forces. He is best known for his brilliant conquest of Scinde in 1843 and laconic telegram to announce the victory: 'Peccavi' ('I have Scinde').

66. (p. 222) This paragraph, and the two dialogues between Trelawny and Byron that follow, were added in 1878.

67. (p. 223) Sir William Curtis (1752–1818), Lord Mayor of London and a well-known Tory M.P.

68. (p. 224) Matthew Gregory Lewis (1752–1818), author of *The Monk*, a Gothic novel full of ghosts and horrors.

69. (p. 224)

> Oh! wonder-working LEWIS! Monk, or Bard
> Who fain would make Parnassus a church-yard!
> Lo! wreaths of yew, not laurel, bind thy brow,
> Thy Muse a Sprite, Apollo's sexton thou!
>
> *English Bards and Scotch Reviewers.*

70. (p. 228) The dialogue between the Captain, Fletcher, Byron and Trelawny that follows is expanded from this short passage in the *Recollections* of 1858:

> Fletcher, Byron's 'yeoman bold', as was his custom in the afternoon, was squatted under the lee of the caboose, eating his supper and drinking bottled porter which he dearly loved. I said, 'You are enjoying yourself, Fletcher.'
>
> 'Yes,' he answered, 'and you had better do so whilst you can: my master can't be right in his mind.'
>
> 'Why?' I asked.
>
> 'If he was, he would not have left Italy, where we had everything, and go to a country of savages; there is nothing to eat in Greece, but tough Billy Goats, or to drink, but spirits of turpentine. Why, Sir, there is nothing there but rocks, robbers, and vermin.' – Seeing his master coming up the companion ladder, he raised his voice – 'I defy my Lord to deny it – you may ask him.'
>
> 'I don't deny it,' said Byron; 'what he says is quite true to those who take a hog's eye view of things. But this I know, I have never been so happy as I was there; and how it will be with me now that my head is as grey, and my heart as hard, as the rocks I can't say.'
>
> I followed Fletcher's advice and example in regard to the supper . . .

This is an instance when Trelawny would have been wise to let well alone. The earlier text is much better than the inflated later version. Of Fletcher Byron once wrote during their first visit to Greece in 1809:

> F. is a poor creature, and requires comforts that I can dispense with. He is very sick of his travels, but you must not believe his account of the country. He sighs for ale, idleness, and a wife, and the devil knows what besides.

See also Byron's letter to his mother, dated 12 November 1809, printed in Moore's *Life of Lord Byron*, from which Trelawny might conceivably have obtained the substance of this conversation.

71. (p. 232) Trelawny was quite mistaken to think that Moore had not read Byron's memoirs. A letter to him from Mary Shelley, dated 28 July 1824 remarks:

> . . . it is conjectured that notwithstanding he (Moore) had the MS in his possession, that he never found time to read it . . . There was not much in

them I know, for I read them some years ago at Venice, but the world fancied that it was to have a confession of the hidden feelings of one, concerning whom they were always passionately curious.

But John Cam Hobhouse, one of those chiefly responsible for the burning of Byron's memoirs, has an entry in his unpublished journals which shows that Moore did read them:

> Moore also told me that the first part of the Memoirs contained nothing objectionable except one anecdote – namely that Lord B. *had* Lady B. on the sofa before dinner on the day of their marriage – and Moore actually showed this to Lady Burghersh and others!

> (15 May 1824)

Again Trelawny was wrong to blame Moore for the destruction of the memoirs. In fact Moore made strenuous efforts to save them but yielded to heavy moral pressure exerted by Hobhouse, Byron's friend and executor, John Murray, his publisher, and the representatives of Byron's wife and sister. Hobhouse and Murray, who had not read the autobiography, were the two most determined on its destruction. Moore was not only manoeuvred into acquiescing to the burning of the MS. but into paying Murray 2,000 guineas (with interest) for it – because the memoirs were Moore's property, given to him by Byron, and represented security for a loan that Murray had made to Moore. On top of that Moore found that he had to shoulder the obloquy of being principally responsible for destroying Byron's memoirs. In blaming him Trelawny was repeating a generally held belief. See the very interesting account in the first chapter of Doris Langley Moore's *The Late Lord Byron*.

72. (p. 237) The next sentence and following paragraph were added in 1878.

73. (p. 239) Charles Barry was Byron's banker at Genoa; Douglas Kinnaird and John Hansom were his London bankers.

74. (p. 240) Trelawny gives more details about this jacket in a letter to William Rossetti dated 14 January 1878. It is probably the one now exhibited in Newstead Abbey.

75. (p. 242) Odysseus (or Ulysses) Androutzos. See pp. 24–5.

76. (p. 242) Trelawny is probably referring to the Kaffir War of 1834–6 in Cape Colony.

77. (p. 246) Trelawny gave a different answer in the *Recollections* of 1858. In the earlier book this sentence continues:

> ... the great mystery was solved. Both his feet were clubbed, and his legs withered to the knee – the form and features of an Apollo, with the feet and legs of a sylvan satyr.

Perhaps Trelawny changed this dramatic description in the effort to be more precise. R. Glynn Grills prints in an appendix to her *Trelawny* (1950) an unpublished letter from him to Monckton Milnes, dated April 1858, soon after the publication of the *Recollections*:

My anxiety to avoid being tedious may have made me obscure and doubtless there are many errors but in the oft vext question of Byrons unfortunate feet I am positive I have made no mistake.

He bathed in trowsers that had been expressly made to conceal his legs and sometimes when he & I were alone & he had them not, I knowing his sensitiveness, gave him a wide birth (sic) – I was always first in the water – I knew there was a deficiancy (sic) in the size of the calves of his legs – that his feet were stunted his toes too broad & heels too narrow – that when standing or walking he had difficulty in balancing his body – in fencing or sparring he remained stationary & merely used his arms – it was mere childs play a make believe – at that period I had a very vague notion of club feet I did not know that the heels being elevated by the contraction of the tendon Achilles or by other muscles of the leg constituted club feet.

Julius Millingen, one of Byron's doctors at Missolonghi (see Introduction, p. 26), remarked in his *Memoirs of the Affairs in Greece* (1831): 'we could not but admire the perfect symmetry of his body ... which might have vied with Apollo himself' (a phrase echoed by Trelawny in the *Recollections*). Millingen goes on to say that its only blemish 'was the congenital malformation of his left foot and leg. The foot was deformed, and turned inwards, and the leg was much smaller and shorter than the sound one ... there can be little or no doubt, that he was born club-footed.' Trelawny, who certainly read Millingen's book, is just as certainly not rehashing Millingen's description of Byron's deformity. In any case Millingen was wrong in one cardinal particular: it was Byron's right, not his left, foot that was malformed.

Millingen's description is of the corpse *before* the autopsy, which was brutally thorough. Harold Nicolson describes it thus in *Byron; The Last Journey*:

For over an hour the five of them hacked and sliced and weighed and dumped things in separate pails. The brain and skull interested them particularly; the *dura mater*, it appears, was firmly attached to the internal wall of the cranium; they had to tug and lever between them to get the two apart ... When it was all over they put him more or less together again and fitted the parts back into each other, and sent for the undertaker.

It seems odd that if Trelawny really saw Byron's corpse, he should not have noticed or reported the effects of this autopsy. Yet Hobhouse, when Byron's body arrived in England preserved in spirits, and he had to identify it, does not mention them either. But he remarks that the face

'did not bear the slightest resemblance to my dear friend – the mouth was distorted & half open showing those teeth in which poor fellow he once prided himself quite discoloured by the spirits – his upper lip shaded with red mustachios which gave a totally new character to his face . . .'

(Hobhouse's Diary for 2 July 1824)

78. (p. 248) The rest of this sentence does not appear in the *Recollections* of 1858. Instead there is this paragraph which Trelawny must have thought best to omit in 1878:

While saying this, Fletcher, without making any remark, drew the shroud and pall carefully over the feet of his master's corpse – he was very nervous and trembled as he did it; so strongly had his weak and superstitious nature been acted upon by the injunction and threats of his master, that, alive or dead, no one was to see his feet, for if they did, he would haunt him, etc. etc.

79. (p. 248) These particulars do not appear in the *Recollections* of 1858.

80. (p. 255) This paragraph was added in 1878. See p. 26.

81. (p. 256) Trelawny obviously has his knife into William Parry, who published *The Last Days of Byron* in 1825. This is a remarkably good book and contains a scarifying account of Byron's sufferings at the hands of his doctors. Parry's references to Colonel Stanhope are scathing; so are his remarks about Trelawny's hero, Odysseus. This may be one reason why Trelawny attacks him. The conversation between Trelawny and Parry may be imaginary, for it seems they could not have met. In his book Parry says he left Missolonghi on 21 April; Trelawny, according to his own account, did not arrive till 24 or 25 April. The 'conversation' could have been concocted from the details in Parry's book. Little is known about Parry, who was a rough diamond but the one man in Missolonghi on whom Byron was able to rely – a fact that Trelawny tries to discredit. Unfortunately Trelawny is right in saying that Parry died in a madhouse. The London Library copy of Parry's book carries an inscription by the superintendent of Hanwell Lunatic Asylum to the effect that it had been presented to him by Parry's son, and that its author 'was after a long residence in other institutions, received into this'.

82. (p. 256) The remainder of this chapter was added in 1878.

83. (p. 261) The following three paragraphs about Byron and tobacco were added in 1878.

84. (p. 262) The paragraph following was added in 1878.

85. (p. 263) The paragraph following was added in 1878.

86. (p. 264) The paragraph following was added in 1878.

87. (p. 264) The remainder of this sentence, and the sentence following it, was added in 1878.

88. (p. 265) The paragraph following was added in 1878.

89. (p. 267) Including Tersitza Kamenou, Odysseus's half-sister, whom Trelawny married. See Introduction, pp. 27–8.

90. (p. 272) In the 1858 *Recollections* Trelawny supplies the Major's name, which was Bacon.

91. (p. 276) Odysseus had been captured by his erstwhile Greek friends in April 1825, and was a prisoner in the Acropolis.

92. (p. 277) In the *Recollections* of 1858 the sentence reads:

In the latter end of May 1825, a young Englishman named Whitcombe came to me from Racora, in Boeotia, where he had been serving with the Greek troops.

93. (p. 277) The sentence following was added in 1878.

94. (p. 278) The next few sentences are an expansion of the text of the 1858 *Recollections*, which reads:

The Hungarian, always prompt, was quickly at his post on the upper terrace, and hearing I was shot, instantly killed Fenton. Whitcombe attempted to escape . . .

95. (p. 278) The sentence following was added in 1878.

96. (p. 281) The 1858 *Recollections* gives his rank: Capt. W. A. Humphreys.

97. (p. 283) Dr Tindal was Dr Millingen's assistant at Missolonghi.

98. (p. 284) The paragraph following was added in 1878.

99. (p. 286) As J. E. Morpurgo remarks in his edition of Trelawny's *Recollections of the Last Days of Shelley and Byron* (The Folio Society, 1952):

It is surprising that Trelawny allows these charges to pass unchallenged, and even compliments the author on his general accuracy. Much that Gordon implies about Odysseus is true, though the extent of his 'treachery' was his animosity for the central Government and an intention to make a three-months' local truce with the Turks (no uncommon occurrence at the time) in order to give himself time to settle, to his own satisfaction, his disputes with Mavrocordato. But Trelawny had gone out of his way to dissuade Odysseus from dealing with the Turks, an action which he felt to be both unworthy and unwise.

100. (p. 290) The Turks had landed an expeditionary force in Greece early in 1825, and recaptured Missolinghi after a long and bitter siege. In June 1827 Athens surrendered except for a small garrison that held out on the Acropolis. But on 20 October 1827, a combined English, Russian and French fleet under Admiral Codrington destroyed the Turkish fleet at the Battle of Navarino.

101. (p. 292) Present-day Nauplia.

102. (p. 294) The letter that follows was added in 1878.

103. (p. 296) Ruppenthal was a banker. This letter, and the one that follows, was added in 1878.

104. (p. 298) The letter that follows was added in 1878.

105. (p. 299) This Appendix was added in 1878.

106. (p. 308) Shelley wrote: 'demokratikos philanthropotatus kai atheos'.

MORE ABOUT PENGUINS
AND PELICANS

Penguinews, which appears every month, contains details of all the new books issued by Penguins as they are published. From time to time it is supplemented by *Penguins in Print*, which is a complete list of all available books published by Penguins. (There are well over four thousand of these.)

A specimen copy of *Penguinews* will be sent to you free on request, and you can become a subscriber for the price of the postage. For a year's issues (including the complete lists) please send 30p if you live in the United Kingdom, or 60p if you live elsewhere. Just write to Dept EP, Penguin Books Ltd, Harmondsworth, Middlesex, enclosing a cheque or postal order, and your name will be added to the mailing list.

Note: *Penguinews* and *Penguins in Print* are not available in the U.S.A. or Canada

LORD BYRON · SELECTED PROSE

Edited by Peter Gunn

During his short and intense life Byron was an inveterate 'scribbler' in prose and verse. His verse no longer occupies the pinnacle it once held throughout Europe, but he remains a superb prose-writer, unrivalled in fluency and forcefulness, in the subtlety of his rhythms and the perfection of his diction. In private journals and magnificent letters to intimate friends he recorded with passion, wit and total honesty his reactions to the many crises of his life, to his lovers, friends and enemies, and to his varied experiences as writer, traveller, notorious philanderer and, finally, soldier.

This selection from Byron's letters and journals, with its biographical commentary, enables the reader to follow them in the context of his life. They reveal the complex personality of the man himself – generous, caustic, ironic, playful, passionate for justice, one of the most noble and lovable of English writers.

POET TO POET

The response of one poet to the work of another can be doubly illuminating. In each volume of this new Penguin series a living poet presents his own edition of the work of a British or American poet of the past. By their choice of poet, by their selection of verses, and by the personal and critical reactions they express in their introductions, the poets of today thus provide an intriguing insight into themselves and their own work whilst reviving interest in poetry they have particularly admired.

CRABBE SELECTED BY C. DAY LEWIS

'As his poetry displays a balance and decorum in its versification, so his moral ideal is a kind of normality to which every civilized being should aspire. This, when one looks at the desperate expedients and experiments of poets (and others) today, is at least refreshing.'

HENRYSON SELECTED BY HUGH MACDIARMID

'There is now a consensus of judgement that regards Henryson as the greatest of our great makars. Literary historians and other commentators in the bad period of the century preceding the twenties of our own century were wont to group together as the great five: Henryson, Dunbar, Douglas, Lyndsay, and King James I; but in the critical atmosphere prevailing today it is clear that Henryson (who was, with the exception of King James, the youngest of them) is the greatest.'

Also available

WHITMAN selected by Robert Creely
WORDSWORTH selected by Lawrence Durrell
HERBERT selected by W. H. Auden
TENNYSON selected by Kingsley Amis